MITCHELL ZUCKOFF

Lost in Shangri-La

Escape from a Hidden World

A TRUE STORY

Harper
Press

Harper*Press*
An imprint of HarperCollins*Publishers*
77–85 Fulham Palace Road
Hammersmith, London W6 8JB
Visit our authors' blog at www.fifthestate.co.uk

This Harper*Press* paperback edition published 2012
1

First published in Great Britain by Harper*Press* in 2011

A catalogue record for this book
is available from the British Library

ISBN 978-0-00-741095-8

Set in Sabon with Requiem display by
G&M Designs Limited, Raunds, Northamptonshire
Printed and bound in Great Britain by
Clays Ltd, St Ives plc

MIX
Paper from
responsible sources
FSC™ C007454

FSC™ is a non-profit international organisation established to promote the responsible management of the world's forests. Products carrying the FSC label are independently certified to assure consumers that they come from forests that are managed to meet the social, economic and ecological needs of present and future generations, and other controlled sources.

Find out more about HarperCollins and the environment at
www.harpercollins.co.uk/green

For Gerry

CONTENTS

A NOTE TO THE READER

NEAR THE END OF THE SECOND WORLD WAR, A US Army plane flying over the island of New Guinea crashed in an uncharted region inhabited by a prehistoric tribe.

In the weeks that followed, reporters raced to cover a tale of survival, loss, anthropology, discovery, heroism, friendship, and a near-impossible rescue mission. Their stories featured a beautiful, headstrong corporal and a strapping, hell-bent paratrooper, stranded amid tribesmen reputed to be headhunters and cannibals. They told of a brave lieutenant grieving the death of his twin brother; a wry sergeant with a terrible head wound; and a team of Filipino-American soldiers who volunteered to confront the natives despite knowing they would be outnumbered more than a thousand to one. Rounding out the true-life cast were a rogue filmmaker who had left Hollywood after being exposed as a jewel thief; a smart-aleck pilot who flew best when his plane had no engine; and a cowboy colonel whose rescue plan seemed designed to increase the death toll.

Front pages blazed with headlines about the crash and its aftermath. Radio shows breathlessly reported every development en route to an astonishing conclusion.

But the world was on the brink of the Atomic Age, and a story of life and death in the Stone Age was soon eclipsed. In time, it was forgotten.

I came across an article about the crash years ago while searching newspaper archives for something else entirely. I set it aside and found what I thought I was looking for. But the story stayed with me. I began doing what reporters call 'collecting string' – gathering pieces of information wherever possible to see if they might tie together.

News reports and official documents can talk about the past, but they cannot carry on a conversation. I dreamed of finding someone who had been there, someone who could describe the people, places and events firsthand. More than six decades after the crash, I located the sole surviving American participant, living quietly on the Oregon coast with vivid memories and an extraordinary story.

That discovery, and the interviews that followed, led to an explosion of string that wove itself into a tapestry. Among the most valuable items was a daily journal kept during the weeks between the crash and the rescue attempt. A lengthy diary surfaced, along with a trove of priceless photographs. Three private scrapbooks followed close behind, along with boxes of declassified Army documents, affidavits, maps, personnel records, military bulletins, letters, and ground-to-air radio transcripts. Relatives of more than a dozen other participants supplied more documents, photos, letters and details. Perhaps most remarkably, the trail led to several thousand metres of original film footage of the events as they unfolded.

Next came a trip to New Guinea, to learn what had become of the place and the natives; to find old men and women who had witnessed the crash as children; and to walk to the top of a mountain where pieces of the plane still rest, along with bones and belongings of some of those who died there.

As I write this, on my desk sits a melted piece of metal from the plane that resembles a gnarled human form. It's a tangible reminder that, as incredible as this story seems, every word of it is true.

MITCHELL ZUCKOFF

A NOTE ON THE TEXT

THE EVENTS DESCRIBED IN THIS BOOK TOOK PLACE on the western half of the island of New Guinea in 1945. At that time, that portion of the island was known as Dutch New Guinea and its capital, on the northern coast, was called Hollandia. The area known at the time as Hidden Valley or Shangri-La is located approximately 240 kilometres southwest of Hollandia. Today, the former Dutch New Guinea is a province of Indonesia called Papua (not to be confused with Papua New Guinea, which is an independent country on the eastern portion of the island). Hollandia is now the city of Jayapura. Shangri-La or Hidden Valley is called the Baliem Valley.

Quoted material throughout the book has been left in its original form; in most cases, that means US spellings and units of distance and measure.

ILLUSTRATIONS

One

Missing

On a rainy day in May 1945, a Western Union messenger made his rounds through the quiet village of Owego, in upstate New York. He turned on to McMaster Street, a row of modest, well-kept homes on the edge of the village, shaded by sturdy elm trees. He slowed to a stop at a green house with a small porch and empty flower boxes. As he approached the door, the messenger prepared for the hardest part of his job: delivering a telegram from the United States War Department.

Directly before him, proudly displayed in a front window, hung a small white banner with a red border and a blue star at its centre. Similar banners hung in windows all through the village, each one to honour a young man, or in a few cases a young woman, gone to war. American troops had been fighting in the Second World War since 1941, and some blue-star banners had already been replaced by banners with gold stars, signifying a permanently empty place at a family's dinner table.

Inside the blue-star home where the messenger stood was Patrick Hastings, a sixty-eight-year-old widower. With his wire-rim glasses, neatly trimmed silver hair, and the serious set of his mouth, Patrick Hastings bore a striking resemblance to the new president, Harry S. Truman, who had taken office a month earlier upon the death of Franklin Delano Roosevelt.

A son of Irish immigrants, Patrick Hastings grew up a farm boy across the border in Pennsylvania. After a long engagement, he married his sweetheart, schoolteacher Julia Hickey, and they had moved to Owego to find work and raise a family. As the years passed, Patrick rose through the maintenance department at a local factory owned by the Endicott-Johnson Shoe Company, which churned out combat boots and officers' dress shoes for the US Army. Together with Julia, he reared three bright, lively daughters.

Now, though, Patrick Hastings lived alone. Six years earlier, a fatal infection struck Julia's heart. Their home's barren flower boxes were visible signs of her absence and his solitary life.

Their two younger daughters, Catherine and Rita, had married and moved away. Blue-star banners hung in their homes, too, each one for a husband in the service. But the blue-star banner in Patrick Hastings' window wasn't for either of his sons-in-law. It honoured his strong-willed eldest daughter, Corporal Margaret Hastings of the Women's Army Corps, the WACs.

Sixteen months earlier, in January 1944, Margaret Hastings walked into a recruiting station in the nearby city of Binghamton. There, she signed her name and took her place among the first generation of women to serve in the United States military. Margaret and thousands of other WACs were dispatched to war zones around the world, mostly filling desk jobs on bases well back from the front lines. Still her father worried, knowing that Margaret was in a strange, faraway land: New Guinea, an untamed island

Corporal Margaret Hastings of the Women's Army Corps, photographed in 1945.

just north of Australia. Margaret was based at a US military compound on the island's western half, an area known as Dutch New Guinea.

By the middle of 1945, the military had outsourced the delivery of bad news, and its bearers had been busy: the combat death toll among Americans neared three hundred thousand. More than one hundred thousand other Americans had died non-combat deaths. More than six hundred thousand had been wounded. Blue-star families had good reason to dread the sight of a Western Union messenger approaching the door.

On this day, misery had company. As the messenger rang Patrick Hastings' doorbell, Western Union couriers with nearly identical telegrams were en route to twenty-three other star-banner homes with loved ones in Dutch New Guinea. The messengers fanned out across the country, to rural communities and urban centres including New York, Philadelphia, and Los Angeles.

Each message offered a nod towards sympathy camouflaged by the clipped tone of a military communiqué. Signed by Major General James A. Ulio, the Army's chief administrative officer, Patrick Hastings' telegram read:

> THE SECRETARY OF WAR DESIRES ME TO EXPRESS HIS DEEP REGRET THAT YOUR DAUGHTER, CORPORAL HASTINGS, MARGARET J., HAS BEEN MISSING IN DUTCH NEW GUINEA, THIRTEEN MAY, '45. IF FURTHER DETAILS OR OTHER INFORMATION ARE RECEIVED YOU WILL BE PROMPTLY NOTIFIED. CONFIRMING LETTER FOLLOWS.

When Owego's newspaper learned of the telegram, Patrick Hastings told a reporter about Margaret's most recent letter home. In it, she described a recreational flight up the New Guinea coast and wrote that she hoped to take another sightseeing trip soon. By mentioning the letter, Patrick Hastings' message was clear: he feared that Margaret had gone down in a plane crash. But the reporter's story danced around that worry, offering vague optimism instead. 'From the wording of the [telegram] received yesterday,' the reporter wrote, 'the family thinks that perhaps she was on another flight and will be accounted for later.'

When Patrick Hastings telephoned his younger daughters, he did not hold out false hope about their sister's fate. Outdoing even the Army for brevity, he reduced the telegram to three words: Margaret is missing.

Two

Hollandia

ELEVEN DAYS BEFORE THE MESSENGER APPEARED AT her father's door, Margaret Hastings awoke as usual before dawn. Already the moist, tropical heat had crept under the flaps of the cramped tent she shared with five other WACs. She dressed alongside her tent mates in the Army-issued khakis she had cut down to match her petite frame. At first, Margaret wrote to a friend back in Owego, the uniforms 'fit me like sacks'. But after a few failed alteration efforts, she boasted in the letter: 'I got hold of a pair of men's trousers that were miles too big for me, and used the material. They really turned out quite well, considering.'

The date was 13 May 1945. It was Sunday, so the bugler had the day off from his usual five-thirty a.m. reveille. Not that Margaret could sleep in. The working week was seven days long at Base G, a sprawling military installation built around the town of Hollandia, on Dutch New Guinea's northern coast. By eight o'clock, Margaret was due at her post, a metal desk with a clackety typewriter where daily she proved that war wasn't just hell, it was hell with paperwork.

Tents for members of the Women's Army Corps in Hollandia, Dutch New Guinea, during the Second World War.

Margaret was thirty years old, lithe and beautiful. She had alert blue eyes, alabaster skin, and long, light-brown hair she wore in a stylish, figure-eight bun. At just 1.56 metres and barely 45 kilos, she could still slip in to her high school wardrobe. Her teenage nickname, 'Little girl' remained an apt description. But Margaret's size was deceptive. She carried herself with style; shoulders back and chin up, the lasting effects of drama club performances, violin lessons, and what her youngest sister called a feisty, 'take-charge' nature. She met strangers with a sidelong glance and a half smile that dug dimples beneath her high cheekbones. Somewhere between sly and sexy, the look suggested that Margaret had a secret that she had no intention of sharing.

As a girl growing up in Owego, Margaret bicycled to the local swimming hole, hitchhiked when she wanted to explore beyond the village, did well in school, and read books under the covers late at night. As she grew older and prettier, she became one of the most sought-after girls in town. She enjoyed the attention but didn't depend on it. Margaret considered herself an independent young woman who, as she put it, 'drank liquor, but not too much' and 'liked the boys, but not too much'.

Even after her younger sisters married, Margaret held out beyond the limit of her twenties. She wasn't interested in the men of Owego, but she didn't blame them, either. 'To tell the truth,' she told an acquaintance, 'I'm not sure I go for the kind of man who's supposed to make a good husband.'

After graduating from high school and bouncing through several jobs, Margaret found work as a secretary at a local factory owned by Remington Rand, a company that turned steel into everything from typewriters to .45 calibre pistols. She liked the work, but it bothered her that she had never been farther from home or anywhere more exciting than Atlantic City. It sounded corny, but Margaret wanted to see the world, serve her country, and find out what she was made of. Joining the Women's Army Corps gave her the chance to do all three.

As Margaret got ready for work, families across the United States were preparing for Mother's Day. This time, though, a mother's love wasn't the only cause for celebration. Five days earlier, Germany had surrendered unconditionally. Reports were trickling out that Adolf Hitler had killed himself in his bunker. Other Nazi leaders were in custody. Concentration camps were being liberated, their horrors fully exposed. After a terrible toll of 'blood, toil, tears and sweat', victory had finally arrived in Europe. In fact, 13 May 1945 marked five years to the day since Winston Churchill had uttered that phrase to the British people to rouse them for the fight ahead.

To mark the success of the war in Europe, the dome of the US Capitol building, which had been blacked out since Pearl Harbor, again gleamed under the glow of floodlights. As President Truman put it: 'The western world has been freed of the evil forces which for five years and longer have imprisoned the bodies and broken the lives of millions upon millions of free-born men.' House Speaker Sam Rayburn hailed the news in Europe but added two sombre notes. He lamented the passing of President Roosevelt weeks before V-E Day. Then he noted that the war wasn't over: 'I am happy but also sad, because I cannot help but think of those thousands of our boys who are yet to die in the far-flung Pacific islands and the Far East in order that victory may come to our armies, and that the glory of America may be upheld and peace and an ordered world may come to us again.'

News from the Pacific was encouraging, though fierce engagements continued there. For the previous six weeks, ferocious fighting had been under way on the island of Okinawa, which American generals intended to use as a springboard for an invasion of Japan. Few relished that idea, yet optimism ran high. That morning, the *New York Times* declared that final victory was assured, whether by negotiated surrender or outright defeat. The paper told its readers, 'It will be a busy summer for the Japanese enemy, and Hirohito can be confident that the "softening-up" period, now started, will be followed by lethal blows.'

That confident inevitability might have been plain to editors of the *Times* and to policy makers in Washington. But the war in the Pacific remained a moment-by-moment struggle. Between sunrise and sunset on 13 May 1945, more than 130 US fighters and bombers would attack troops, trains, bridges, and other Japanese 'targets of opportunity' in south and east China. Ten B-24 Liberators would bomb an underground hangar on a dot of land called Moen Island. Nine other B-24s would bomb an airfield on a lonely speck in the northern Pacific called Marcus Island. On Borneo, B-24s would bomb two airfields. To the east, B-25 Mitchell bombers and P-38 Lightning fighters would support ground forces on Tarakan Island. The US 7th Marine Regiment would burst through Japanese defences on Okinawa to capture Dakeshi Ridge. In the Philippines, the 40th Infantry Division would capture Del Monte airfield, and bombers and fighters would pound targets on Luzon Island.

Those were the major events of the day, to be catalogued, analysed and recounted in countless books and films about The Big War. Another incident on 13 May 1945 would escape the notice of historians and filmmakers: a C-47 transport plane carrying two dozen officers, soldiers and WACs would disappear during a flight over the mountainous jungles of New Guinea.

US military map of New Guinea during the Second World War, with Hollandia on the northern coast at roughly the midpoint of the island. The mapmaker was unaware of a large valley some 240 kilometres southwest of Hollandia, in the mountain range that crosses the island's midsection.

Located between Australia and the Equator, New Guinea was a largely uncharted tropical island 2500 kilometres long and nearly 800 kilometres wide at its centre. The world's second-largest island, after Greenland, it was a gift-box assortment of inhospitable environments. Much of the coastline featured barely habitable lowlands, swamps, and jungles. In the great middle were soaring limestone mountains covered by impenetrable rainforests and topped by snow or rocky outcroppings. The New Guinea terrain was so forbidding that the most common experience for its inhabitants was isolation. Pockets of humanity carved out small places to survive, fighting with anyone who came near and often among themselves. As a result, the island evolved into a latter-day Babel. New Guinea's natives spoke more than one thousand languages, or about one-sixth of the world's total – despite accounting for less than one-tenth of one per cent of the global population.

Inhabited by humans for more than forty thousand years, New Guinea passed the millennia largely ignored by the rest of the world. Lookouts on European ships caught sight of the island early in the sixteenth century. In 1545, the Spanish explorer Yñigo Ortiz de Retez named the island Neuva Guinea after an African country 16,000 kilometres away, because the natives he saw on the coast had black skin. For another two centuries, New Guinea was left mostly to itself, though trappers stopped by to collect the brilliant plumes of its birds of paradise to make hats for fashionable Sri Lankan potentates. In the eighteenth century, the island became a regular landing spot for French and British explorers. Captain Cook visited in 1770. Scientists followed, and the island drew a steady stream of field researchers from around the globe searching for discoveries in zoology, botany and geography.

In the nineteenth century, New Guinea caught the eye of traders seeking valuable raw materials. No precious minerals or metals were easily accessible, but the rising value of coconut oil made it worthwhile to plant the flag and climb the palm trees along the coastline. European powers divided the island roughly in half, and the eastern section was cut in half again. Over the years, claims of sovereignty were made by Spain, Germany, the Netherlands, and Great Britain. Nevertheless, even well-educated Westerners had a hard time finding it on a map.

After the First World War, New Guinea's eastern half was controlled by Britain and Australia. The island's western half was controlled by the Netherlands – and was henceforth known as Dutch New Guinea – with Hollandia as its capital. Unprecedented attention was drawn to the island as the Second World War unfolded, because of its central location in the Pacific theatre.

Japan invaded in 1942, planning to use New Guinea to launch attacks on Australia, just over 160 kilometres away across the Torres Straits. In April 1944, US troops executed a daring strike called 'Operation Reckless' that scattered the Japanese troops and won Hollandia for the Allies. The Americans turned it into an important base of their own, and General Douglas MacArthur, Supreme Commander of Allied Forces in the Southwest Pacific, built his headquarters there before moving on to the Philippines.

In New Guinea as elsewhere, Margaret Hastings and other WACs filled strictly non-combat roles, as expressed by their slogan, 'Free a Man to Fight'. An earlier motto, 'Release a Man for Combat', was scratched because it was feared it might feed suspicions among the WACs' detractors that their secret purpose was to provide sexual distractions for soldiers in the field. MacArthur was not among those critics. He liked to say the WACs were 'my best soldiers' because they worked harder and complained less than male troops. Eventually, more than one hundred and fifty thousand women served as WACs during World War II, making them the first women other than nurses to join the US Army.

Margaret arrived in Hollandia eight months after the success of Operation Reckless. By then, little of the war's bloody drama was playing out in that corner of the Pacific. Thousands of Japanese troops remained armed and in hiding on the island, but few were believed to be in the immediate vicinity of Hollandia. Nevertheless, sentries patrolled the sea of tents and one-storey buildings on the Army base. WACs were routinely escorted under armed guard, and women's tents were ringed by barbed wire. One WAC explained that the highest-ranking woman in her tent was given a sidearm to keep under her pillow, with instructions to kill her tent mates then herself if Japanese troops attacked. New Guinea natives also raised concerns, though the ones nearest Hollandia had grown so comfortable with the Americans they would call out, 'Hey Joe – hubba, hubba – buy War Bonds.' Australian soldiers who had received help from the natives during battles with the Japanese nicknamed them 'Fuzzy Wuzzy Angels'.

Some WACs thought the safety precautions' real aim wasn't to protect them from enemies or natives, but from more than one hundred thousand US soldiers, sailors and airmen in and around Hollandia. Some of those fighting boys and men hadn't seen a Western woman in months.

Almost immediately upon her arrival in Hollandia, Margaret became a focus of lovelorn soldiers' attentions. 'I suppose you have heard about blanket parties,' she wrote to a friend in Owego in February 1945. 'I know I did and was properly shocked. They are quite the thing in New Guinea. However, they are not as bad as they seem and anyway, nothing can be done on a blanket that can't be done in the back seat of a car.

'You see, we have no easy chairs and Jeeps are not too easy to sit in. So you just take your beer, or at the end of the month when the beer is all gone, your canteen of water and put it in a Jeep and ride all around until you find some nice place to relax. The nights are lovely over here and it's nice to lay under the stars and drink beer and talk, or perhaps go for a swim ... With the surplus of men over here, you can't help but find some nice ones. I have had no difficulty along that line at all.'

Far from home, Margaret indulged her adventurous impulses. 'One night,' she wrote, 'six of us went out in a Jeep without any top and drove all over the island. We travelled on roads where the bridges had been washed away, drove through water, up banks, and almost tipped over about ten times.' The letter didn't give away military secrets, only personal ones, so it slipped untouched past the base censors.

Margaret's great friend was a pretty brunette sergeant named Laura Besley. The only child of a retired oil driller and a homemaker, Laura hailed from a small town in Pennsylvania, 144 kilometres from Pittsburgh. She had spent a year in college before enlisting in the WACs in August 1942.

Laura was taller and more full-figured than Margaret, but otherwise the two WACs were much alike. Laura was thirty-one, single, with a reputation among her family for being a 'sassy' young woman who did as she pleased.

When they were not working, blanketing or joyriding, Margaret, Laura and the other WACs made their quarters as plush as possible. 'It is really quite homelike, and I am lucky enough to be in with five exceptionally nice girls,' Margaret wrote another friend at home. They furnished their 3.5-metre-square canvas home with small dressing tables made from boxes and burlap. They sat on chairs donated by supply officers who hoped the gifts would translate into dates. A small rug covered the concrete pad that was the floor, mosquito netting dangled over their

Sergeant Laura Besley of the Women's Army Corps.

cots, and silky blue parachute cloth hung as decoration from the tent ceiling.

A single bulb illuminated the tent, but a kind lieutenant named John McCollom who worked with Margaret's boss gave Margaret a double electric socket. The coveted device allowed her to enjoy the luxury of light while she ironed her uniforms at night. Quiet and unassuming, John McCollom was one of a pair of identical twins from Missouri who served together in Hollandia. He was single and could not help but notice Margaret's good looks, yet he did not try to convert the gift into the promise of a date. His good manners made Margaret appreciate it all the more.

The wildlife of New Guinea was not so unassuming. Rats, lizards, and hairy spiders the size of coffee saucers marched boldly into the WACs' tents, and mosquitoes feasted on any stray arm or leg that slipped out from under the cots' protective netting. Even the precautions had vivid side effects. Bitter-tasting Atabrine tablets warded off malaria, but the pills brought on headaches and vomiting, and they turned soldiers' and WACs' skin a sickly shade of yellow.

A lack of refrigeration meant most food came three ways: canned, salted, or dehydrated. Cooking it changed the temperature but not the flavour. WACs joked that they had been sent to the far reaches of the South Pacific to 'Get skinny in Guinea'. To top it off, Hollandia was paradise for fungus. The weather varied little – a mixture of heat, rain, and humidity – which left everyone wet and overripe. Margaret showered at least twice a day using cold water pumped from a mountain stream. Still, she perspired through her khakis during the boiling hours in between. She relied on Mum deodorant, as well as 'talcum, foot powder, and everything in the books in order to keep respectable', she wrote in a letter home. 'It is a continuous effort to keep clean over here. There are no paved roads and the dust is terrible, and when it rains there is mud.'

An American military officer described Hollandia vividly: 'There was "jungle rot" – all five types. The first three were interesting to the patient; the next two were interesting to the doctor and mostly fatal to the patient. You name it – elephantiasis, malaria, dengue fever, the "crud" – New Guinea had it all. It was in the water in which you bathed, the foliage you touched – apparently the whole place was full of things one should have cringed from. But who has time to think when there are enemy snipers hanging dead, roped to their spotter trees; flesh-eating piranhas inhabiting the streams; lovely, large snakes slithering nearby; and always the enemy.'

Yet there was great beauty, too, from the lush mountains to the pounding surf; from the sound of the wind rustling through the leaves of coconut palms to the strange calls and flamboyant feathers of wild birds. Margaret's tent was some fifty kilometres inland, near Lake Sentani, considered by its admirers to be among the world's most picturesque bodies of water. Small islands that looked like mounds of crushed green velvet dotted its crystalline waters. On long work days, Margaret relieved her tired eyes by looking up from her desk to Mount Cyclops, its emerald flank cleaved by the perpetual spray of a narrow waterfall. She described the sight as almost enough to make her feel cool.

Mostly, though, Hollandia was a trial. The WACs' official history singled out Base G as the worst place in the war for the health of military women: 'The Air Surgeon reported that "an increasing number of cases are on record for nervousness and exhaustion," and recommended that personnel be given one full day off per week to relieve "nervous tension."'

Margaret's boss took such warnings to heart, and he searched for ways to ease the stress among his staff.

Margaret was one of several hundred WACs assigned to the Far East Air Service Command, an essential if unglamorous supply, logistics and maintenance outfit known as 'Fee-Ask'. Just as in civilian life, Margaret was a secretary. Her commanding officer was Colonel Peter Prossen, an experienced pilot and Fee-Ask's chief of maintenance.

The early hours of 13 May 1945 were quiet in the big headquarters tent at Fee-Ask. Colonel Prossen spent part of the morning writing a letter to his family back home in Texas: his wife Evelyn, and their three young children, sons Peter and David, and daughter Lyneve, whose name was an anagram of her mother's.

Prossen was thirty-seven, stocky, with blue eyes, a cleft chin, and thick brown hair. A native of New York from an affluent family, he joined the military so he could fly.

Prossen had spent most of his children's lives at war, but his elder son and namesake knew him as a warm, cheerful man with a love of photography. He would sing 'Smoke Gets in Your Eyes' loudly and out of tune while his wife played flawless piano. After visits home, Prossen would fly over their house and tip his wings, to say goodbye.

In a letter to his wife a day earlier, addressed as always to 'My dearest sweetheart', Prossen commented on the news from home, counselled her to ignore slights by his

Colonel Peter Prossen with his sons,
David and Peter.

sister, and lamented how long it took for photos of their children to reach him. He told her to save the stuffed koalas he had shipped home until their baby daughter's second birthday. He asked her to watch the mail for a native axe he had sent home as a souvenir.

A dozen years in the military hadn't diminished Prossen's tenderness to his family. He sent his wife love poems and heart-filled sketches on Valentine's Day, and he pined for them to be reunited. Despite the harsh conditions he endured in Hollandia, Prossen commiserated sincerely with his wife about the hardships of gas rationing and caring for their children without him there.

The morning of 13 May 1945, for Mother's Day, he wrote to Evelyn in his cribbed handwriting: 'My sweet, I think that we will be extra happy when we get together again. Don't worry about me ... I am glad that the time passes fairly quickly for you – hope it does till I get home. Then I want it to slow down.'

Later in the letter, Prossen described a poem he had read about two boys playing 'make-believe'. It made him wistful for his own sons. Sadness leaked through his pen as he wrote that their son Peter would take his First Communion that very day without him: 'I'll bet he is a nice boy. My, but he is growing up.' Prossen signed off, 'I love you as always. Please take good care of yourself for me. I send all my love. Devotedly, Pete.'

Lately, Prossen had been anxious about the toll Dutch New Guinea was taking on the hundred or so men and the twenty-plus WACs serving directly under him. He wrote to his wife that he tried to relieve the pressures shouldered by junior officers, enlisted men, and WACs, though he didn't always succeed. 'I lose sight of the fact that there is a war going on and it's different,' he wrote. 'My subordinates are also depressed and been here a long time.' He wanted to show them he valued their hard work.

Prossen wheedled pilots flying from Australia to bring his staff precious treats: Coca-Cola syrup and fresh fruit. Lately, he had been offering even more desirable rewards – sightseeing flights up the coastline. On this day, 13 May 1945, Colonel Prossen had arranged the rarest and most sought-after prize for his staff, one certain to boost morale: a trip to Shangri-La.

Three

The Hidden Valley of Shangri-La

A YEAR EARLIER, IN MAY 1944, COLONEL RAY T. Elsmore heard his co-pilot's voice crackle through the intercom in the cramped cockpit of their C-60 transport plane. Sitting in the left-hand seat, Elsmore had the controls, flying a zigzag route over and through the mountainous backbone of central New Guinea.

Elsmore commanded the 322nd Troop Carrier Wing of the US Army Air Forces. On this particular flight, his mission was to find a place to build a landing strip as a supply stop between Hollandia, on New Guinea's northern coast, and Merauke, an Allied base on the island's southern coast. If that wasn't possible, he hoped to discover a more direct, low-altitude pass across the Oranje Mountains to make it easier to fly between the two bases.

The co-pilot, Major Myron Grimes, pointed at a mountain ahead: 'Colonel, if we slip over that ridge, we'll enter the canyon that winds into Hidden Valley.'

Grimes had made a similar reconnaissance flight a week earlier, and now he was showing Elsmore his surprising discovery. On his return from that first flight, Grimes claimed to have found a mostly flat, verdant valley some 150 air miles (240 kilometres) from Hollandia, in a spot where maps showed only an unbroken chain of high peaks and jungle-covered ridges. Mapmakers usually just sketched a string of upside-down 'Vs' to signify mountains and stamped the area 'unknown' or 'unexplored'. One imaginative mapmaker claimed that the place Grimes spotted was the site of an 'estimated 14,000-foot peak'. He might as well have written: 'Here be dragons.'

If a large, uncharted, tabletop valley really existed in the jigsaw-puzzle mountain range, Colonel Elsmore thought it might make a good spot for a secret air supply base or an emergency landing strip. Elsmore wanted to see this so-called Hidden Valley for himself.

On Grimes's signal, Elsmore pulled back on the C-60's control wheel. He guided the long-nosed, twin-engine plane over the ridge and down into a canyon. Easing back the plane's two throttle levers, he reduced power and remained below the billowing white clouds that shrouded the highest peaks. Pilots had nightmares about this sort of terrain. An occupational hazard of flying through what Elsmore called the 'innocent white walls' of clouds was the dismal possibility that a mountain might be hiding inside. Few pilots in the Army Air Forces knew those dangers better than Elsmore.

At fifty-three years old, energetic and fit enough to pass for a decade younger, Elsmore resembled the actor Gene Kelly. The son of a carpenter, he had been a flying instructor during the First World War, after which he had spent more than a decade delivering air mail through the Rocky Mountains. With the Second World War looming, Elsmore returned to military service and, when the war started, he immediately proved his worth. In March 1942, Elsmore arranged General MacArthur's evacuation flight from the

Colonel Ray Elsmore.

besieged island of Corregidor in Manila Bay to the safety of Australia. Later he became director of air transport for the Southwest Pacific, delivering troops and supplies wherever MacArthur needed them in New Guinea, the Philippines, the Dutch East Indies, Borneo, Australia, and the western Solomon Islands.

As Elsmore and Grimes flew deeper into the canyon, they could see the walls growing steeper and narrower, steadily closing in on the plane's wingtips. Elsmore steered around a bend, trying to stay in the middle of the canyon to maximize clearance on both sides of the twenty-metre wingspan. Straight ahead he saw a horrifying sight: a sheer rock wall. Elsmore grabbed both throttle levers. He began to thrust them forward, trying to gain full power as he prepared to veer up and away. But Grimes urged otherwise.

'Push on through,' the major said. 'The valley is just beyond.'

Surveying the situation with only seconds to spare, travelling at more than 320 kilometres per hour, Elsmore chose to trust his twenty-four-year-old co-pilot. He followed Grimes's instructions, slicing his way over the onrushing ridge and just beneath the overhanging clouds.

Safely in the clear, Elsmore saw a break in the puffy clouds. Spread out before them was a place their maps said didn't exist, a rich valley Elsmore later called 'a riot of dazzling color'. The land was largely flat, giving him a clear view of its full breadth – nearly forty-eight kilometres long and in places more than twelve kilometres wide, running northwest to southeast. Much of the valley was carpeted by tall, sharp kunai grass, waist-high in spots, interrupted by occasional stands of trees. Surrounding it were sheer mountain walls with jagged ridges rising to the clouds.

At the southeastern end, a river cascaded over a cliff to enter the valley. More than thirty metres wide in spots, it snaked through the valley, interrupted by occasional rapids before, at the valley's northwestern end, the cocoa-coloured river disappeared into an enormous hole in the mountain wall that formed a natural grotto, its upper arch some ninety metres above the ground.

Even more remarkable than the valley's physical splendour were its inhabitants: tens of thousands of people who lived as their ancestors had since the Stone Age.

Peering down through the cockpit windows, Elsmore and Grimes saw several hundred small, clearly defined native villages. Surrounding the native compounds were carefully tended gardens, with primitive but effective irrigation systems, including dams and drainage ditches. 'Crops were in full growth everywhere and, unlike the scene in most tropic lands, the fields were literally alive with men, women, and children, all hard at work,' Elsmore marvelled.

Men and boys roamed naked except for hollowed-out gourds covering their genitals; women and girls wore only low-slung fibre skirts. As he flew on, mesmerized by the scene below him, Elsmore watched the natives scatter at the sight and sound of the roaring airplane, 'some crawling under the sweet potato vines and others diving into the drainage ditches'. Pigs wandered around the compounds, and Elsmore caught sight of a few black dogs lazing about.

At the edges of large, open fields, Elsmore noticed spindly towers made from lashed-together poles rising some nine metres or more above the valley floor. Each tower had a platform for a sentry near the top, and some towers had small grass roofs, to shelter the sentries from the sun. Elsmore pushed the control wheel forward, to guide the plane lower for a better look. He guessed, correctly, that they were watchtowers to guard against marauding

A native village photographed from the air by Colonel Ray Elsmore.

enemies. As the C-60 flew on, the thrumming noise of its twelve-hundred-horsepower engines bounced off the valley floor and mountain walls. Frightened sentries abandoned their posts, climbed down the towers, and ran to nearby huts. Elsmore saw wooden spears more than four metres long leaning against those huts.

Elsmore snapped a few photographs, focusing on the people and their huts, some of them round like toadstools or thatched-roof 'igloos', he thought, and others long and narrow like boxcars. 'The panorama of these hundreds of villages from the air is one of the most impressive sights I have ever seen,' he wrote afterwards.

He and Grimes had a mission to complete, so Elsmore pulled back on the control wheel and roared up and out of the valley. He pointed the plane southeast and flew some 320 kilometres to another potential site for a landing strip, in an area called Ifitamin.

Several days later, Elsmore wrote a secret memo on his findings to his commanding officer, General George C. Kenney. The memo described the survey flights and paid special attention to the valley and the people in it. Major Grimes had called his discovery 'Hidden Valley', but in the memo Elsmore referred to it in less poetic terms. He called it the 'Baliem Valley', using the name of the river that flowed through it.

One concern Elsmore expressed to General Kenney about building a landing strip was the reaction of the natives. 'There is no access into this valley ... except by air, and for that reason very little is known of the attitude of the natives. It is known that there are headhunters in many of the adjacent regions and there is a suspicion that the natives in the Baliem Valley may also be unfriendly,' he wrote. Also in the memo, Elsmore issued an ominous warning to fellow pilots who might follow him there. He described at length how treacherous it could be to fly through the cloud-covered pass into the valley, especially 'for a pilot unfamiliar with this canyon'.

As it turned out, by any name Hidden Valley or Baliem Valley was unsuitable for a military landing strip. At 1600 metres above sea level, surrounded by mountains reaching 4000 metres and higher, it was too dangerous and inaccessible. Also, there was a better alternative. Elsmore learned that an Australian missionary had found the natives at Ifitamin to be friendly and eager to be put to work. This was more suitable for Elsmore's plan. 'Not only were we anxious to avoid incidents and bloodshed' – believed to be a strong possibility with the natives of Hidden/Baliem Valley – 'but we wanted to employ native labor on the construction project.'

Although the valley could serve no military purpose, news of its discovery spread quickly around Hollandia and beyond. Interest heightened when Elsmore began telling people that he thought the valley's inhabitants looked much taller and larger than any other New Guinea natives he had seen. Elsmore's impressions contributed to fast-spreading stories, or more accurately, tall tales, that Hidden Valley was populated by a previously unknown race of primitive giants. Some called them black supermen – handsome models of sinewy manhood standing over two metres tall. Soon the natives were said to be headhunters and cannibals, savages who practised human sacrifice on stone altars. The pigs the natives raised were said to be the size of ponies. The bare-breasted native women were said to resemble the curvaceous pin-up girls in soldiers' barracks, especially the exotic, sarong-wearing actress Dorothy Lamour, whose hit movies included *The Jungle Princess*.

In time, the stories multiplied, largely because no one could contradict any claim, no matter how outlandish. And it seemed as though the stories would remain unchallenged.

No one in Hollandia had any reason to hike 240 kilometres, past untold Japanese troops in hiding, over mountains, and through swamps and jungles. And no planes could safely land in the valley – the ground was too soft, uneven and grassy for a natural runway – and helicopter blades could not generate enough lift in the thin, high-altitude air to clear the surrounding mountains. Above all, the soldiers at Base G had a war to fight, not an anthropological expedition to mount.

Still, the valley captivated Elsmore. He asked around among Dutch and Australians whom he considered to be experts on New Guinea and found no evidence that any outsider had ever set foot in the valley.

As the stories spread, sightseers clamoured to see Hidden Valley with their own eyes. Over flights became a perk for officers, WACs, and enlisted men. Some returned with exciting stories of natives firing arrows and throwing spears at their planes. The more adventurous among them dreamed of touching the valley floor, even if it meant crash landing. 'I suppose I would have regretted it,' a lieutenant named William J. Gatling Jr wrote to his family in Arkansas, 'but I feel I would have liked to have been forced down simply to get a good first-hand idea of the whole area. Flying over was like holding candy just out of reach of a baby.'

Gatling's letter continued:

> Quite a number of us were skeptical of what we had heard before we made the trip but our skepticism had all vanished by the time we returned. Some will and some will not believe this story ... Beyond what has been observed from the air, it is believed nothing first-hand is known of these primitive people and their habits and customs. Sealed as they are in their Hidden Valley, they appear to be wholly

> self-supporting and self-sufficient. It is possible, of course, that they have some hidden footpath out of there, but such has not been located from the sky. Even if they could leave their valley, they would face a one-hundred-fifty-mile trek through almost impenetrable rainforest-type jungle to reach the Pacific coast in the north, or would encounter one-hundred-fifty miles of impassable, unexplored swamp extending between them and the Arafura Sea to the south.

After describing all he had seen during his flight, Gatling concluded his letter home with a philosophical thought: 'Probably after the war the Dutch government will send an expedition into the valley or missionaries may penetrate it, so until then the natives ... will know nothing of the white man except that he flies a big bird that makes lots of noise. Who knows, maybe they are much better off the way they are. At any rate, I am sure if they knew of the turmoil in which we are now engaged, they would be much happier to stay ignorant of the "civilized" world.'

The press got wind of the valley, and Colonel Elsmore agreed to take two veteran war reporters with him on one of his frequent flights over the valley, George Lait and Harry E. Patterson. Lait, in particular, had a lot to live up to. His father was Jack Lait, the pugnacious editor of the *New York Mirror*, who as a reporter in 1934 had filed an exclusive, on-scene story describing how the FBI gunned down bank robber John Dillinger. At thirty-eight, George Lait was on the way to matching his old man. As a swashbuckling correspondent for the International News Service, he palled around with legendary reporter Ernie Pyle and gossip columnist Walter Winchell; he was knocked out cold in London when shrapnel hit his helmet during the Blitz; and he had been blown out of a car seat by a German bomb. He had shot pheasants with King George VI, spent eighteen months with the British Eighth Army, and qualified as a paratrooper with the US Army's 11th Airborne. Another reporter once said of him: 'As a war correspondent, George was an inspired writer, fighter and souvenir collector. Where other correspondents might liberate a pistol or a helmet, George liberated machine guns, bazookas, tanks, and once had to be persuaded not to put the snatch on a Messerschmitt. It was a big war, George said, and he wanted something big to prove it.'

A man on his way to having seen it all, George Lait admitted that he had never seen anything quite like the valley. After returning from the flight with Elsmore, he filed a dispatch rich in description though tinged with racial and cultural condescension:

> Skimming less than one-hundred feet over the valley floor, one was able to identify among the native crops banana trees, a water plant (swamp taro), extensive patches of the native sweet potato or yam, and a waist-high plant closely resembling tobacco.
>
> Of animals, only a few dogs and pigs were seen. The pigs, staple meat food throughout New Guinea and religiously revered by most natives of the island, appeared exceptionally large and well kept, and of two varieties – an all-black or dark brown species, and a black and white variety, the latter growing to immense size.
>
> When the plane first roared over the valley, crowds of natives ran from their houses and vanished into the standing crops or clumps of trees. But after flying down the valley several times, their child-like curiosity seemed to overcome their fear of the motors – they cautiously emerged to watch the soaring plane.

Harry Patterson's story of the flight emphasized drama and intrigue: 'Even today, weeks after the discovery that has the whole South Pacific buzzing with speculation, no white man and probably no regular native has set foot in the lost valley ... It is pretty well-known in this part of the world that most of the New Guinea savages were either cannibals or head hunters.' Patterson quoted Colonel Elsmore describing the valley natives as 'taller, more finely built and lighter-skinned than the usual New Guinea fuzzy-wuzzies'.

The colonel, fancying himself an amateur geologist as well as a cockpit anthropologist, speculated that the natives' ancestors came to the valley 'hundreds or thousands of years ago'. 'He thinks that after they settled in this mountain paradise an earthquake or some tremendous upheaval trapped them in the valley,' Patterson reported.

As impressed as they were by what they had seen, Lait and Patterson were disappointed by the name Hidden Valley. Determined to re-christen it, they thought back several years to the Frank Capra movie, *Lost Horizon*, and its source, a 1933 James Hilton novel about a mysterious, peaceful utopia isolated from a war-weary world.

Hilton's story revolves around the crash of a small plane into a Tibetan mountain. The survivors, one of them a woman, are rescued by monks who guide them to a bucolic valley where the inhabitants' lives are long and happy, a land where moderation and tolerance reign supreme. In time, the survivors must choose whether to remain forever in the valley or return to the outside world, knowing that they might never be able to return.

Often read as an adventure tale, Hilton's book is really a meditation on finding peace and preserving humanity in a world spiralling towards self-destruction. Hilton saw 'civilization' trapped in a ruinous cycle, careening from one war to the next, each more deadly and destructive than the last. In a long exchange between two main characters, *Lost Horizon* anticipated a global war of unimaginable proportions. More than a decade before the first atom bomb,

Hilton feared a future in which 'a single-weaponed man might have matched a whole army'.

Describing one especially wise character, Hilton wrote: 'He foresaw a time when men, exultant in the technique of homicide, would rage so hotly over the world that every precious thing would be in danger, every book and picture and harmony, every treasure garnered through two millenniums, the small, the delicate, the defenseless – all would be lost.'

Hilton's frightening prediction didn't escape notice. President Roosevelt quoted that passage from *Lost Horizon* in a 1937 speech in Chicago. Four years before Pearl Harbor, Roosevelt used Hilton's horrifying vision to warn that, in defence of civilization, America might find itself forced to quarantine aggressive nations bent on unleashing a global storm. Roosevelt's warning had proved prescient.

It's no wonder, then, that a pair of veteran war correspondents looked wistfully on a fertile valley, sealed from the outside world, its natives ignorant of war, Nazis and *kamikazes*, and thought of the name that Hilton had given his fictional paradise. Never mind the reports of headhunters and cannibals, of spears and arrows, of watchtowers and sentries and battles among neighbours. Never mind the possibility that the native world glimpsed by Colonel Elsmore and Major Grimes wasn't peaceful at all, but a window into a shared human inheritance, one that suggested that the very nature of man was to make war.

Those questions could wait for another day, perhaps until someone from outside entered the valley and met the natives. In the meantime, George Lait and Harry Patterson bestowed a new name on New Guinea's Hidden Valley: they called it Shangri-La.

Four

Gremlin Special

THE VALLEY'S NEW NAME TOOK HOLD.

A 'Shangri-La Society' was formed for pilots and passengers fortunate enough to fly over it. Each society member received a comically ornate certificate on parchment paper that looked like a hard-earned diploma, complete with blue-and-yellow ribbons affixed by a gold foil seal. Signed by Elsmore and one of his subordinates, the certificates were personalized with the society member's name and the date of his or her special flight.

Reporters couldn't get enough of Elsmore – one dubbed him the 'leading authority on the valley and its people' – and the colonel lapped it up. After Lait and Patterson, other correspondents clamoured to visit the valley, and Elsmore usually obliged. Some who didn't see it for themselves but interviewed Elsmore or Grimes took flights of fancy. One desk-bound reporter gushed about the valley's beauty and called it 'a veritable Garden of Eden'. Then he interviewed Elsmore about fears of headhunters. The colonel played up the danger, with a wink. Elsmore told the reporter that he might drop a missionary into the valley by parachute to show that 'we come as friends and mean no harm. But I'm afraid it would more likely be a case of "head you lose."'

The quotable colonel told a correspondent for The Associated Press that when the war ended, he wanted to be the first white man to set foot in the valley and make contact with, in the reporter's phrase, the 'long-haired, giant natives'. Elsmore said his plan was to land in a glider, 'fully equipped with bargaining trinkets, also weapons if they won't bargain, food and the necessary material for swiftly setting up an airstrip so that transport planes can follow in.'

The AP story appeared in US newspapers on Sunday, 13 May 1945 – the same day that Corporal Margaret Hastings' boss, Colonel Peter Prossen, began rounding up members of the Fee-Ask maintenance division for a trip to Shangri-La.

For official purposes, Prossen described the flight as a 'navigational training' mission. The truth – a Mother's Day sightseeing joyride – wouldn't look nearly as good in a military flight log. Although he had taken his staff on similar recreational flights up and down the New Guinea coast, this would be Prossen's first trip to Shangri-La.

Margaret was at her desk when the invitation came. She had a date after work with a soldier she had been seeing regularly, a handsome sergeant named Walter 'Wally' Fleming. He had managed to get the keys to a Jeep, so they planned a drive to a secluded beach for an ocean swim. Yet Margaret had been desperate to visit Shangri-La since arriving at Fee-Ask five months earlier. Confident that she would be back in time for her date, she leapt at Prossen's offer.

The letter Prossen wrote that morning to his wife apparently put him in a mood to chat about home. He stopped by Margaret's desk and shared amusing news from his wife's last letter, laughingly telling Margaret that the family's new dog – a mutt that his son Peter had named 'Lassie' – was somehow winning prizes at local dog shows.

Margaret rushed to clear Prossen's desk of work by noon. She wolfed down a lunch of chicken, with ice cream for dessert, abandoning her usual practice of savouring each cold spoonful.

Prossen arranged for a truck to take Margaret and eight other WACs to the nearby Sentani Airstrip, named for the lake of the same name, while the men invited on the flight walked or hitched rides there. When the passengers arrived, they found Prossen, his co-pilot, and three crew members mingling outside a transport plane, its engines warming and propellers spinning. In civilian life, the plane was a Douglas DC-3, but once enlisted in the war effort it became a C-47 Skytrain, a workhorse of the wartime skies, with more than ten thousand of them deployed at Allied bases around the world.

Nearly twenty metres long, with a wingspan of more than twenty-nine metres, the C-47 cruised comfortably at

A C-47 in flight during the Second World War.

280 kilometres per hour. At full throttle it theoretically could fly 80 kilometres per hour faster. It had a range of about 2575 kilometres, or about five times as far as the round-trip that Prossen had planned. Most C-47s had twin, twelve-hundred-horsepower Pratt & Whitney engines. Some had guns, but Prossen's plane was unarmed. C-47s were not flashy or fast, but they were reliable and stable in flight. If troops or materials were needed somewhere, a C-47 could be counted on to get them there. Pilots spoke fondly of their signature smell, a bouquet of leather and hydraulic fluid.

Prossen's plane had been built in 1942 at a cost to the military of $269,276. Upon its arrival in Hollandia, the plane had been painted in camouflage colours to blend with the jungle if spotted from above by an enemy fighter or bomber. If the C-47 went down in the dense New Guinea jungle, its paint job would make it nearly impossible for searchers to spot.

To officials, Prossen's plane was Serial Number 42-23952. In radio transmissions, it would be identified by its last three numbers, as '*nine-five-two*'. C-47s were often called 'Gooney Birds', especially in Europe, and individual planes earned their own monikers from their captains and crews. Around the Sentani Airstrip, Prossen's plane was affectionately called *Merle*, though its better-known nickname was the *Gremlin Special*.

The name was ironic at best. Gremlins were mythical creatures blamed by airmen for sabotaging aircraft. The term was popularized by a 1943 book called *The Gremlins*, written by a young Royal Air Force flight lieutenant based in Washington DC named Roald Dahl. In Dahl's story, the first he published, the tiny, horned beasties were motivated to make mechanical mischief as revenge against humans, who had destroyed their primeval forest home to build an airplane factory.

At two o'clock in the afternoon it was time to go. As the passengers lined up outside the *Gremlin Special*, Prossen told them to expect the tour to last three hours.

'Let the girls in first,' Prossen said, 'and then fill it up with any enlisted men and officers who want to go.'

One enlisted man, especially keen to see Shangri-La, grumbled: 'Hey, that's showing partiality.' Prossen ignored the soldier's complaint.

One after another, the nine WACs climbed into the plane through a door near the tail, with Margaret first in line. Once inside, she found bucket seats with their backs against the inner walls of the cabin, so the passengers on one side of the plane would look across a centre aisle at the passengers on the other side.

Like a child playing musical chairs, Margaret ran up the aisle towards the cockpit. She plopped into the bucket closest to the pilots, certain she had picked a winner. But when she looked out the window, she didn't like the view. The C-47's forward cabin windows looked down on to the wings, making it difficult if not impossible to see directly below. Determined to make a full aerial inspection of Shangri-La, Margaret ran back down the aisle towards the tail. She grabbed the last seat on the plane's left side, near the door she had used to come aboard. The view was perfect.

Close behind Margaret was her close friend, Laura Besley. The attractive sergeant sat directly across from Margaret, in the last seat on the plane's right side. The centre aisle of the plane was so narrow the toes of their shoes almost touched. Margaret caught Laura's eye and winked. They were certain to have quite a story to tell.

Sitting next to Laura Besley was Private Eleanor Hanna, a vivacious, fair-skinned farm girl from Pennsylvania. At twenty-one, the curly-haired Eleanor had an older brother in the Army Air Forces and a younger brother in the Navy.

Her father had served in the ambulance corps during the First World War, and had spent time in a German prisoner-of-war camp. Eleanor had a reputation around Fee-Ask for singing wherever she went.

'Isn't this fun!' she yelled over the engines.

On Eleanor Hanna's wrist dangled a decidedly non-military adornment: a souvenir bracelet made from Chinese coins strung together with metal wire. She owned at least two others just like it.

Also on board was Private Marian Gillis of Los Angeles, the daughter of a newspaper publisher. An amateur pilot, she had already lived a whirlwind life, including fleeing from Spain with her mother at the outbreak of the Spanish Civil War. Nearby was Sergeant Belle Naimer of the Bronx, the daughter of a retired blouse manufacturer. She was still grieving the death of her fiancé, an Army Air Forces lieutenant killed months earlier when his plane went down in Europe.

Another WAC searching for a seat was Sergeant Helen Kent of Taft, California. A widow, she had lost her husband in a military plane crash. Bubbly and fun-loving despite her loss, Helen had joined the WACs to help relieve her loneliness. Her best friend at the base, Sergeant Ruth Coster, was supposed to accompany her on the flight. But Ruth was swamped with paperwork for planes that General MacArthur had decreed should be flown to the Philippines. Ruth had urged Helen go ahead and, upon her return, tell her what it was like. Ruth would join the 'Shangri-La Society' another day.

Three more WACs climbed aboard: Sergeant Marion McMonagle, a forty-four-year-old widow with no children from Philadelphia; Private Alethia Fair, a divorced, fifty-year-old telephone operator from Hollywood, California; and Private Mary M. Landau, a single, thirty-eight-year-old stenographer from Brooklyn.

Best friends Sergeant Ruth Coster (left) and Sergeant Helen Kent fooling around for the camera. Ruth wanted to join Helen aboard the *Gremlin Special* but had too much work to do.

Behind them came Colonel Prossen, trailed by his co-pilot, Major George Nicholson. Nicholson was thirty-four, a student of the classics who had graduated from Boston College then received master's degrees from Harvard, in the arts, and Boston University, in education. After several years on the home front in the infantry reserve, during which he taught junior high school, Nicholson joined the Army Air Forces to earn his silver pilot's wings. He had only been overseas for four months, during which he had served under Lord Mountbatten, the Supreme Allied Commander in South East Asia, before transferring to Dutch New Guinea.

Four days earlier, George Nicholson had skipped a 'Victory in Europe' party at the Fee-Ask Officers' Club. He spent the night alone in his tent, writing a remarkable letter to his wife, Alice, a fellow schoolteacher he had married days before reporting for active duty.

In neat script, with a historian's sense of scale and a poet's lyric touch, Nicholson marked the Allied victory over Germany by composing a vivid, fifteen-page narrative of the war in Europe and Africa. His words swept armies across continents, navies across oceans, warplanes across

Major George Nicholson.

unbounded skies. He channelled the emotions and prayers of families on the home front, and the fear and heroism of soldiers, marines, sailors and airmen on the front lines. He tracked the American military's rise from a miscellaneous band of ice cream-eating schoolboys to a juggernaut of battle-tested warriors. He moved Allied men and machines through crushing blows at Dieppe, in France, and the Kasserine Pass, in Tunisia. He roused them to victory on North African soil against the hardened German tank units in the battle at El Guettar. He drove them on to Salerno and 'Bloody Anzio' in Italy.

Nicholson gained momentum, just as the Allies had, as he approached the beaches of Normandy on D-Day. He wrote as if he had been there: 'Then the morning twilight was stabbed by the flashes of ships' guns pounding the invasion coast, and the air was rocked by the explosions of shells from the guns and bombs from the planes. Rockets traced fiery arcs across the sky. The choppy waters of the Channel made many of the troops seasick in the assault boats. German artillery plowed into the water, plowed often into assault boats and larger vessels, blowing them to destruction. Mines exploded with tremendous shock. Beach and boats drew closer. Fear gripped the men but courage welled from within them. The ramps were let down, the men waded through obstacle-strewn water, they reached the beaches. The invasion had begun.'

Four pages later, Nicholson described American troops crossing the Rhine into Germany, American flyers driving the feared pilots of the Luftwaffe from the sky, and Allied forces squeezing the Third Reich by the throat to force its surrender. 'We may have been soft, but we're tough now,' he wrote. 'The battle is the payoff. We beat them into submission.'

Only at the very end did the letter turn personal, as Nicholson expressed his guilt and questioned his own manhood for not having served in Europe with the US Eighth Air Force. Addressing his wife directly, Nicholson confessed: 'This is illogical, I admit, but a man is scarcely a man when he does not desire to pitch in when the combat involves his country and his loved ones. Do not think harshly of me, darling. The proof lies in action; I would have liked to go to the Eighth, but I never requested it.'

Having unburdened himself, Nicholson signed off: 'Darling, I love you.' Then, for the first time in fifteen pages of commanding prose, he repeated himself. 'I love you.'

Along with Prossen and Nicholson came the plane's three other crew members, Staff Sergeant Hilliard Norris, a twenty-three-year-old flight engineer; and two privates, George Newcomer, a twenty-four-year-old radio operator; and Melvin Mollberg, the assistant engineer.

Mollberg, known to his friends as 'Molly', was a muscular, handsome twenty-four-year-old farm boy with thick blond hair and a crooked grin. He was engaged to a pretty young woman from Brisbane, Australia, where he had been stationed before arriving in Hollandia a month earlier. Mollberg was a last-minute substitute on the *Gremlin Special* crew. The assistant engineer whose name initially came up on the duty roster was Mollberg's best friend, Corporal James Lutgring, with whom Mollberg had spent nearly three years in the Fifth Air Force in the South Pacific. But Lutgring and Colonel Prossen did not get along. The source of the tension was not clear, but it might have traced back to Lutgring believing that Prossen played a role in denying Lutgring a promotion to sergeant. Lutgring had no desire to spend his Sunday afternoon flying on the colonel's crew, even if it meant missing a chance to see Shangri-La. Mollberg understood. He volunteered to take his friend's place on the flight.

Corporal James 'Jimmy' Lutgring (left) and his best friend, Private Melvin Mollberg, who replaced Lutgring on the crew of the *Gremlin Special*.

Next to board the plane were the ten male passengers, seven officers and three enlisted men. Amongst them was Tech Sergeant Kenneth Decker of Kelso, Washington. A wiry, laconic draftsman in the command's engineering department, Decker had worked in his father's furniture store before the war. He had been in New Guinea for several months, after being stationed in Australia for more than two years. The flight was a special treat for Decker: he was celebrating his thirty-fourth birthday. On the other hand, seeing Corporal Margaret Hastings on the plane came as an uncomfortable surprise. Weeks earlier, Decker had asked her on a date, only to be refused. A flight over Shangri-La separated by a few seats seemed about as close to Margaret as he would ever get.

Another passenger was Herbert F. Good, a tall, forty-six-year-old captain from Ohio. Good had survived service in the First World War, after which he'd married and returned home to life as an oil salesman and a leader in his Presbyterian church. Then war called again, so again he went.

At the end of the line were identical twins, John and Robert McCollom, twenty-six-year-old first lieutenants from Trenton, Missouri. They were nearly indistinguishable, with sandy blond hair, soulful blue eyes, and lantern jaws. One small difference: John was 1.67 metres and

Tech Sergeant Kenneth Decker.

Robert was a shade taller, a fact that Robert playfully lorded over his 'little' brother. Known to friends and family as 'The Inseparables', the twins' close relationship was forged as toddlers after their mother left them, their older brother, and their father. As eight-year-olds, they dressed in matching outfits and idolized aviator Charles Lindbergh for his solo nonstop flight across the Atlantic. When the twins came home from third grade and gushed about their teacher, Miss Eva Ratliff, their father, a railroad station manager, decided to meet her. John, Robert and their older brother soon had a stepmother.

The McCollom twins became Eagle Scouts together. They were both sports fanatics. They joined the Reserve Officers' Training Corps together and shared a room as aerospace engineering students at the University of Minnesota, where they worked long hours to pay tuition while managing the school's hockey team. They could only afford one set of books, so they shared them. Though alike in most ways, Robert McCollom was quieter, more introverted, while John was the outgoing twin. Robert was always known as Robert, while John was often called 'Mac'.

The McCollom twins' first test apart came two years earlier, on 5 May 1943, when Robert married a young woman he had met on a blind date, Cecilia Connolly, known by her middle name, Adele. In a wedding photo published in a local newspaper, both McColloms are in uniform; the only way to tell them apart is by Adele's winsome smile in Robert's direction. After the wedding, Robert, Adele and John became a threesome, spending evenings together at the Officers' Club. The McColloms earned their pilot's licences together in the service, and with the exception of a brief period apart, were stationed together at several bases stateside. Six months before the flight to Shangri-La, they were sent overseas together to New Guinea.

Lieutenants John (left) and Robert McCollom.

Six weeks before the Mother's Day flight, Adele McCollom gave birth to a girl she and Robert named Mary Dennise and called Dennie. Robert McCollom had yet to see his new daughter.

The McCollom twins wanted to see Shangri-La through the same window of the *Gremlin Special*, but they couldn't find two seats together. Robert McCollom walked towards the cockpit and slipped into an open seat near the front. John McCollom saw an empty seat next to Margaret Hastings, the second-to-last spot on the plane's left-hand side, near the tail.

Margaret knew John McCollom from his regular visits to Colonel Prossen's office. She also remembered how months earlier he had equipped her tent with a double electrical socket.

'Mind if I share this window with you?' he asked.

Margaret shouted her assent over the engines.

The *Gremlin Special* was full. As the door closed, Margaret noticed that the soldier who had complained about the women boarding first was not among them.

Five

Eureka!

AT TWO-FIFTEEN P.M., WITH COLONEL PROSSEN AT the controls, the *Gremlin Special* rumbled past the palm trees lining the runway at the Sentani Airstrip and lifted off into a clear blue sky. As the plane passed over Lake Sentani, the passengers twisted in their seats for a look at the shimmering blue waters and the green hills that rolled down to the lake's edge. Prossen guided the plane towards the Oranje Mountains, setting a course directly to the valley. He announced over the intercom that it would take fifty-five minutes to get there.

A WAC sitting near the cockpit chanted, 'Oh, what is so rare as a June day in May?' invoking a medieval knight's quest for the Holy Grail. Her chant quoted the sentiment if not the exact words of a century-old epic poem, 'The Vision of Sir Launfal', by James Russell Lowell, which asked, 'And what is so rare as a day in June?' Just as appropriate were other lines of the poem, which read:

Joy comes, grief goes, we know not how;
Every thing is happy now,
Every thing is upward striving;
'Tis as easy now for the heart to be true,
As for grass to be green or skies to be blue.

Glued to the window, Margaret looked down through puffy white clouds. She thought the lush jungle below looked as soft as green feathers that would cushion a fall from even that great height. In the distance, the passengers could see snow-topped Mount Wilhelmina, named for the Dutch queen, at 4730 metres the highest peak in the range.

John McCollom was more curious about the *Gremlin Special*'s altitude and directional heading. He estimated that they were flying at about 2000 metres, and he learned from the crew that they were on a heading of 224 degrees, or due southwest from the base. That course would take them to the northwest end of Shangri-La, to the narrow pass through the mountains discovered by Major Grimes a year earlier.

As they cruised towards the valley, Colonel Prossen made a fateful decision: he unbuckled his seat belt and walked back into the cabin. The point of the trip, after all, was to let his staff know that he cared about them and their morale. This was a bonding opportunity, a chance for them to see Shangri-La together. Yet, in light of the uncharted mountains, the changeable weather, and the relative inexperience of his co-pilot, Prossen's move from the pilot's seat was ill-advised.

Both Prossen and Nicholson were making their first flights to Shangri-La. All they knew about the treacherous entrance through the mountain pass was what they had read or heard from other pilots. By leaving the cockpit and trusting the most difficult part of the flight to his co-pilot,

Colonel Peter Prossen.

Prossen was underestimating the risks or disregarding them altogether. Moreover, with Prossen occupied by administrative tasks in his Fee-Ask job, and with Nicholson new to New Guinea, it is not clear how often, if ever, they had previously flown together. Perhaps most troubling of all was that Prossen disregarded Elsmore's warning about the dangers that would confront 'a pilot unfamiliar with this canyon'.

The C-47 had seat belts for passengers, but when the socializing started after take-off at least some were unfastened. Most of the passengers were members of Prossen's maintenance division at Fee-Ask, so they knew each other and fell into easy conversation. Prossen joined the camaraderie, standing in the narrow radio compartment that separated the cockpit from the passenger cabin.

Looking into the cockpit, John McCollom noticed that Helen Kent had walked forward from the cabin. The curvaceous WAC had plopped into the left-hand seat left vacant by Prossen, to enjoy an unobstructed view out the front windscreen. Next to her, the co-pilot, Major Nicholson, was alone at the controls.

Nearly an hour into the flight, the *Gremlin Special* snuck over a ridge, dropped a couple of hundred metres, and entered a narrow valley that was an offshoot of the main valley of Shangri-La. The plane flew at about 2000 metres above sea level, or some 400 metres above the valley floor. Jungle-covered mountains flanked the *Gremlin Special* on both sides. Nicholson eased the control wheel forward, and he guided the *Gremlin Special* down to an altitude of about 300 metres above the valley floor. The drop continued. Soon they were flying at less than 120 metres over the ground.

'Eureka!' cried an over-eager WAC.

The passengers whirled around to the windows and saw a small native village – a cluster of mushroom-shaped huts with thatched roofs, surrounded by carefully marked, well-tended fields of sweet potato. Margaret was thrilled, but she had not seen any natives. Not realizing that this was only a small settlement in a side valley – the huge valley of Shangri-La was another sixteen to twenty-five kilometres ahead – she felt cheated.

Turning to John McCollom, she complained: 'I want to come again!'

McCollom wasn't listening. His head was turned sharply to the left as he stared into the cockpit. Looking through the windscreen, he saw clouds dead ahead. Through the whiteness, he saw snatches of dark green jungle covering a mountain he estimated at 3500 or 4000 metres. In the parlance of pilots, the cloud had a rock in it.

McCollom's body stiffened. 'Give her the gun and let's get out of here,' he shouted towards the cockpit.

Margaret and some of the other passengers thought he was joking. But Major Nicholson knew it was no joke; he had already recognized the risk.

As a licensed pilot, McCollom knew that the first rule of mountain flying was always to be in a position to turn. But this valley was too narrow for Nicholson to try. That left only one option. Nicholson gripped the control wheel and pulled sharply back. With Prossen standing in the radio compartment, and Sergeant Helen Kent still enjoying the view, the young major was on his own.

Nicholson pointed the plane's nose skyward, desperate to clear the fast-approaching ridge. McCollom watched Nicholson thrust the throttles forward, applying full power to climb. As Nicholson strained to gain altitude, McCollom spun around to look out the window by his seat. Through holes in the clouds he glimpsed trees below, their highest branches reaching up towards the belly of the *Gremlin Special*. He was certain that the clouds obstructed Nicholson's view out the front windscreen. He was flying without the aid of his more experienced superior, but he was also guiding the plane blind, relying on the instrument panel arrayed before him. That, and gut survival instinct.

No one can say with certainty what brought the *Gremlin Special* and its twenty-four passengers and crew to this perilous moment. A mechanical malfunction – the work of gremlins – was possible, though that appears highly unlikely. More likely was a combination of factors that included Prossen leaving the cockpit, errors by Nicholson, and the inherent difficulty of flying into the valley called Shangri-La.

Based largely on what John McCollom witnessed and what happened next, it appears that Nicholson, who had learned to fly only three years earlier, grew momentarily disoriented or misjudged the situation when he flew low through the small valley. But the threat to the *Gremlin Special* might have been exaggerated by conditions beyond Nicholson's control.

As Nicholson fought to gain altitude, it is possible a powerful gust of wind swept down on the C-47. Turbulent air was common in canyons and narrow valleys. Winds rushed over one edge and raced down to the valley floor, creating downdraughts, then raced back up the other side, creating updraughts. Sudden, short-lived updraughts and downdraughts often appeared without warning. The high-altitude valleys and canyons of New Guinea were especially treacherous. One reason was the ragged terrain. Another was rapid changes in air temperature, a result of jungle heat rising into the cumulus clouds that routinely formed over and around the peaks in mid-afternoon.

If a downdraught did occur at that moment, the twenty-four people aboard the *Gremlin Special* might have been in mortal danger no matter who was at the controls. An official military account of the flight later suggested that 'a sudden down-draft of air current' apparently stymied the pilots' effort to gain altitude.*

As Nicholson struggled and McCollom worried, Margaret felt no sense of danger. She had been so engrossed in the sight of the native huts that she had not noticed that Colonel Prossen had given his seat to Helen Kent and was standing outside the cockpit. Margaret felt the nose of the plane rise, but she was unaware that Nicholson was flying alone. She thought that Prossen was merely gaining altitude to fly through a high pass between the mountains that she had glimpsed earlier.

* However, the account was incomplete. It made no mention of Prossen's absence from the cockpit or the apparent mistakes by Nicholson.

At the controls, Nicholson could not make the plane bend to his wishes. The *Gremlin Special* began to shear the tops of giant tropical evergreens, their limbs and leaves scratching and smacking and cracking against the plane's camouflage-painted, sheet-metal skin. Even if Prossen grasped what was happening, as he surely must have, he had no time to race back to his seat, evict Helen Kent, and take over.

Still, Margaret remained calm. Her confidence in her boss was so complete that for a split-second she thought Prossen had buzzed the treetops to give his passengers a thrill – flying 'flat on the deck' as pilots called it.

John McCollom knew better. He grabbed Margaret's arm.

'This is going to be darn close,' he told her, 'but I think we can get over it.'

His optimism was misplaced. Shortly after three o'clock in the afternoon on Sunday, 13 May 1945, Major George Nicholson's desperate struggle to gain altitude ended. The distance between the C-47 and the unforgiving terrain closed to zero. To the ear-splitting din of metal twisting, glass shattering, engines groaning, branches snapping, fuel igniting, bodies tumbling, lives ending, the *Gremlin Special* plunged through the trees and slammed into the jungle-covered mountainside.

The cabin crumpled forward towards the cockpit. The walls of the fuselage collapsed as though sucked inward. Both wings ripped away. The tail section snapped off like a balsa-wood toy. Flames shot through the wreckage. Small explosions rang out like gunshots. Black smoke choked off the light. The air grew bitter with the stench of burning metal, burning leather, burning rubber, burning wires, burning oil, burning clothes, burning hair. Burning flesh.

One small mercy was that Nicholson had managed to point the nose of the plane skyward in his attempt to clear the ridge, so the C-47 hit the mountain at an upward angle instead of head-on. As a result, although fire rushed through the cabin, the *Gremlin Special* didn't explode on contact. Anyone not immediately killed or mortally wounded might stand a chance.

When the plane burrowed through the trees, John McCollom flew across the centre aisle, from the left side of the plane to the right. He lurched forward, turning somersaults as he fell, and momentarily blacked out. When he came to, he was on his hands and knees halfway up the cabin towards the cockpit, surrounded by flames. Driven by instinct, he searched for an escape route. He saw a flash of white light where the tail had been. The roof of the cabin had flattened down like a tin can, so he was not able to stand. He crawled towards the light, landing on the scorched earth of the mountain jungle, disoriented but with barely a scratch.

McCollom began to comprehend the horror of what had happened. He thought about his twin brother and the twenty-two others on board – all trapped inside and dead, he believed. As he rose to his feet outside the broken plane, he told himself: 'This is a heck of a place to be, a hundred-and-sixty-five miles from civilization, all by myself on a Sunday afternoon.'

Margaret bounced through the cabin like a rubber ball. Her first impulse was to pray. But that felt like surrender, and Margaret was not the surrendering type. She grew angry. She knew this was not rational, but as she tumbled she took it personally, indignant that her trip had been spoiled by a plane crash. And she still had not seen any natives.

When she stopped tumbling and regained her senses, Margaret found herself lying on top of a motionless man. Her fall had been cushioned by his body. She tried to move, but before he died the man had somehow wrapped his thick arms around her. Whether he had tried to save her or simply grabbed on to whatever was closest to him was not clear. Either way, Margaret was locked in a dead man's grip. She felt flames licking at her face, feet and legs. The air filled with the acrid scent of sizzling hair. Again Margaret thought of relaxing, giving up. Then her fury returned, and with it her strength.

She pried loose the man's hands and began to crawl. She had no idea whom she was leaving behind or which way she was heading – back to the missing tail or ahead to the crushed cockpit and into the inferno. As she crawled towards her hoped-for salvation, she didn't see anyone else moving or hear anyone speaking or moaning inside the burning cabin. Whether by luck or divine intervention, she chose the right direction for escape.

Margaret stumbled out the torn-open rear end of the fuselage on to the jungle floor.

'My God! Hastings!' called John McCollom, who had come out the same way less than a minute earlier.

Before Margaret could answer, McCollom heard a WAC scream from inside the plane: 'Get me out of here!'

The *Gremlin Special* was now fully aflame. McCollom doubted it would explode but he could not be sure. Without hesitating, he scrambled back inside, crouching beneath the smoke and fire, avoiding and ignoring the heat as best he could. He inched his way along, following the WAC's pleading voice.

'Give me your hand!' he ordered.

A moment later, Margaret watched as McCollom led out her friend Laura Besley. McCollom placed the WAC sergeant on the fire-seared ground, turned around, and headed back inside the burning fuselage.

He fought his way through the smoke towards Eleanor Hanna, who had sat next to Laura Besley directly across from him and Margaret. Eleanor had been badly burned, far worse than Margaret or Laura. Her hair still crackled with burning embers when he carried her out.

By now, McCollom's hands were scorched and his hair was singed from rescuing the two WACs. Otherwise, remarkably, he remained unhurt. Still, it was not possible to go back for a third rescue mission – the fire raged higher and hotter, and one explosion after another echoed from inside the wreckage. He doubted anyone inside could still be alive.

Startled by a movement, McCollom looked up and saw a man walk woozily towards him from around the right side of the plane. Any hope that it was his twin brother quickly faded. He recognized Sergeant Kenneth Decker – McCollom supervised Decker's work in the drafting room of the Fee-Ask maintenance department. Decker was on his feet but dazed and badly hurt. Margaret saw a bloody gash several inches long on the right side of Decker's forehead, deep enough to expose the grey bone of his skull. Another cut leaked blood on the left side of his forehead. Burns seared both legs and his backside. His right arm was cocked stiffly from a broken elbow. Yet somehow Decker was on his feet and moving towards them.

'My God, Decker, where did you come from?' McCollom asked.

Decker couldn't answer. He would never regain any memory of what happened between take-off at the Sentani Airstrip and when he crawled out from under the plane to his deliverance in the jungle. Later, McCollom would find a hole on the side of the fuselage and conclude that Decker had escaped through it, though he also thought it possible that the sergeant had been catapulted through the cockpit and out through the windscreen.

As he walked unsteadily towards McCollom and Margaret, Decker repeatedly muttered, 'Helluva way to spend your birthday.'

Margaret thought he was talking gibberish from the blows he had taken to the head. Only later would she learn that Decker was born on 13 May 1911, and this really was his thirty-fourth birthday.

Turning back to the three surviving WACs, McCollom saw Margaret standing fixed in place, apparently in shock. He set aside his hollowness, his feelings of unspeakable grief at being alone for the first time in his life. The situation was clear. McCollom was the least injured among the five survivors, and though he was only a first lieutenant, he outranked Decker and the three women. McCollom steeled himself and assumed command.

He snapped: 'Hastings, can't you do something for these girls?'

Laura Besley and Eleanor Hanna were next to each other, lying on the ground where McCollom had placed them. Margaret knelt by Eleanor. She did not seem to be in pain, but Margaret knew it was too late to help her. The fire had seared off all Eleanor's clothes, leaving her with vicious burns across her body. Only her cherubic, fair-skinned face was unscarred.

Eleanor looked up with pleading eyes and offered Margaret a weak smile.

'Let's sing,' she said. They tried, but neither could make a sound.

Laura Besley was crying uncontrollably, but Margaret and McCollom couldn't understand why. She seemed to have suffered only superficial burns.

McCollom heard someone yell. He scrambled around the right side of the plane to a spot where he could see another officer, Captain Herbert Good, lying on the ground. McCollom knew that he was the reason that Good was aboard the *Gremlin Special*. That morning, McCollom had bumped into Good at the base in Hollandia. Affable as always, McCollom asked Good, a member of General

MacArthur's staff, whether he had afternoon plans. Good was free, so McCollom invited him to join in the fun on a trip to Shangri-La.

Captain Good looked unhurt, so McCollom beckoned him to join the other survivors. Good didn't seem to hear him, so McCollom started fighting through the smouldering undergrowth in his direction. Decker followed, not fully alert but instinctively wanting to help and to stay close to McCollom.

As they edged closer to Good, flames exploded from fuel tanks in the torn-off wings, which had remained close to the fuselage. When the flames subsided, McCollom rushed to Good but it was too late – he was dead. When McCollom reached Good's body, he learned why the captain had not moved when McCollom first called: his foot was tangled in the roots of a tree.

There was nothing they could do. They left Good's body where it fell, hunched on the ground amid brush and branches a metre or so from the wrecked plane, his head tilted awkwardly to one side. Good's right arm, bent at the elbow, reached downward towards the moist ground.

No one else emerged alive from the C-47 *Gremlin Special*, bound for Shangri-La on a Sunday afternoon pleasure flight.

Gone was Colonel Peter J. Prossen, who'd begun that day worried about his wife and children in Texas and his staff in Dutch New Guinea. In a few days, the letter he'd written that morning would arrive in San Antonio – his family would receive Mother's Day greetings from a dead man.

Gone was the co-pilot, Major George H. Nicholson Jr, a Massachusetts junior high school teacher who days earlier had written so elegantly to his wife about battles in Europe that he'd never seen.

Gone was WAC Sergeant Helen Kent of Taft, California, who'd left behind her dear friend Ruth Coster. When she

The body of Captain Herbert Good, photographed approximately two weeks after the crash.

learned what happened, a devastated Ruth would find it tragically appropriate that Helen had died in the pilot's seat, just as Helen's husband Earl had perished when his plane went down eighteen months earlier over Europe.

Gone, too, was Sergeant Belle Naimer of the Bronx, who joined her fiancé as a casualty of a wartime air crash. Gone were four other WACs: Sergeant Marion W. McMonagle of Philadelphia; Private Alethia M. Fair of Hollywood, California; Private Marian Gillis of Los Angeles; and Private Mary M. Landau of Brooklyn.

Gone were the plane's three enlisted crew members: Sergeant Hilliard Norris of Waynesville, North Carolina; Private George R. Newcomer of Middletown, New York; and Private Melvin 'Molly' Mollberg of Baudette, Minnesota, who'd volunteered to take his best friend's place on the flight crew.

Gone were the male passengers: Major Herman F. Antonini, twenty-nine years old, of Danville, Illinois; Major Phillip J. Dattilo, thirty-one, of Louisville, Kentucky; Captain Louis E. Freyman, who would have turned twenty-nine the next day, of Hammond, Indiana; First Lieutenant Lawrence F. Holding, twenty-three, of Raleigh, North Carolina; Corporal Charles R. Miller, thirty-six, of Saint Joseph, Michigan; and Corporal Melvyn Weber, twenty-eight, of Compton, California.

The bodies inside the *Gremlin Special* were cremated by the flames, making the wreckage a funeral pyre and a mass grave for the passengers and crew killed inside the cockpit and cabin.

Yet amid the ashes, a gold wedding ring with a white inlay somehow survived intact. Inscribed on the inside of the band were two sets of initials, 'CAC' and 'REM'. When the ring was discovered years later inside the wreckage, it provided final proof of John McCollom's agonizing realization during those first minutes in the mountain jungle. After twenty-six inseparable years, his twin brother was dead.

Six

Charms

MOURNING WOULD WAIT. AS MCCOLLOM AND Decker stood over Good's body, the exploding fuel tanks spread the fire closer to the three surviving women, threatening to trap them in a ring of flames.

Margaret saw the impending danger. She yelled to McCollom, who was still being shadowed by the woozy Decker: 'Lieutenant McCollom, we have to get out of here. We're going to be surrounded by fire if we don't.'

Even as he hurried, searching for a path to safety, McCollom fought to maintain composure. No one under his command would panic. He responded calmly: 'You're all right.'

Margaret saw a small rock ledge at the edge of a cliff, some twenty metres down the jungle-covered mountain from the wreckage. She clawed her way towards it. From the sky, the rainforest had looked to Margaret like an inviting green cushion, but now on the ground she discovered it was something else entirely – a botanist's dream and a crash survivor's nightmare.

Covering its rocky, muddy, uneven floor was a snarling mesh of giant ferns, vines, shrubs, fallen tree trunks, and spongy mosses, always wet. Thorns and spines and saw-toothed leaves ensnared her legs and tore her clothes and skin. Huge rhododendron bushes filled the spaces where light shone through a multilayered canopy of leaves. Above her head was a jumble of trees – giant eucalyptus, banyan, palm, bamboo, yoli myrtle, scrub oak, pandanus, tropical chestnut, soaring araucaria pines, evergreen casuarina, and hundreds of other species – some more prominent at higher altitudes, some at lower, the tallest of them reaching more than thirty metres into the sky.

Gnarled webs of thick, woody vines, heavy beards of lichen, spindly climbers, and aptly named strangler figs knitted the trees to one another and hung from branches like beaded curtains. Orchids sprouted everywhere, in hundreds of species, with flaming colours and strange, erotic shapes. The lush flora created a luxuriant bouquet, as the jungle carried out its endless cycle of birth, growth, decay, death, and new birth.

In the skies and the trees were hawks, owls, parrots, rails, swifts, flycatchers, warblers, and perhaps the most wondrous avian creatures in Shangri-La: colour-drenched birds of paradise. The jungle had no predatory mammals, but rodents and small marsupials scurried in the under-brush. Salamanders, lizards, and snakes worthy of Eden, notably a python that grew to four and a half metres or more, represented the reptile kingdom.

Many of the natural wonders had never been seen by anyone other than natives. Margaret could have discovered new species simply by reaching out her hand. But in a diary Margaret began to keep shortly after the crash, she admitted that she was too preoccupied to appreciate the show. 'Everything in the jungle had tentacles,' she wrote, 'and I was too busy fighting them to enjoy nature.'

As Margaret climbed over the fat trunk of a tree mowed down by the plane, it dawned on her that she was not wearing shoes – they had either been blown off or burned away. She stopped in her tracks, sat down on the tree's jagged stump, and took stock. She pulled off her half-socks to inspect her feet. Her right foot was badly cut and bleeding. To her surprise, her left sock didn't have a mark on it, but the sole of her left foot was burned – heat had passed through the fabric to sear her skin. Both legs had deep burns, and her right hand was cut and bloody. The left side of her face had blistered from the heat.

Margaret pulled off her khaki shirt. After that came her cotton bra. She put her shirt back on, then tore the bra in half and tried to bandage her feet, though it did little good. Margaret unbuttoned her trousers, slipped them down her burned legs, and set them aside. She bent over and pulled off the mud-brown Rayon underwear that was standard issue for WACs – white underwear was banned by the Army, out of fear that it would attract enemy bombers when hanging out to dry on jungle clotheslines. Margaret pulled her trousers back on over her naked bottom. She intended to use her panties' silky fabric to make bandages for herself and the other survivors.

As she finished dressing, Margaret saw McCollom leading the way down the rough path she had followed minutes beforehand, carrying Eleanor Hanna on his back, her arms draped over his shoulders. Eleanor's clothes had been burned off, but somehow her Chinese coin bracelet still dangled from her wrist. On the way down, McCollom lost his footing, slipped, and landed awkwardly on a small tree. He picked himself up, brushed himself off, and pulled Eleanor on to his back once more. McCollom emerged from the crash unhurt, but he had just suffered his first injury: a broken rib. He told no one.

Ken Decker and Laura Besley trailed close behind. When all five survivors were together, Margaret still wasn't thinking clearly. Although she had removed her underpants to make bandages, she immediately forgot about that plan. She asked McCollom for a handkerchief, which she used to wrap her lacerated hand, binding it tight to stem the bleeding.

As they walked on, Decker tried to help McCollom with Eleanor Hanna. When they reached the ledge Margaret had seen, the five of them sat, catching their breath, collecting themselves and thinking about what had happened – to them, to their friends, and in McCollom's case, to his beloved twin. They were about 2700 metres above sea level, and as they sat there, the late afternoon temperature began to fall. Rain followed, and they learned firsthand why the jungle was called a rainforest. Small trees gave them some cover, but after a short time their clothes soaked through to their skin, chilling them to the bone and compounding their misery.

After a brief rest, McCollom and Decker left the three women on the ledge and climbed back up towards the wreckage. McCollom's survival training kicked into gear. He hoped to find supplies to build a shelter, and also food, clothing and weapons. He had a lighter and a small pocketknife he carried everywhere, but those would not be much use if they ran into the giant, spear-carrying natives they had expected to see only from the air.

McCollom recalled that one of the plane's crew members carried a .45 calibre pistol. He had also noticed that the plane carried blankets, jugs of water, and crates of Cracker Jack-sized boxes of 'K' rations. The ready-to-eat meals might include dishes such as ham and cheese, or beef and pork loaf; hard biscuits or crackers; bouillon cubes; instant coffee; powdered lemon drinks; heat-resistant chocolate bars; hard candy; small packs of cigarettes, books of matches, and chewing gum. Some K rations might contain one of the greatest military luxuries of all: toilet paper.

But when McCollom and Decker reached the plane, they knew none of those items could be salvaged. The cockpit and much of the cabin were still on fire. Fed by the plane's fuel, the wreckage would burn until the middle of the next day. The fire guaranteed that nothing would be left intact that had not already been destroyed by a series of explosions following a 320-kilometres-per-hour crash into a tree-covered mountain. As McCollom surveyed the scene, he understood that in one sense they had been lucky. On one side of the wreckage was a 4.5-metre boulder; if they had hit the rock head-on, no one would have survived.

Another piece of relatively good news was that the *Gremlin Special*'s tail section, after separating on impact, had not caught fire or exploded. The tail rested at an odd angle by a ravine, jammed against a tree stump and swathed in vines at the edge of a steep drop. The jagged opening where the tail had torn away from the rest of the plane pointed upward towards the sky, like the hungry mouth of a baby bird.

McCollom climbed up to the tail's opening and pulled himself inside. He found a duffel bag with a bright yellow self-inflating life raft, two heavy tarpaulins designed as covers for the open raft, and a few basic supplies. He tossed the bag outside and climbed out. He inflated the life raft and took inventory of the supplies. He counted several small tins of water and a First-Aid kit with bandages, a few vials of morphine, vitamins, boric acid to disinfect wounds, and sulphathiazole tablets to fight infection. The only food was 'Charms', fruit-flavoured sucking sweets made from sugar and corn syrup that were a staple of soldiers' rations. McCollom found a signalling mirror and, even better, a signal pistol he could use to draw the attention of searchers. There was just one problem: he could not find any flares.

McCollom and Decker hauled the life raft and supplies over towards the ledge. Along the way, the raft snagged on something sharp and deflated. When they reached the women, they cleaned and bandaged their wounds and gave them shots of water to wash down the anti-infection tablets. McCollom put the flattened life raft under Laura Besley and Eleanor Hanna and covered them with a tarpaulin. As he tucked them in, Eleanor smiled. Again, she said, 'Let's sing.' McCollom gave her morphine, hoping it would help her to sleep.

The ledge was too small for all five survivors to stretch out, so Margaret and the two men moved a few metres away to another ledge. Exhausted, they wrapped themselves in the second tarpaulin. A pack of cigarettes had survived the crash in McCollom's pocket, so he flicked his lighter and they shared a few drags in silence. As darkness fell, they could see through the hanging vines and thick foliage that the plane was still aflame. They huddled together, bracing for a cold, wet night.

Several times that first night in the jungle, they heard a plane overhead and caught a glimpse of signal flares. But they had no way to let the searchers know they were alive under the thick canopy. Margaret wasn't even sure the lights were flares; they were so far off she thought they might be lightning. They talked hopefully about rescue. Privately, McCollom had already started to contemplate the challenge of walking the 240 kilometres to Hollandia.

Now and then, in the inky black night, the jungle erupted with noises that sounded to the survivors like the yaps and barks of wild dogs.

The next morning, McCollom rose first and went to check on Eleanor Hanna and Laura Besley. As he knelt by the injured WACs, he was not surprised by what he found.

'Eleanor's dead,' he said quietly.

McCollom carefully wrapped her body in a tarpaulin. They had no tools for burial, and no energy to try, so he laid the remains of Eleanor Hanna at the base of a nearby tree.

The silence was broken by Laura Besley, who had sat next to Eleanor on the plane and slept beside her all night: 'I can't stop shaking,' she said.

Hurt and in shock, chilled and wet, thirsty and hungry, sore and tired, Margaret and Decker realized that they were shaking, too.

They couldn't do anything about Eleanor, and there was little they could do for themselves or each other. McCollom resolved to ration their water, so they each took a few sips with a vitamin pill and a few Charms to tide them over. Their shaking continued.

After their paltry breakfast, McCollom and Decker returned to the plane. Back in the tail section, they found two cots, another life raft, two more large yellow tarps and one small one, two compasses, a heavy cotton flying suit, more First-Aid kits, another signalling mirror, and seventeen cans of water, each one containing about one cup of liquid. Decker dug into a tool kit and brought out a roll of black electrical tape and a pair of pliers. They carried their bounty back to the ledge.

Laura's crying and shaking continued, though she didn't complain of being in pain. McCollom gave her the flight suit for warmth and told her to lie on one of the cots. She was thirsty and wanted water, but each time she drank she would spit it up. She looked fine, and her burns seemed superficial. McCollom feared she had suffered internal injuries.

Margaret took a closer look at her legs and discovered rings of burned skin, three to six inches wide, around each calf. To her surprise, they weren't as painful as they looked. Her bandaged feet, however, hurt more with every step on the jungle floor. Margaret asked Laura if she could borrow her shoes while Laura rested. Laura gave them to her.

In Margaret's diary, written in secretarial shorthand on scraps of paper and cardboard from their supplies, she confessed that she did not want to return her friend's shoes. Later, upon rewriting and expanding the diary, she wrote: 'Secretly, I wondered if – without shoes – I would ever be able to keep up with the others. I would have to give Laura's shoes back to her before we started down the mountain. I was frightened that I would never be able to make it through the jungle in feet covered only by half sox and a layer of cotton bandage.'

The survivors had felt confident that Army search planes would be dispatched when the *Gremlin Special* failed to return to Sentani Airstrip as scheduled. That belief had been confirmed the night before when they heard a plane flying somewhere above them. But McCollom knew they were not visible in their current location. Their plane was a demolished, camouflage-painted speck in a dense swath of trees and vines. Still visible on the detached tail section was a five-pointed white star – the signature emblem of a United States military plane. But the leaves and fronds overhead made it impossible to see except from a short distance. From the air, the star was as inconsequential as a flower petal in the ocean.

Smoke from the wreckage might help to place the survivors' location, but only if searchers spotted it before the flames died. Complicating matters was the fact that although Prossen's flight plan listed his destination as Shangri-La, the *Gremlin Special* crashed into a mountain miles from the pass that led into the valley. Alone at the controls and consumed by trying to keep the plane aloft, Nicholson had not placed a Mayday call. In fact, no radio communication was exchanged between the plane and ground controllers at the base at any time after Prossen took off from the Sentani Airstrip.

Decker's wristwatch had fared better than his skull, so they knew how slowly time was passing. At about eleven o'clock on Monday morning, less than twenty-four hours after the crash, they heard the distinctive sound of an engine. McCollom grabbed the signalling mirror and worked it furiously to flash snatches of sunlight skyward. It was no use. The engine sound grew faint as the plane flew away.

Still, McCollom considered it a hopeful sign. 'Don't worry,' he assured his companions. 'I don't know how, but they'll get us out.'

Mist settled over the mountain by mid-afternoon, and with it came steady rain. They talked about their families, and Margaret dreaded to think how her father would take the news that her plane had crashed and she was missing. Margaret told her diary she felt relieved that her mother had been spared the anxiety of learning that her eldest daughter was lost in Dutch New Guinea. It was the first time she had felt at peace with her mother's death.

Margaret's middle name was Julia – her mother's first name. Margaret's youngest sister believed that Margaret was their mother's favourite. In a school essay, Margaret described her mother as 'the sweetest, kindest and the most lovable little woman who ever lived. My father, my two younger sisters and I all lived at home, and she was the very hub of our existence. At fifty-five she was a tiny woman, with silvery white hair, pink and white skin, fine features – much prettier than any of her daughters.'

In the essay, Margaret described how she'd learned from a doctor that her mother was seriously ill and would live no more than a year. 'Onto my shoulders, so unaccustomed to responsibility, was thrown suddenly the problem of deciding how this crisis should be met. Should I tell my younger sisters, my father and my mother's brothers and sisters? For days I debated the question pro and con, and finally decided to act in the way which would cause Mother the least unhappiness. I was sure she didn't want to die – not when she was having so much fun for the first time in her life. I didn't feel sure that I could rely on my sisters to act normally if they knew the truth, so I told only my father. To this day I don't know whether I was right or wrong, but the decision was mine to make, and I did what I thought best.'

Her mother died three months later.

At about three that afternoon, the four remaining survivors felt exhausted from their injuries, the lack of food, and the little sleep they had managed the night before. They set up the two camp beds.

Margaret and Laura shared one, pulling a tarp over themselves and hugging tightly to keep from falling off. Margaret lay there, trying to sleep while at the same time listening for search planes overhead. Laura couldn't stop tossing, so McCollom gave her morphine and tucked the tarp tightly around her. Margaret's eyes burned from fatigue and she was eager to sleep, but even after the morphine Laura remained restless. Her squirms on the narrow camp bed kept Margaret awake.

Hanging in the air was a rhetorical question Laura had posed to McCollom as he had tucked her in. Looking up from the camp bed, she had asked: 'Everyone else is dead and we're very lonely, aren't we?'

Eventually, Margaret drifted into a fitful sleep. When she awoke around midnight, she felt an unexpected stillness. Laura had stopped fidgeting. Now, pressed against Margaret on the camp bed, Laura seemed too quiet. Margaret put her hand on Laura's chest. Nothing. She searched her friend's neck for a pulse. Again nothing.

Margaret screamed: 'Please, McCollom, please come. Laura has died!'

Roused from much-needed sleep, McCollom suspected that Margaret was overreacting. Clearly Laura was hurt, and her inability to keep down water was a bad sign. But he thought her injuries weren't life-threatening. Decker was doubly sure, and he did not hide his annoyance.

'Don't be a dope, Hastings,' Decker replied. 'She's all right.'

McCollom walked to the cot and felt Laura's hands. Doubt crept into his mind. He searched in vain for a pulse. Margaret was right.

Without a word, McCollom lifted Laura Besley's body from the cot. He wrapped her remains in one of the tarps and placed it alongside Eleanor Hanna's corpse at the foot of a tree.

Even in their grief Margaret and McCollom knew how fortunate they had been. Margaret had changed seats for a better view, and McCollom had boarded too late to sit alongside his brother. They ended up in the last two seats on the left side of the plane. They lived. Laura Besley and Eleanor Hanna, who had sat across from them, died.

'I ought to have cried,' Margaret wrote in her diary. 'I ought to have felt some kind of terrible grief for this dear friend. But all I could do was sit on the cot and shake. I couldn't even think that Laura was dead. I just sat there and shook and all I could think was: "Now the shoes belong to me."'

The death toll had reached twenty-one. The survivors of the *Gremlin Special* were down to three: McCollom, at twenty-six years old, was the youngest of the three, but he held the highest rank and suffered the fewest injuries. Combined with his quiet competence, those qualities made him the group's natural leader.

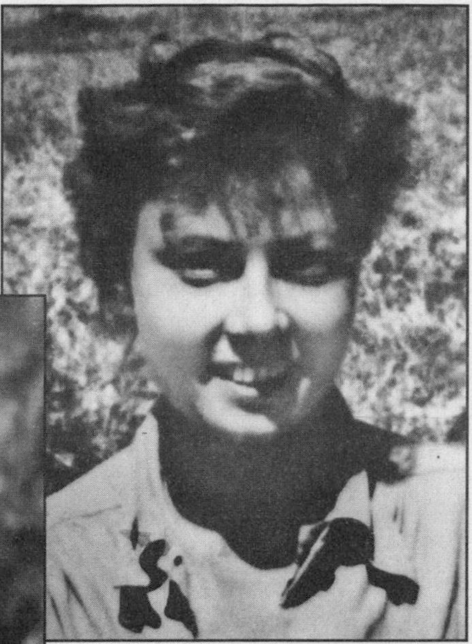

After the crash: Margaret Hastings, Kenneth Decker and John McCollom.

The three survivors had known each other casually around the base, but were hardly close friends. As they rested in the shadow of their burning plane, they considered themselves no more than comrades and acquaintances who had shared a horrible experience. For the time being, they would follow Army protocol and call each other by rank, last name, or both, but not by first name.

But women in the military were still a novelty, and calling a woman by her last name didn't always come naturally. Unless McCollom was giving her an order or Decker was needling her, 'Corporal Hastings' soon became 'Maggie'. The truth was, she preferred to be called Margaret – she hated the nickname Maggie. But she never complained or corrected them.

After wrapping Laura Besley's body, McCollom returned to Margaret, who had remained fixed on the camp bed. He lit a cigarette and handed it to her. Then he sat next to her to share it. She wrote in her diary: 'No night will ever again be as long as this one.'

As the hours passed, McCollom lit several more cigarettes, the smouldering orange tip moving back and forth between them in the darkness. He remained with her until dawn. They did not speak.

Seven

Tarzan

THE NEXT MORNING, MCCOLLOM CONTINUED HIS treks between the rock ledge and the wreckage. On one trip, he climbed a tree and surveyed the area. He saw what looked like a clearing several kilometres away. Using a compass he had found in the plane's detached tail, McCollom plotted a course they could follow to reach it. With his companions' injuries festering, and with little water and no food but hard sucking candies, they needed to get to the clearing as soon as Margaret and Decker felt strong enough to walk.

Plane crash survivors are usually told to remain with the wreckage to increase their likelihood of being found. But the usual rules rarely applied in New Guinea. McCollom recognized that if they remained where they were, hidden under the jungle canopy, they faced certain death. Even if they reached the clearing, the likelihood of rescue seemed slim.

New Guinea's jungles were boundless cemeteries of unmarked military graves. In April 1944, when the wife of a missing Army Air Forces pilot sought information about her husband's prospects, an officer wrote back with unusual candour: 'It is necessary to cross high mountain ranges on practically every flight made on the island. Thick jungle growth goes right up to the tops of the peaks and entire squadrons could completely disappear under this foliage. No matter how thorough the search is, the possibility of locating the plane is rather remote. We have had numerous other instances of like nature and no word has come concerning those crews or airplanes. The weather and terrain account for more airplanes than combat flying.'

More than six hundred Allied planes had crashed on the island since the start of the war, some in combat but many from rough weather, mechanical failures, pilot error, uncharted mountains hiding in clouds, or some combination. Hundreds more planes from Japan, Australia, Great Britain, New Zealand and the Netherlands had crashed on New Guinea, as well. Some were located after they went down, but many were concealed by the emerald-green rainforests. By 1945, New Guinea was home to more missing aeroplanes than any country on earth.

Two and a half years earlier, in November 1942, a severe downdraught struck an American C-47 delivering troops and supplies to another part of the island. The plane crashed into a mountain at 2700 metres, into conditions almost identical to those encountered by the survivors of the *Gremlin Special*. Search planes flew one sortie after another, but found no trace of the C-47, which was nicknamed the *Flying Dutchman*.

Seventeen of the twenty-three men aboard survived the crash, though some had severe injuries. When no rescuers arrived, eight men felt fit enough to attempt to walk out of the jungle. They split up, leaving the crash site in two groups of four. On the fifth day of their trek, the first group came to a narrow gorge with a fast-moving river. It was not possible to cross, so they tried to ride logs down the rapids. Two drowned. The other two eventually met friendly natives, who guided them from village to village. After thirty-two arduous days, they arrived at an Allied base. The second group had an easier time. They received help from natives after ten days, and within a month all four were safely out of the jungle.

The reappearance of survivors from the *Flying Dutchman* triggered a new search for the injured men left behind, but that failed, too. As a last-ditch effort, a reward was offered to any natives who discovered the wreck. More than sixty days after the crash, a group of natives came across a cluster of decaying bodies and a lone survivor, an Army chaplain described in one account as 'blind from malnutrition and so light that he "felt like a baby"'. Around him was a bare semi-circle of dirt – near the end of his ordeal, he had sustained himself by eating mountain moss within his reach. The natives offered him cooked banana, but he died in their arms. They left his body, but brought back his Bible as proof that they had located the *Flying Dutchman*.

Long after, searchers returned to the wreck and found a rear cargo door where the survivors had kept a makeshift diary written in charcoal. The first entries were simple reports with an almost military tone. Each entry was a few words long, noting when the crash occurred, when each group of healthy survivors left, how the remaining men had tried to launch a balloon to attract searchers, and what food they had found and eaten. The rationing of one chocolate bar and a single can of tomato juice took up five days' worth of entries.

After a while, when food, tomato juice, and cigarettes were gone, the entries scratched on the cargo door turned personal, revealing hope, fear, and occasional flashes of grim humour. On Friday, 27 November 1942, seventeen days after the crash, an entry read: 'Buckets full [of] water this morn ... still got our chin up.' Two days later: 'Boy we're getting weak.' But the diarist added, 'Still have our hope.' The next day: 'Still going strong on imaginary meals.' On Monday, 7 December, the first anniversary of Pearl Harbor, the entry read: 'Year ago today the war started. Boy, we didn't think of this then.' Two days later, a month after the crash: 'Just thirty days ago. We can take it but it would be nice if someone came.' A week later, as thoughts turned to Christmas: 'Running out of imaginary meals. Boys shouldn't be long in coming now – 6 more shoping [sic] days.' Six days later: 'Tonite is Christmas eve. God make them happy at home.' Six days later: 'Johnnie died today.'

The entries petered out after two more days, seven weeks after the crash. The final entry noted that it was New Year's Eve. The three remaining survivors signed their names: Pat, Mart and Ted. Days later, the natives found the wreckage – and Captain Theodore Barron, the blind, malnourished, moss-eating chaplain, known to his friends as Ted.

At daylight on Tuesday, 15 May 1945, the second day after the *Gremlin Special* crash, McCollom announced that he had changed his mind. They could not wait for Margaret and Decker to feel stronger before starting their trek to the clearing he had spotted from the tree.

With soiled and soggy bandages on their burns, McCollom feared his companions would get worse before they got better. Already they moved slowly, as though swimming through honey, a side effect of their injuries, sleeplessness, empty stomachs, and the thin air at such high altitude, more than 1600 metres above sea level. A native would have considered the rainforest a mess hall overflowing with fruits and roots, birds and small mammals, but for the survivors it was as mysterious as a menu in Mandarin. The only nourishment they trusted was their boiled sweets.

McCollom assembled most of their supplies in one of the remaining yellow tarpaulins. He packed a smaller one for Decker and gave Margaret a pail that he had found in the plane's tail. Rattling around in it were her day's rations: two tins of water and a few cellophane-wrapped sweets.

McCollom returned to Laura Besley's body for a grisly but necessary task. He unwrapped the tarpaulin and removed the flight suit he had given her for warmth. Just as Margaret had shortened her Army-issue uniforms when she had first arrived in Hollandia, McCollom used his pocket-knife to slice twelve inches of fabric from each cuff so Margaret could wear the flight suit without tripping over herself.

When McCollom brought her the suit, Margaret knew that it came from the body of her good friend but she was glad to have it nonetheless, just as she knew that wearing Laura's shoes might be the difference between life and death. Margaret still had the Rayon underwear she had stripped off after the crash intending to make bandages. Now she tore the pants in half and used the fabric to cover the burns on her legs, so the rough flight suit wouldn't scrape against her charred skin.

Later, writing in her diary, Margaret wished that before they left the crash site they had said a prayer, built a cross, or laid some kind of marker for the twenty-one friends, comrades, and McCollom's twin. Even a moment of silence would have made her feel better about their departure. But at the time, their only focus was on reaching a place where they might be spotted from the air.

'Let's go,' McCollom ordered his two-person platoon. He took the lead, Margaret followed close behind, and Decker brought up the rear.

They first had to climb up from the ledge where they had spent the previous two nights and make their way past the wreckage. The growth was so thick that they made the

The detached tail section of the *Gremlin Special*.

most progress by crawling on their hands and knees. In a few places, a wrong step would mean a fall into a rocky ravine. In others, it would mean a deadly plunge over a cliff. It took an exhausting thirty minutes just to get twenty-five metres past the plane.

Margaret tried to tie back her hair, which fell halfway down her back. But it was no use. It kept getting caught in the clawing vines and branches that surrounded them. They repeatedly had to halt their crawl-march to untangle it. In desperation, Margaret shook loose her hair and declared: 'Please, McCollom, hack it off.'

The lieutenant used his pocketknife to saw through chunks of Margaret's thick hair, dropping the cuttings where they stood. After working his way around Margaret's head, McCollom fashioned what Margaret called 'a rather sad, three-inch "feather" bob'. They started out again, but still the jungle tore at her.

'For goodness sake, McCollom, I've got to get rid of this hair!' she yelled.

McCollom cut it even shorter.

Margaret's burns made each step painful. Decker, worse off, still unsteady from his head injury, moved stiffly but never complained.

As they inched their way through the mud and brush on the jungle floor, the trio stumbled upon what Margaret considered a miracle: a dry creek bed, or gully, that formed a narrow path down the mountain. To view this as miraculous mostly reveals how difficult the jungle was by contrast. The gully cut into the mountain at a sharp angle, in some places forcing them to climb, slide or jump down the rocky slope. The footing was unstable even along the flatter sections of the path, with loose stones that slid out from under them. In other places they had to climb over boulders and old tree trunks. But it was a trail nonetheless.

'It is foolish to think that we could have cut our way out of that dense, clinging jungle with a pocketknife our only weapon,' Margaret wrote in her diary. 'The gully promised two things: a foothold in the jungle, precarious though it was, and eventual water.'

Even as they followed the dry stream, the survivors had to stop and rest every half-hour. After two breaks they noticed trickles of icy water draining into the gully. At first, they were delighted. Margaret and Decker, aching with thirst, announced that they intended to fill their stomachs as soon as the water became deep enough to collect. McCollom warned against it, worrying that waterborne germs would torture their bowels. But they were too excited to listen. In no time, the tributaries grew larger and they had more water than they wished for. It rose over their shoe tops and kept rushing into the gully, threatening to sweep them down the mountain with the swift-moving stream.

They navigated the rougher spots by sliding along on their bottoms, getting soaked in the process. In the steepest places, waterfalls cascaded from one to three metres down. The jungle bordered closely on both sides of the gully, so fallen logs rested in some of the waterfalls. Whenever possible, they used those logs as ladders or poles to climb down. When no logs were available, McCollom led the way, climbing down the falls hand over hand, the water pouring over his head. He stood at the bottom, under the rushing water, as Margaret made her way down far enough to stand on his shoulders. Then she slid into his arms, and McCollom placed her in shallower water. When she was safe, he returned to help Decker.

They came to a three-metre waterfall, too high and too steep to try McCollom's shoulder trick. Margaret and Decker rested at the side of the stream while McCollom fought his way into the encroaching jungle to search for a way around. But the growth was especially thick there, so he returned with a new idea.

McCollom grabbed a thick vine that hung from a tree alongside the falls. After testing it with his weight, he held tight to the vine, took a running jump, and swung over and beyond the falls. When he cleared the cascading water, he let himself down at the bottom. He tossed back the vine and told the others to follow.

Margaret didn't hesitate. She grabbed the vine and launched herself into space. When she cleared the falls, McCollom caught her as she let go of the vine. Next came Decker, who followed suit.

When he was safely beside them, the sergeant smiled drily: 'Damned if I ever thought I'd understudy Johnny Weissmuller.' Decker's mention of the vine-swinging movie star who played 'Tarzan' made Margaret laugh, though she overlooked the obvious implication: that made her Jane.

As they trudged onward, Margaret felt worse with each step. She was cold, wet and exhausted. Her whole body ached. Tears welled in her eyes, but she was determined not to cry.

From time to time they heard search planes overhead. As the thrum of each plane's engines grew closer, McCollom frantically worked the signal mirror. But he knew that the foliage canopy made the effort useless. Still, the sound alone was enough to revive their confidence that there was still a possibility, no matter how remote, that they would be found.

McCollom's plan was to walk until early afternoon then set up camp when the daily mist and rain rolled in. But the jungle bordering the stream was so relentless they couldn't find a spot on the bank large enough to stretch out. They kept moving until they could go no farther, eventually settling on a location that was far from ideal.

McCollom placed one tarpaulin on the sodden ground and draped the other over them as a cover. They ate a few Charms, then bunched together to keep warm as they slept. McCollom slid between Decker and Margaret, so he could care for them both if needed. Decker thought McCollom displayed 'the old mother hen instinct', but he appreciated it and kept quiet.

Their campsite slanted sharply towards the stream, and several times during the night the trio rolled in a heap down the bank into the icy water. Each time they dragged out the tarpaulins and their soggy selves and tried again to sleep.

Also disturbing their sleep was something they had seen earlier in the day. While walking through the stream, they noticed an unmistakable sign that they were not alone: outlined in the mud was a fresh human footprint. That night they heard strange barking sounds in the distance.

As far as the three survivors knew, they were the first outsiders to trek through this part of New Guinea's mountainous rainforest. But they were mistaken. That distinction belonged to a wealthy, amateur American zoologist who seven years earlier led an expedition to New Guinea in search of undiscovered flora and fauna.

One unfortunate result of that 1938 expedition was an act of deadly violence. The question now was whether that legacy would threaten the three survivors of the *Gremlin Special*.

Eight

Gentleman Explorer

COLONEL RAY ELSMORE BASKED IN PUBLIC ACCLAIM as the valley's self-styled discoverer. Unbeknownst to him or anyone else in the Army, Elsmore was the New Guinea equivalent of Antarctic explorer Robert Falcon Scott. In other words, Elsmore was the second outsider to discover Shangri-La, third if proper consideration were given to Major Byron Grimes.

The valley's true Western discoverer was Richard Archbold, a young man who enjoyed the good fortune of being born exceedingly rich. And unlike Elsmore and Grimes, Archbold had visited the valley on the ground.

Archbold's inherited wealth flowed from his grandfather, John D. Archbold, a president of Standard Oil and a partner of John D. Rockefeller. The family's millions guaranteed that Richard Archbold would never be required to earn his living by holding a traditional job. This was convenient, given his less than glittering performance at any of the private schools he attended. Skinny, shy and socially awkward, with piercing eyes and a brusque manner, there was only one subject to which Archbold did apply himself: the great outdoors. In 1929, Archbold's father, hoping to set Richard on a productive path, agreed to help finance a joint British, French and American research expedition to Madagascar. The elder Archbold had one condition: along with his money came his underachieving twenty-two-year-old son. The expedition's organizers were delighted by the cash but not quite sure what to do with young Archbold, who had reached adulthood as a tall, thin, moderately handsome man with a shock of wavy black hair, a thick moustache, and a partiality for bow ties.

After initially planning to use Archbold as a photographer, one of the expedition's senior scientists suggested: 'Why don't you collect mammals?' So he did.

Archbold practised collecting at the family's Georgia estate – something akin to a big-game hunter preparing for a safari at a zoo – and learned from his many mistakes. But once in Madagascar, he stoically suffered the bites of land leeches and mosquitoes, the many discomforts of camp life in the wild, and the stigma among serious scientists of being the rich kid along for the ride. Along the way, he found his calling as a biological researcher.

Upon his return from Madagascar, Archbold learned that his father had died. He collected his inheritance and with it a Manhattan apartment on Central Park West. He took a low-level job down the street, as a research associate in the mammal department at the American Museum of Natural History, where his grandfather had been a major benefactor.

Working in an office across the hall on the museum's fifth floor was a young ornithologist from Germany named Ernst Mayr, who later became a legend in evolutionary biology. Archbold's new acquaintance encouraged him to focus on the wilds of New Guinea, where Mayr had spent months studying bird life. Archbold put his inheritance to work by organizing, funding and leading several major expeditions there under the auspices of the museum. From the outset, his plan was nothing less than 'a comprehensive biological survey of the island'. Unlike Mayr, who had done his work among small groups of scientist-explorers, Archbold assembled a veritable research army to attempt the ambitious task.

Archbold enjoyed notable success on his first two New Guinea journeys, one begun in 1933 and another in 1936, as he and his well-funded teams reached previously unexplored territory and supplied the New York museum with numerous new plant and animal species. But Archbold grew frustrated by the logistical challenges posed by the enormous island, not least of which was the inhospitable terrain and the lack of native pack animals. Napoleon said armies march on their stomachs; the same could be said for large, exotic scientific expeditions. Archbold's journeys in New Guinea depended on efficient supply lines, which meant that someone or something needed to carry tons of provisions to explorers and assistants cut off from civilization for months on end.

In the absence of horses, mules, oxen or camels, and in light of the impossibility of using trucks in the roadless interior, human bearers were the only land-based option. But Archbold learned that New Guinea natives couldn't be relied upon. One reason was fear, not of the explorers but of each other. The island's innumerable tribes and clans were usually at war with one another, so the instant a native bearer left his home territory he had reason to fear death at the hands of a neighbour.

Archbold concluded that the best way to conquer New Guinea, scientifically at least, would be with air support. He became a pilot and began buying aeroplanes. In early 1938, he purchased the largest privately owned plane in the world – the first commercial version of a US Navy patrol bomber known as a PBY. With a wing span of more than thirty metres, a yawning cargo bay, and a range exceeding 6500 kilometres, Archbold's PBY fit his needs perfectly. Its greatest appeal to him, however, was the PBY's design as a 'flying boat'. Fitted with pontoons, it could take off and land on bodies of water, including the high-altitude lakes and rivers of New Guinea. Archbold added special navigation and communications equipment, then named his plane after a native word for a powerful storm: *Guba*. With *Guba* at his disposal, Archbold could ferry supplies, personnel and specimens wherever needed, making possible his third and most ambitious expedition to New Guinea.

Explorer Richard Archbold in 1938, standing on the *Guba* after landing in what was then known as Challenger Bay in Hollandia.

Archbold obtained approval and support from the Dutch government, which controlled the area he wanted to explore. The government's motivation was that the expedition would provide authorities in the Netherlands with hitherto unknown details about their colony, including not just the flora and fauna in Archbold's sights, but also the people and the resources hidden within.

In April 1938, Archbold's team established a base camp in Hollandia with nearly two hundred people, including scientists from the American Museum of Natural History; seventy-two Dyak tribesmen brought from the neighbouring island of Borneo as bearers; two cooks; a backup pilot; a navigator; a radioman; and two mechanics. The Dutch government contributed nearly sixty soldiers, including a captain and three lieutenants. Also on hand, courtesy of the Dutch, were thirty political prisoners – anti-colonial activists, mostly – pressed into duty as 'convict carriers'.

The expedition focused on collecting mammals, birds, plants and insects at a range of altitudes – from sea level to the barren, 3500-metre peaks in the least-studied area of New Guinea, the north slope of the Snow Mountains, one of several ranges in the island's interior. With *Guba*, the Dyak bearers, and the convicts carrying supplies to keep them fed, Archbold and his team of scientists gathered a trove of remarkable specimens, including tree-climbing kangaroos, metre-long rats, and a previously unknown songbird with a fly-catcher beak. But nothing was as startling as what they encountered on the morning of 23 June 1938.

Archbold was piloting *Guba* towards Hollandia after a reconnaissance flight when the plane broke through thick clouds surrounding the 4730-metre-high mountain named for Dutch Queen Wilhelmina. Ahead, Archbold saw a wide, flat, heavily populated valley that appeared nowhere on his maps and was unknown except to its inhabitants. He estimated that the valley was roughly 64 kilometres long by 16 kilometres wide. Later, adopting patrician nonchalance and the detached language of science, he downplayed his shock and called it 'a pleasant surprise'.

A Dutch soldier on board *Guba* called the area a *Groote Vallei*, or Grand Valley, and Archbold declared that that would be its name.

He initially placed the population at sixty thousand people, though in fact it was perhaps double that, including natives who lived in the surrounding mountains. Even at Archbold's estimate, that was enough people immediately to establish the valley as the most densely populated area in all of Dutch New Guinea.

It almost defied belief. New Guinea was remote, but hardly unknown. Explorers had penetrated large parts of the island's interior on foot, and mountaineers had climbed its highest peaks. Separate expeditions in 1907, the early 1920s, and 1926 came close to Archbold's Grand Valley and made contact with some travelling natives, but they never found the valley itself. One group of explorers, the Kremer Expedition of 1921, reached a nearby area called the Swart Valley. The anthropologist Denise O'Brien, who studied the Swart Valley some forty years later, wrote that when they first encountered Kremer and his team, the natives 'were puzzled as to why the light-skinned men, who must really be ghosts or spirits, had no women with them. Finally they decided that the spirits' women were carried in containers, containers that the spirits also used for carrying and cooking food. Sometimes the spirit women came out of the containers, and to the (natives) they looked like snakes as they slithered along the ground, but to the spirit men they looked like women.' The natives' overall reaction, O'Brien wrote, was fear, compounded by a severe epidemic of dysentery after the explorers left.

Even if land-based surveyors missed the valley, surely a military or commercial pilot should have spotted an area of more than 1,000 square kilometres filled with hundreds of villages, inhabited by tens of thousands of men, women and children. Not to mention pigs. Yet some of the world's most celebrated aviators missed it. In July 1937, a year before Archbold's discovery, Amelia Earhart flew over part of New Guinea as she attempted to circumnavigate the globe. Her last known stop was at an airstrip in the town of Lae, at New Guinea's eastern edge, after which her plane disappeared somewhere in the Pacific. But she, too, never saw the Grand Valley.

By the late 1930s, most anthropologists believed that every significant population centre on the planet had been discovered, mapped, and in most cases, modernized to some degree by missionaries, capitalists, colonizers or a combination of the three. No one doubted that pockets of undisturbed aborigines still roamed the rainforests of the Amazon and elsewhere. But the people of Archbold's Grand Valley were stationary farmer-warriors, living in clearly defined villages, in a wide-open area, covered only by the clouds above. Sixty years later, mammalogist and environmental scientist Tim Flannery, an authority on the natural wonders of New Guinea, declared that Archbold's find represented 'the last time in the history of our planet that such a vast, previously unknown civilization was to come into contact with the West'.

One explanation is that an unusual combination of forces kept the valley off the map. When Archbold described his find for *National Geographic Magazine*, an editor there tried to make sense of it, writing: 'Forestation is so heavy and terrain so rugged that earlier explorers passed on foot within a few miles of the most thickly populated area without suspecting the existence of a civilization there.' The surrounding mountains played an important role, as well, discouraging flights overhead and commercial incursions by land. The valley natives were self-sufficient farmers, as opposed to hunter-gatherers or traders who might travel far and wide to feed themselves and obtain needed goods. Their stay-at-home tendency was cemented by their wars, which ensured that most spent their lives within short, relatively safe distances of their huts.

When Archbold first saw the valley, rough weather prevented him from changing course or dipping *Guba* low for a better look. But in the weeks that followed, he flew several reconnaissance missions, photographing the valley and sending pigs and their owners running for cover – just as Colonel Elsmore's flights would do six years later.

Archbold's chief botanist, L.J. Brass, described what they saw from the air:

> The people were living in compact, very orderly and clean, fenced, walled or stockaded villages of about three or four to about fifty houses. Dwellings were of two types, built with double walls of upright split timbers, grass-thatched, and without floors. The men's houses were round, ten to fifteen feet in diameter, with dome-shaped roof; the women's houses long, narrow and rectangular. The everyday dress of the men consisted of a penis gourd, and perhaps a hair net of looped string. The women affected either short skirts of pendent strings, worn below the buttocks, or an arrangement of cords around the thighs, and always one or more capacious carrying nets hung over the back from the forehead. As arms and implements they had bows, arrows of several kinds, spears, stone adzes, and stone axes.

Archbold seemed only mildly interested in the people, but he was fascinated by their farming methods. Unlike all other known tribes on New Guinea, natives of the valley grew sweet potatoes – their staple food – in clearly defined plots of land, with labyrinthine drainage ditches and surrounding walls. Archbold said it reminded him fondly of the farm country he had seen on holiday in central Europe.

Archbold's assistants established a camp some twenty-four kilometres west of the valley on a body of water called Lake Habbema, where *Guba* could set down and take off. One day, two natives presented themselves to the outsiders. 'One was evidently a man of some importance,' Archbold wrote. 'The other, who was younger, perhaps a bodyguard, remained very much on the alert. They squatted on their haunches, their backs toward home, their bows and arrows handy, while we sat down on the camp side of them.'

Archbold gave the two men bead-like cowrie shells – small, pearly white, naturally smooth shells that are widely used as currency and jewellery in Africa and elsewhere. He plied them with sugar, cigarettes, and dried fish. The two men accepted the gifts, but after a polite period of time, handed them back, a gesture that Archbold interpreted 'as a sign of independence'. He noted, however, that the more senior man did accept a few draws from the cigar of the senior Dutch officer on the expedition, a captain named C.G.J. Teerink. After a fifteen-minute visit, the two natives left the explorers' camp.

Subsequently, Archbold dispatched two exploration teams, each consisting of Dutch soldiers, convict carriers, and Dyak tribesmen trained to collect flora and fauna. The teams, one led by Captain Teerink and the other by a lieutenant named J.E.M. Van Arcken, started their treks at opposite ends of the valley, the plan being to meet roughly in the middle.

In August 1938, the two teams marched through the valley's high grasses, past one village after another. If the outsiders had been tribesmen from other parts of the valley, such an incursion likely would have been greeted with spears and arrows. But the white explorers and their bearers were so strange and exotic, so far removed from the day-to-day warfare among the tribes, they were met by little more than curiosity from the native men and shyness from the women and children. The explorers saw signs that the natives practised cannibalism, but the heavily armed Dutch army troops felt they had nothing to fear.

Occasionally some tribesmen would discourage the explorers from travelling to the next village – placing sticks in their path, pantomiming the firing of arrows, and standing arm in arm as a human blockade. Language barriers prevented Captain Teerink or Lieutenant Van Arcken from getting a full explanation, but the acts seemed to Teerink more protective than hostile. The natives apparently did not want their new acquaintances to be harmed by enemies who lived in the next village.

This pattern remained in place until 9 August 1938, when a patrol from Van Arcken's exploration team neared the Baliem River in the valley's centre. They were met by tribesmen 'in large numbers' carrying spears and bows and arrows. 'We apparently were not to be trusted because we had come from the direction of enemy territory,' Van Arcken wrote in his daily log. He defused the confrontation with a few cowrie shells. Later that night, four natives came into his camp asking to sleep among the soldiers. 'These gentlemen were sent packing,' Van Arcken wrote, 'after a shot in the air to scare them off.'

The next day, Van Arcken found that the patrol's trail had been 'closed off with tree branches, behind which some youths with spears took cover'. His troops brandished their weapons and the young natives fled. As the column of soldiers moved forward, bringing up the rear were two soldiers, one of them a corporal named Pattisina. Van Arcken wrote that two natives grabbed Pattisina from behind. When the other lagging soldier came to Pattisina's aid, one of the natives 'wanted to spear the corporal with his lance, whereupon said native was shot by the corporal'. In short, Van Arcken's report revealed that Pattisina had killed a native, and the official version was that he had done so in self-defence.

Captain Teerink, the highest-ranking Dutch officer on the expedition, didn't buy the explanation. Teerink, who was leading the other patrol, wrote a critical addendum to Van Arcken's report that suggested he held a more humane view of the natives: 'In my view, this fatal shot is to be regretted. Corporal Pattisina should have fired a warning shot first. It has been my experience that with tribes like this, a warning shot is usually sufficient. It is requested that you issue instructions to this effect to your men.'

Even before he returned to the United States, Archbold published articles about the expedition in the *New York Times* and elsewhere. In March 1941, he wrote a long piece for *National Geographic Magazine*. In it, he described a number of encounters with natives, most of them friendly though a few laced with tension. He seemed most surprised when his expedition passed villages and the natives paid them little mind: 'Here the natives seemed to take our party for granted. Some stood by and watched the long line of carriers file by, while others, digging in the gardens of rich black earth, did not even look up.'

But in none of his accounts did Archbold describe what the natives must have considered the most awful moment of the outsiders' visit.

Four years after the shooting, in June 1942, Archbold finally acknowledged that an incident had occurred between the natives and Van Arcken's patrol that day near the river. But the way he described it and the publication he chose guaranteed that the significance would be overlooked. Writing in the Bulletin of the American Museum of Natural History, Archbold described how on 10 August Van Arcken's patrol encountered a trail barricaded with branches and guarded by men with spears. Archbold wrote: 'Here occurred the one incident of the whole expedition where more than a show of force was necessary.' Without stopping to explain what he meant, much less acknowledge and discuss the gunshot death of a native, Archbold forged ahead to report the time of day that the patrol reached the river and the precise width of the river's floodplain.

Van Arcken took an even more misleading approach when he created the first known map of the valley. On it, he drew an arrow to the spot of the 10 August 1938 confrontation and wrote: 'Location where one native died due to a lance attack.' Unless a map reader knew better, Van Arcken's note seemed to suggest that the explorers had witnessed a fatal duel between two natives.

Elsewhere in Archbold's report to the museum, he outlined his overall philosophy where natives were concerned. There he whitewashed the shooting entirely: 'In venturing into an unknown area, the kind of reception the natives will extend is unpredictable. Certain it is that natives in general tend to be more friendly toward a large, well-armed party than toward a small, weak one. Our parties inland were usually of the former category and no unpleasant incidents of importance arose in our contacts with the people.'

Archbold apparently had no interest in determining whether the natives considered the Grand Valley's first fatal gunshot to be 'unpleasant' or an 'incident of importance'.

Archbold's expedition and his writings about the valley went unnoticed by Colonel Elsmore. When initially told about Archbold after the crash of the *Gremlin Special*, Elsmore brushed it off, certain that his Hidden Valley, his

Shangri-La, was distinct from Archbold's Grand Valley. After all, New Guinea was so huge and unexplored, who could say how many isolated, undiscovered valleys might still exist?

But the Grand Valley and Shangri-La were one and the same. And the first known contact between its natives and the outside world had been marked by blood.

Nine

Guilt and Gangrene

After seeing the native footprint, the three survivors spent what Margaret described as 'this aching, miserable night' on the sloped, muddy banks of the mountain stream. Soggy and exhausted from their repeated rolls into the cold water, they woke in the dim predawn light on Wednesday, 16 May, to resume their trek towards the clearing that McCollom had spotted farther down the slope.

As Margaret tried to stand, pain racked her body, and with it came fear. Overnight, her joints had stiffened, and the burned skin on her legs had tightened around her muscles. The burns choked off blood flow, starving healthy flesh. It hurt even to think about walking and sliding farther downstream. She couldn't straighten up. She wrote in her diary, 'My legs were so stiff they were a sickening sight.'

A quick inspection showed that infection had set in. She downplayed the gory details in her diary – the oozing pus, the blue-black hue of dead tissue. But she had a sickening idea of the causes and the dangers of what she described as 'big, evil-smelling, running sores'.

New Guinea teemed with bacteria, and the combination of burned flesh, unsanitary conditions, and swarming bacteria was a recipe for gangrene. Unless treated, the dread condition meant the death of a damaged body part and ultimately an entire body. Gangrene comes in two varieties, wet and dry. Both are awful, but wet gangrene is worse. Dry gangrene usually appears gradually as a result of blocked blood flow through the arteries. Decades of smoking might lead to dry gangrene and the slow death of a smoker's feet. Margaret's infected injuries were ripe for fast-moving, fast-killing wet gangrene. The longer her wounds went untreated, the greater the chance that her legs would have to be amputated. Even such a radical step as this might not be enough. Wet gangrene can lead to the blood infection called sepsis. In the jungle, sepsis is fatal. The only question is whether it takes its victim in hours or days.

Margaret steeled herself and struggled upright on to her tender feet. She walked in agony, back and forth on the inclined bank, trying to loosen her joints to enable her to continue the journey. She glanced at Decker, knowing that he must have been in at least as much pain. She admired how stoic he remained.

McCollom looked at his two companions. He felt responsibility for them, but also respect and growing admiration. Affection, too. During all the walking, all the sliding downstream, all the discomforts, Decker hadn't complained once about his gaping head wound or his other injuries. And this petite WAC corporal turned out to be much tougher than he had expected. Not only was she soldiering on with gangrenous wounds on her legs and hand, but the burns on the left side of her face had darkened. It occurred to him that other WACs he had known, as well as some male soldiers, would not have survived half of what she had already been through.

Yet as their injuries worsened and infections took hold, McCollom could see his companions' strength ebbing. He felt certain that both already suffered from full-blown wet gangrene, and he feared that if the search planes did not find them soon, he would be the only one left alive.

McCollom would not reveal it to Margaret or Decker, but he was fighting back fear. Later, he explained: 'We were in what was thought to be headhunter territory, we had no medical supplies, no shelter. We were in the middle of nowhere. I knew my twin brother was dead in the wreckage. I had to take care of the others. I didn't want to think about being out there all by myself, so I did what I could as much for myself as for them.'

Though determined to save Margaret and Decker, McCollom made a private resolution: if the searchers gave up before spotting them, he would somehow find a navigable river and build a raft, or if need be, keep walking. He would float or walk all the way to the ocean 240 kilometres away, if that was what it took to get out of there. He would return to Hollandia, and after that to his family. He could not save his brother, but he was determined to save himself and keep watch over his brother's infant daughter.

He would do everything in his power to help Decker and Margaret. But if gangrene got the best of them, McCollom would go it alone.

Breakfast was water and more boiled sweets, still their only food on the third day after the crash. They separated the Charms by colour, eating the red ones until they tired of them, moving on to yellow, and so on. Decker jokingly called the colour-by-colour approach a good way to vary their diet. They had cigarettes, but McCollom's lighter was dry and their matches were wet. As they prepared to resume their trek, rolling their supplies into the yellow tarpaulins, their thoughts turned to coffee.

'I'd love to be back in the mess hall having some of that delicious battery acid,' Decker said.

'Me, too!' Margaret said. She did not understand why, but despite not eating since her lunch of chicken and ice cream three days earlier, she did not feel especially hungry.

The stream bank was too steep for them to walk on, and the jungle foliage gave no quarter. They gingerly stepped down the 2.5-metre bank, back into the mountain stream, to resume their soaking march. Again they clambered over fallen logs and slid on their bottoms down waterfalls. Tears filled her eyes as Margaret fought to keep up. Her feet throbbed with each step. Decker hung back with her. McCollom marched on, eager to reach the clearing. He got so far ahead they lost sight of him.

Margaret teetered on the edge of panic.

'McCollom has gone off and left us, and he's got all the food,' she cried to Decker. 'And we're going to starve to death.' She plopped down in the stream. It was the closest she had come to giving up since the thought of surrender flickered through her mind in the burning plane.

Decker, usually the quiet man among the three, had heard enough. He wheeled around like a red-faced drill sergeant. Margaret would not recount his full tirade in her diary, but she sheepishly admitted that he called her 'a piker' and 'a quitter'. Whether he did it as a motivating technique or in real anger, Decker had found the exact right words.

'I got so mad I wanted to kill him,' she wrote. 'But I got on my feet and stumbled downstream once more. Pretty soon we caught up with McCollom.'

Margaret was not someone who easily admitted that she was wrong, but almost immediately she felt regret. McCollom had been steadfast and strong, guiding and helping them even as he suppressed his emotions about his brother's death, which Margaret suspected hurt more deeply than her burns. She told her diary: 'It shames me to the core to think that even in hysteria, I doubted him for a moment.'

Back in Hollandia, the *Gremlin Special*'s failure to return to Sentani Airfield sent shock waves through the headquarters. The plane's absence and the lack of radio communication almost certainly meant a crash, and a crash meant a search. From the outset, the mindset at Fee-Ask was a 'rescue' mission, based on the hope of finding survivors, as opposed to a 'recovery' effort, aimed at returning remains to families.

As a unit on a large air base, Fee-Ask had almost unlimited access to pilots and planes. The fact that the missing crew and passengers were colleagues, friends and subordinates of the Fee-Ask brass made it doubly certain the search organizers would have whatever they needed. Raising the ante further were nine special circumstances: the WACs on board.

There's no evidence to suggest that Colonel Ray Elsmore and the other officers at headquarters would have been any less aggressive if everyone aboard was male. But transport planes crashed regularly during the war with little notice from the press. Elsmore must have known that the WACs aboard the *Gremlin Special* would attract special interest.

Several hundred US women had already died during the course of the war, but the accurate numbers are hard to come by in part because some were civilians working with the Red Cross and other relief organizations, and some died in transit to war zones and in accidents on US soil. Of the women who died serving non-combat military roles, many were nurses, including decorated heroes such as Lieutenant Aleda Lutz, an Army flight nurse who took part in nearly two hundred missions. In November 1944, she was aboard a C-47 hospital plane evacuating wounded soldiers from a battlefield in Italy when it ran into rough weather and crashed, killing everyone aboard. Thirty-eight US military women who died were members of the Women's Auxiliary Ferrying Squadron, the WAFS, and the Women Airforce Service Pilots, the WASPs, who flew military aircraft on non-combat missions to keep male pilots fresh and available for battle.

Each female death drew attention, but in most cases the deaths came singly or in pairs. Exceptions included six nurses killed by German bombing and strafing of a hospital area during the battle on Anzio. And just two weeks before the *Gremlin Special* crash, six nurses were among twenty-eight crew members killed when a Japanese *kamikaze* pilot slammed into the US Navy hospital ship *Comfort* off Leyte Island, between Guam and Okinawa.

The base at Hollandia had suffered only one previous WAC death, in February 1945, when a private drowned while swimming in the Pacific. On the day before her burial, her distraught friends wanted to honour her by flying the WAC flag – a banner of gold and green satin, with a fringe at the edge, its centre adorned by the profile of the Greek war goddess Pallas Athena. No such flag existed anywhere in New Guinea. As one Hollandia WAC put it, the materials needed to make one were 'as out of their reach as a handful of icicles'. Regardless, a group of WACs stayed awake past four in thc morning, fashioning a flag from Australian bed sheets, coloured with dyes made from yellow Atabrine anti-malaria tablets and red Merthiolate antiseptic ointment pilfered from the infirmary. For the image of Pallas Athena, they used green India ink from the drafting department. For a fringe, they used old parachute cords. Bleary-eyed, they finished in time for the funeral. They ignored their flag's blotchy colours and irregular size, its makeshift fringe and rough edges, saluting proudly as it waved in the warm breeze for their lost friend.

That was the reaction to the death of one drowned Hollandia WAC. Now nine Hollandia WACs were missing and feared dead in the island's wild interior.

After the *Gremlin Special* missed its estimated return time, calls were made to Allied landing strips throughout the region to see if Colonel Prossen and Major Nicholson had unexpectedly landed the C-47 elsewhere. That proved fruitless, so Fee-Ask planners hauled out their admittedly inadequate maps and divided the island into sectors where the pilots might have made what they euphemistically called 'a forced landing'.

Though hampered by incessant rain, airborne searchers spent three days scouring those sectors. In all, twenty-four planes took part – a squadron of C-47s, a C-60 transport plane, and a flock of heavy bombers, including B-24 Liberators, B-25 Mitchells, and a B-17 Flying Fortress. A volunteer crew member on one of the search planes was Corporal James Lutgring, hoping against hope that he might rescue his best friend, Melvin Mollberg, who had taken his place on the *Gremlin Special*.

Overseeing the rescue effort was Colonel Elsmore, who knew the area around the Shangri-La Valley better than anyone in the US military.

At around eleven a.m. on Wednesday, 16 May, after five hours of trudging through the stream, McCollom climbed up the 2.5-metre bank.

'Come on,' he called, 'this is it.'

Decker scrambled up, dragging Margaret behind him. On flat ground at the top, she fell face-forward on to the earth, unable to take another step. Decker and McCollom went ahead while she crawled after them on her hands and knees. A half-hour later, she reached the spot fifty metres from the stream where Decker and McCollom lay panting on the ground. Margaret sprawled next to them, catching her breath. Feeling the warmth of the sun's rays, she noticed that for the first time in days she could see a wide expanse of sky. They had reached their goal, a clearing in the rainforest atop a small knoll.

Within minutes, the survivors heard the roar of four powerful engines. They looked up to see a B-17 bomber, its unmistakable shape silhouetted high overhead against the blue sky. The trio waved to draw its attention, but the pilot of the Flying Fortress flew away without spotting them. They rested and ate what passed for lunch, disappointed by the near miss but heartened by the sight of the plane.

An hour later, either the same B-17 or another just like it made another pass over the clearing. This time McCollom was not taking any chances. He jumped to his feet.

'Get out the tarps!' he shouted.

McCollom and Decker raced to untie their supplies and spread out the yellow tarpaulin covers they had salvaged from the *Gremlin Special*'s life rafts. The B-17, with Captain William D. Baker at the controls, was flying over the jungle at high altitude. Along with his usual crew, Baker had brought along an unusual passenger for a heavy bomber: Major Cornelius Waldo, the Catholic chaplain at the Hollandia base.

Margaret worried that the pilot would miss them again and declare that sector of the mountain fully searched, with no sign of wreckage or survivors. She begged her companions to hurry.

Just when it seemed that the B-17 was about to fly away, Captain Baker turned the big bomber and circled back over the clearing. Still, Baker gave none of the traditional signs that he had seen them. McCollom called to the sky:

'Come on down, come on down and cut your motors,' he cried. 'Cut your motors and dip your wings.'

Margaret chimed in: 'I know they see us, I know they do.'

Decker added a note of optimism: 'They see us by now.'

Even though Baker was flying high above the clearing, he could not mistake the survivors for any natives that might be around. One obvious distinction was that all three wore clothing. But the real giveaway was the tarp. Less than five minutes after the survivors spotted the B-17, the B-17 returned the favour. Baker raced his engines. He dipped his wings.

They had been found.

McCollom had made the right call when he had ordered them to leave the crash site and march down the mountain and through the icy stream. As one pilot experienced in jungle searches described it, 'An airplane going into the trees makes a very small gash in a limitless sea of green.' By leading them to a clearing and laying out the bright yellow tarpaulin, McCollom had given them a shot at being rescued.

Later, a funny thought struck him: a life raft designed for ocean survival had saved them in the middle of a jungle.

Unbeknownst to the survivors, they were not alone. Hiding in the nearby jungle was a group of native men and boys from a nearby village, among them a boy named Helenma Wandik. 'I watched them,' he recalled. 'I saw them in the clearing, waving.'

Barely able to stand just a short time earlier, now Margaret, McCollom and Decker jumped up and down. They danced and screamed and waved their weary arms. For the first time since they had sat in the *Gremlin Special*, they laughed.

Baker wagged the B-17's wings again to be sure they had seen him. He logged their position by longitude and latitude, then had his crew drop two life rafts as markers as close as possible to the clearing. With a violent thunderstorm moving towards the valley, no more flights could be made at least until morning. As Baker flew out of sight, heading towards the island's northern coast, he radioed a message to the Sentani Airstrip: three people in khaki, waving, spotted in a small clearing on the uphill side of a forested ridge, about 1800 metres from the valley floor.

'We'll probably be back in Hollandia by Sunday,' said Decker, who by then had dropped back to the ground.

'Hollandia, here I come,' Margaret replied.

She wrote in her diary that she daydreamed about her beau Wally Fleming. She fantasized about him sitting adoringly at her hospital bedside, holding her hand and telling her how brave she had been. Knowing that she would be teased, she did not share that vision with McCollom or Decker.

Meanwhile, Decker displayed a dry wit. Affecting a glum tone, he told McCollom, 'I suppose one of us will have to marry Maggie and give this adventure the proper romantic ending.'

McCollom joined the act. He appraised the injured, worn, and tired WAC. After looking her up and down, he delivered the punchline: 'She'll have to put on more meat before I'm interested.'

Margaret puffed herself up and defended her injured pride: 'I wouldn't marry you if you were the last man in the world. I'm going to marry Decker!'

Decker, who had been turned down by Margaret for a date weeks before their flight, would not give her the last word. But stumped for a snappy comeback, he blurted: 'The hell you are!'

Relieved, they sat together on the ground and wondered how long it would take until more planes returned with supplies. Above all, Margaret wanted real food, so they could throw away 'the damn hard candy'.

As the survivors lounged and chatted in the clearing, the thought occurred to Margaret that the jungle had not spontaneously stopped growing there. Someone had painstakingly cut down the trees and cleared the area for cultivation. They were sprawled in a mountainside garden of sweet potato, or camote, mixed with a smattering of wild rhubarb.

Eventually, the garden's owner or owners would come to tend or harvest it, and that could mean trouble. But returning to the stream wasn't an option, and neither was leaving the place where they had been spotted by the B-17. They would hunker down and pray for the best. Maybe the gardeners lived far away and only rarely visited this particular field. They had no choice but to wait and hope.

Their wait did not last long.

An hour after the B-17 flew off, the jungle came alive. They heard again the sounds they had thought were the yaps and barks of a faraway pack of dogs.

'Do you hear something funny?' Decker asked.

The sounds grew closer. The creatures making them were human.

The survivors had been intimidated by the prospect of fighting off a pack of wild dogs. But they preferred that option to the two-metre, flesh-eating, headhunting, human-sacrificing natives they had expected to see only from the air, through the windows of the *Gremlin Special*.

Their assets and weaponry consisted of a lanky sergeant with painful burns and gaping head wound, an undersized WAC with gangrenous burns, and a hungry lieutenant with a broken rib and a Boy Scout knife. It would not be much of a fight.

It seemed to Margaret that more voices joined the strange chorus. The survivors told each other optimistically that maybe the yapping was the noise that native children made when they played. Or maybe the people making the sounds would continue on their way in the jungle and pass them by altogether. But Margaret worried that the rising number of voices meant that 'the signal had spread that a tasty dinner was waiting in the camote patch'.

Still they saw no one, even as the sound was upon them. No longer did it seem to come from everywhere. It rose from the far edge of the garden clearing, across a gully some twenty-five metres away.

The jungle rustled and shook. As the survivors stared helplessly in that direction, their fears took human form: dozens of nearly naked black men, their eyes shining, their bodies glistening with soot and pig grease, their hands filled with adzes made from wood and sharpened stone, emerged from behind the curtain of leaves.

Ten

Earl Walter, Junior and Senior

GOOD NEWS RACED THROUGH THE RANKS AT Fee-Ask.

Word that Captain Baker had spotted survivors in the jungle near the Shangri-La Valley sent Colonel Elsmore and his Hollandia staff into high gear. Baker had only seen three khaki-clad people in the clearing, but his B-17 was only over the area for a few minutes, flying at high altitude. He had not been able to communicate with the people he saw, and he didn't spot any wreckage. There was room for optimism. If three were alive, why not all twenty-four?

Maybe Colonel Prossen had somehow been able to set down the *Gremlin Special* intact in an emergency landing. Maybe the three survivors that Baker saw were an advance party, and others who had been aboard the C-47 were hurt but alive at the crash site. Or maybe they had split up, as the *Flying Dutchman* survivors had done, with some heading in another direction in search of help.

Those hopes found expression in material form. Elsmore's team assembled what one observer called 'enough equipment to stock a small country store'. Supply crews attached cargo parachutes to crates filled with essentials such as ten-in-one food rations, blankets, tents, First-Aid kits, two-way radios, batteries, and shoes. Having spotted what looked like a WAC on the ground, they included less conventional jungle survival necessities including lipstick and safety pins. Not knowing how many among the crew and passengers had survived, the would-be rescuers assembled enough provisions to feed, clothe and temporarily house all twenty-four.

Excitement aside, Elsmore and his command staff knew they faced a serious problem: they had no idea how to reach the survivors, and worse, they had no idea how to get them out. If there had been a way to land a plane in Shangri-La and take off again, Elsmore almost certainly would have done so already. He probably would have brought reporters along, to record him subduing or befriending the natives, possibly both, perhaps while planting a flag with his family crest to claim the valley as his sovereign territory.

Dutch and Australian authorities, who had been in contact with Elsmore throughout the search, offered help and expertise outfitting an overland trek. But this idea was dropped when it became apparent that such an expedition would require scores of native bearers and an undetermined number of troops to defend against hostile tribes and thousands of Japanese soldiers hiding in the jungles between Hollandia and the survivors. Even more problematic than the cost in manpower and equipment, it might take weeks for marchers to reach the valley, and by then any survivors might be dead from their injuries or at the hands of natives or enemy troops. Even if the crash victims survived the wait, they might lack the strength for a month-long trek over mountains and through jungles and swamps back to Hollandia.

Helicopters were raised as a possibility, but were almost as quickly shot down. As far as the Fee-Ask planners knew, they would not be able to fly at the necessary altitudes – the air was too thin for their blades to generate the necessary lift to carry them over the Oranje Mountains.

Other rescue plans still under consideration included those using pilots from the US Navy who could land a seaplane on the Baliem River. Also on the drawing board were plans worthy of Jules Verne involving lightweight planes, dirigibles, gliders, and Navy PT boats that could operate in shallow water and might reach the interior by river. If a submarine had been available or remotely feasible, someone on Elsmore's team no doubt would have suggested that, too.

But every idea had logistical flaws, some worse than others, so a rescue plan would have to wait. Elsmore's immediate concern was getting the survivors help on the ground. Presumably some were wounded, so they needed medical care. Equally urgent, considering the stories about the natives, the survivors needed protection. One solution was to drop in a team of heavily armed paratroopers, soldiers as well as medics – to prevent the survivors being horribly outnumbered by what they presumed were cannibalistic native 'savages'.

One challenge would be finding volunteers for such a mission. A bigger problem would be availability. Infantry-trained paratroopers were in the thick of the fight. As far as Elsmore and his staff knew, none were anywhere near Hollandia.

The Southwest Pacific region hosted two storied airborne units, the 503rd and the 511th Parachute Infantry Regiments. Both had played major roles in the Pacific war, most notably and heroically in the Philippines. Three months earlier, in February 1945, the 503rd had recaptured the island of Corregidor and helped General MacArthur make good on his promise to return to the Philippines. That same month, on the island of Luzon, the 511th had carried out a lightning raid thirty-nine kilometres behind enemy lines that freed more than two thousand Allied civilians, including men, women and children, from the Los Banos Internment Camp.

Both airborne regiments were still committed to combat in the Philippines, and winning the war took precedence over fetching a handful of survivors from a sightseeing crash in the New Guinea jungle.

When it looked as though they had run out of paratrooper options, an idea struck one of Elsmore's planners, a bright young officer named John Babcock.

Before the war, Babcock taught biology and chaired the science department at a private military high school in Los Angeles. When the US entered the war in December 1941, he traded his chalk for the rank of lieutenant colonel in the US Army. His science background led to his assignment as Fee-Ask's chemical warfare officer.

A few weeks before the crash, Babcock learned that one of his former students was based in Hollandia. Babcock knew two things about this particular young man: first, he had been expelled from school as a troublemaker, and second, he was now an infantry-trained paratrooper, frustrated about being stuck in Hollandia.

C. Earl Walter's boyhood revolved around his father and namesake, C. Earl Walter Sr. Most of that boyhood was spent in the Philippines, where the elder Walter had moved his wife and toddler son from Oregon to take a job as a timber company executive. Before the boy was nine, his mother fell ill with malaria. She returned to the United States for treatment, but she so missed her husband and son she took the next boat back to the Philippines. She died several months later.

That left just C. Earl Walter, senior and junior. Neither cared for the name Cecil, so both went by Earl. In the midst

Captain Earl Walter.

of the Depression, father and son lived on the southern Philippines island of Mindanao, in a big house with a full-time cook and a couple of native houseboys who saw to their every need. The younger Earl Walter had a small horse and his own little boat, and lots of friends who lived in the barrio near his home. He was smart, but with so many distractions and a busy father, school was a low priority. So low, in fact, that for two years Earl Junior did not attend. He preferred to go with his father into the wild reaches of the island on timber surveying trips. His favourite boyhood memory came from one of those trips.

'We had been hiking all day, and we found this little glade in the forest, and there was a little creek that had formed a pool,' Walter recalled. 'So he and I took our clothes off and we got in the water and splashed around just to get rid of the sweat. We were both naked, and when we got out of the water, it was so funny because the natives were standing two or three deep around the pool. Dad asked our guide what that was all about, and he said, "They're just curious to see if you're white all over."'

By the time he was fourteen, the tall, handsome white boy with wavy brown hair, blue-grey eyes, and a well-off father was even more of a curiosity, especially among the local girls. 'At that age you're old enough to wonder about women,' Walter explained. 'You wonder what it's like.'

Walter's father saw where things were headed, and worried that his only child was not getting much of an education. He had remarried after his wife's death. His new wife's mother, who lived in Portland, Oregon, was willing to take charge of the boy. Among other benefits, the move would give Earl a chance to catch up in school. It is possible that his father had other concerns, too. Even before Pearl Harbor, the elder Walter feared a Japanese invasion. 'When I was growing up with Dad, he used to say, "I'm going to put a machine gun over there, and a machine gun over there, and when the Japs come, we'll be ready for them."'

Earl Walter returned to the United States, first to his step-grandmother's house and then to the care of his paternal grandmother, who did her best to spoil him. His father decided that a firmer hand was needed: 'I think Dad felt that I needed a military school to go to, and that might straighten me out.'

The teenage boy was sent to Black-Foxe Military Institute in Los Angeles, a high-toned private academy complete with a polo team. Located between the Wilshire Country Club and the Los Angeles Tennis Club, Black-

Foxe provided a useful place for movie stars to stash their wayward sons. At various times, the Black-Foxe student body boasted the sons of Buster Keaton, Bing Crosby, Bette Davis, and Charlie Chaplin. Chaplin's son Sydney once described Black-Foxe as 'a sleep-away school for the sons of Hollywood rich people'.

There, Earl Walter grew into his full height of 1.93 metres and became an All-American swimmer, backstroking his way on to a record-setting relay team. One class he especially liked was biology, which meant that he skipped it less often than the others. His biology teacher was a future Army lieutenant colonel named John Babcock.

For the most part, the plan to discipline Earl Walter failed. He was not a malicious teen, but he found endless ways to avoid studying: 'It didn't straighten me out. In fact, I learned more bad habits there than I did anywhere.'

His stepmother had made the mistake of setting up a generous allowance to ease the transition into a new school. Black-Foxe administrators controlled the money, but Earl found a clever way around that barrier. He spent lavishly at the school store on notebooks and other supplies. Then he would sell them for half price to other students, for the cash. Even with the discounts, 'I had more money than I knew what to do with.'

'What kind of trouble did I get into? Well, I was always looking for female companionship,' the younger Earl Walter recalled. 'I had a bosom buddy named Miller, and we would go downtown Los Angeles, just hitchhike down to the bars. If you had money in those days and you were tall enough, they served you liquor. So I'd always have a couple of gin drinks. There was one area of LA where the burlesque shows were. Miller and I liked to look at naked women, so that's where we'd go.'

Black-Foxe decreed that young Earl was a 'bad influence' on the other boys and kicked him out. He returned to his grandmother's house and finished high school in Portland. By then he was nearly twenty. 'I heard that quite a few parents told their girls to stay away from Earl Walter because, what the hell, I was old enough to chase women and liked it.'

One girl he dated introduced him to her friend Sally Holden. Her mother was not keen on Earl, but Sally was. 'She was a beautiful gal,' he said, 'and we mutually fell in love. Once we started going steady, I had no interest in anybody else.'

Earl spent two semesters at the University of Oregon before being drafted in August 1942, when he was twenty-one. He went to Officer Candidate School and underwent parachute training at Fort Benning, Georgia. However, just before he was due to set sail for the European front, as a junior officer in the infantry, he received unexpected news about his father. The last he had heard from Earl Senior was a letter in 1941, just before Pearl Harbor, in which his father wrote that he would 'most likely stay on in the islands in the event that war came'.

As a US territory, the Philippines sent a Resident Commissioner to Washington to represent its interests, without a vote, in Congress. At the time, the Resident Commissioner was Joaquin Miguel 'Mike' Elizalde, a member of one of the Philippines' richest families. The Elizaldes held an interest in the lumber company where the elder Earl Walter was an executive. Mike Elizalde learned that Earl Senior had followed through on his plan to remain in the Philippines when war came. Rather than surrender and face internment or death, or attempt to flee to Australia or the United States, Earl Senior took to the jungles of Mindanao. There he had led a resistance force of Filipino guerrilla fighters against the invading Japanese army.

Earl Walter with his father and namesake.

A book about a fellow guerrilla leader in the Philippines described the elder Walter as a 'tough, no-nonsense warrior' and 'a leathery man in his fifties ... ready with his fists'. It said he had been honoured for bravery under fire in the First World War and picked up where he left off during the Second. Walter and his guerrilla troops 'mounted as vicious a close-in infantry action as men have fought' – ambushing Japanese soldiers along a coastal road and patrolling the streets of Japanese garrison towns at night.

Mike Elizalde, the Philippines' Resident Commissioner in Washington, sent word to the younger Walter to let him know that his father was alive, well, and fighting the Japanese. Walter told a lieutenant colonel, one of his commanding officers at the time, that Elizalde 'gave me enough information of my father to at least stop my fears for his safety and make me proud of his work'.

The news about his father had another effect: C. Earl Walter Jr lost interest in battling Germans and Italians in Europe. In a report filed at the time, the lieutenant colonel quoted Walter as saying that although he did not know many specifics of his father's guerrilla fighting, it was 'enough to make me envy the type of work he was doing'.

With help from Elizalde, Lieutenant Walter volunteered for a special commando and intelligence unit, the 5217th Reconnaissance Battalion, made up almost entirely of Filipino-American volunteers. The idea was to insert Filipino-American soldiers on to one of the Japanese-held islands by submarine or parachute, under the theory that they could immediately blend in among the native civilians. Once there, members of the unit would direct guerrilla operations and direct supply drops for resistance fighters.

Having grown up in the Philippines, Walter knew the culture and the Visayan dialect, which made him an ideal officer for the 5217th. As a qualified paratrooper, he was a natural to establish a jump school for the battalion outside Brisbane, Australia, known as 'Camp X'. Best of all, he thought, when he got to the Philippines, he could fight alongside his father. That was the plan, at least.

After marrying Sally, Walter shipped out in early 1944 and got to work turning members of the 5217th Recon into qualified paratroopers – occasionally with amusing results. The Army used large parachutes, and many of the Filipino-American soldiers weighed less than 55 kilos. After jumping, they would float around in the air currents. 'This one little guy kept yelling, "Lieutenant, I'm not coming down!"' Eventually he did, and afterward one of Walter's sergeants fitted smaller men with weighted ammunition belts to speed their descent.

In July 1944, upon his arrival in the South Pacific, Walter filled out a duty questionnaire for officers. He immediately sought a 'special mission' in the Philippines prior to the anticipated Allied invasion. He explained his reasoning more fully in a long memo to his new commanding officer.

In it, he detailed his upbringing in the Philippines and his knowledge of the islands and its languages, and described his father's work and his own ambitions. 'In short,' he wrote, 'I have an intense hatred for the Jap and came to this theater hoping to join a combat parachute unit and do my bit in their extermination.'

Later in the memo, Walter wrote that he would perform to the best of his ability in a non-combat intelligence or propaganda mission, but only if he were denied a posting in the heart of the action. Though he had yet to fire a shot in anger, Walter believed he was certain how he would react if and when the opportunity arose. Despite his discipline and training, Walter wrote, he might not be able to restrain his trigger finger in a non-combat assignment. 'My only desire is that I be given a job which would involve possible contact with the enemy, as I am afraid my liking for combat with the Jap might run away with itself when it should be curbed.'

His thirst for battle notwithstanding, Walter's unit was left out of the invasion of the Philippines and MacArthur's return to the islands in October 1944, which came some three months after Walter had appealed for a role in the fight. Even as the battle for control of the Philippines continued, Walter and his men remained at ease. Ill at ease would be more accurate.

While suppressing his frustration and biding his time for a meaningful assignment, Walter worked with members of the battalion who were secretly brought to the islands by submarine for intelligence missions. One submarine trip was to the island of Mindanao, and Walter went along. When he arrived at the landing place, he climbed out of the sub to find a surprise: his father was waiting there to greet him. Walter was thrilled – he hadn't seen Earl Senior for seven years, since he'd been sent to the United States to finish high school far from the Filipinas.

But his happiness was short-lived. The elder Walter told his son that he didn't want him taking part in more secret missions, by submarine or any other conveyance. Earl Senior also said that he intended to let higher-ups in the Army know his wishes. As far as C. Earl Walter Sr was concerned, the Allies would have to win the war without the help of his son.

Eleven

Uwambo

WHEN CAPTAIN BAKER AND HIS B-17 CREW reported seeing three survivors in a jungle clearing, they didn't mention any natives nearby. Even if they had spotted the tribesmen approaching Margaret, McCollom and Decker from the surrounding jungle, they could not have done anything about it. To start shooting was unthinkable, they could not land, and they had neither paratroopers nor weapons to drop to the trio.

The *Gremlin Special* survivors were on their own, and they were about to experience a first encounter with the people of Shangri-La.

The survivors of the *Gremlin Special* had crash-landed in a world that time had not forgotten. Time never knew it existed.

In their isolation, the people of this so-called Shangri-La followed an idiosyncratic path. They tamed fire but hadn't discovered the wheel. They carved bows and arrows but not bowls or utensils. They caked their bodies with clay when mourning but never developed pottery. They spoke complex languages – the verb that meant 'hit' or 'kill' could be inflected more than two thousand ways – but had a single word that could describe both time and place: 'O'. Their only numbers were one, two, and three; everything beyond three was 'many'. In a world awash in colour, they had terms for only two: *mili*, for black, dark browns, greens and blues; and *mola*, for reds, oranges, yellows, light browns and reddish-purples.

They ornamented themselves with necklaces and feathers but created no art. They believed the moon was a man and the sun was his wife, but they ignored the canopy of stars that hung low in the night sky. Four hundred years after Copernicus had declared that the earth revolved around the sun, people in and around the Baliem Valley thought the sun revolved around them. They believed it crossed the sky by day, spent the night in a sacred house, then travelled underground to its starting place at dawn. The moon had a house of its own.

They feared the ghosts of their ancestors but worshipped no gods. They were gentle with children but hacked off girls' fingers to honour dead relatives. They treated pigs as family – women nursed piglets when needed – but slaughtered them without remorse. They built nine-metre-tall watchtowers but their only furniture was a funeral chair for the dead. They grew strong tobacco but never distilled their crops into liquor. They practised polygamy but men and women slept apart. They valued cleverness but not curiosity. Loyalty had special significance. To greet close friends and relations, they said *hal-loak-nak*: 'Let me eat your faeces.' Its true meaning: 'I will do the unthinkable for you.'

The sixty thousand or so natives in the main valley, and tens of thousands more in the surrounding areas, organized themselves into communities consisting of small, fenced villages or hamlets. Most had thirty to fifty people living communally in huts arranged around a central courtyard, though larger villages might have several times that number. Men of the hamlet usually slept together in a round hut that was off-limits to women. Women lived with children in other round huts and worked together in a long, oval cooking house. Pigs lived in the huts, too, to keep them from wandering at night or being stolen by enemies.

When they referred to themselves, the natives of the valley might say they were *ahkuni*, or people. Their enemies were *dili*. Sometimes they would identify themselves by the name of their neighbourhood or clan, or by the name of the big man, or *kain*, who held sway over the military confed-

Dani tribesmen, photographed by Earl Walter in 1945.

eration to which their district belonged. They might describe themselves in relation to the river that wound through the valley: *Nit ahkuni Balim-mege*, or 'We people of the Baliem.' Although they were members of the Yali tribe or the Dani tribe, tribal affiliation was less important than district, clan and alliance loyalties. Different clans and districts within the same tribe were often enemies, and Yali and Dani people routinely crossed tribal lines to fight shared enemies.

A walk of a few minutes to an hour might take a resident of any one hamlet to ten or fifteen similar hamlets that comprised a district. Several districts that joined together for war made a confederation, and several confederations constituted an alliance of four to five thousand people. Native wars, called *wim*, were fought between alliances. Despite shared language, ethnicity and culture, alliances nurtured deep, longstanding hostilities towards one another, the original source of which was often unknown. They had always been enemies, and so they remained enemies.

Indeed, hostility between alliances defined the natives' lives. If covered by a glass roof, the valley would have been a terrarium of human conflict, an ecosystem fuelled by sunshine, river water, pigs, sweet potatoes, and war among neighbours.

Their ancestors told them that waging war was a moral obligation and a necessity of life. Men said, 'If there is no war, we will die.' The permanence of war was even part of the language. If a man said 'our war', he structured the phrase in the same way he would describe an irrevocable fact, such as the names of his parents. If he spoke of a possession such as 'our wood', he used different parts of speech. The meaning was clear: ownership of wood might change, but parents and wars were forever.

When compared to the Second World War, the motives underlying native wars were difficult for outsiders to grasp.

They did not fight for land, wealth or power. Neither side sought to repel or conquer a foreign people, to protect a way of life, or to change their enemies' beliefs, which both sides already shared. Neither side considered war a necessary evil, a failure of diplomacy, or an interruption of a desired peace. Peace was not waiting on the far side of war. There *was* no far side. War moved through different phases in the valley. It ebbed and flowed. But it never ended. A lifetime of war was an inheritance every child could count on.

In the Baliem Valley, the inexhaustible fuel for war was a need to satisfy spirits or ghosts, called *mogat*. No one ever saw the *mogat*, yet the living built huts for them, so the spirits would have a place to rest and a hearth to light their tobacco. The living also designed rituals to please them, believing that the *mogat* could choose either to help or hurt them, so they best be kept happy. When a person died in war, his or her friends and family sought to mollify his or her spirit. That required killing a member of the hated enemy – a male warrior, a woman, an elder, even a child. It could happen on the battlefield or in a raid on a sweet potato patch. Until the spirit was satisfied, the survivors believed that their souls were out of balance, and the *mogat* of the fallen would torment them with misfortune. Once they settled the score, they would celebrate with dancing and feasting. Sometimes those rituals included cooking and eating the flesh of their enemies. While the successful warriors and their families celebrated, their enemies cremated their dead, held elaborate mourning rituals, and began plotting a turn of events. Because combatants on both sides shared the same spiritual beliefs, one side or the other always had a death to avenge, a retaliatory killing to plan, a ghost to placate. An eye for every eye, *ad infinitum*.

Pacifying ghosts was the main rationale for war, but it was far from the only one. In an isolated valley where people enjoyed generally good health and abundant food and water, a place with temperate climate and no seasons, where nothing seemed to change, war animated communities and bound people to one another. It satisfied a basic human need for festival. War deaths and their resulting funerals created obligations and debts, shared enmities and common memories. Occasionally, war led to changes among allies, which freshened everyone's outlook, for good or ill. War also had a practical benefit for some: warrior deaths meant fewer men, which allowed male survivors to take multiple wives without creating villages filled with unhappy bachelors.

The practice of war in the valley was as unusual as its principles. Battles were arranged by calling out an invitation to the enemy across a no-man's land. If the enemy declined, everyone went home. They fought only by day, to prevent mischievous night spirits from getting involved.

Dani tribesmen, photographed by Earl Walter in 1945.

They cancelled battles in bad weather, lest the rain smear their war paint. Their war whoop wasn't a predator's cry but the hoot of a cuckoo dove. They put feathers in their hair but not on their arrows; when fired, the arrows traced jagged patterns, like birds in flight. During breaks in battle, warriors lounged, sang, and gossiped. They knew details about their enemies' lives, and hurled insults across the front lines. A nasty remark about an enemy's wife might reduce both sides to belly laughs. Then they would pick up their spears and try again to kill one another.

Because success in war was seen as necessary for the well-being of the community, men who succeeded in battle gained social standing. Skilled warriors had access to more potential wives. This was especially valuable in a culture in which married couples routinely abstained from sex for up to five years after the birth of a child. But it would be wrong to overstate the link between war, polygamy, and abstinence. For many men, war was its own reward, a source of pleasure and recreation, a platform on which to find excitement and camaraderie. Paradoxically, when not waging war, village life tended to be serene, punctuated by occasional conflicts over pig theft and marital discord. Among friends and family, the most common way of coping with conflict was not violence but avoidance – one party would simply move away.

War had few apparent benefits for women. It hung over every journey her male kin made from their village and each trip she and her daughters made to the gardens or to the brine pools to collect salt, where an enemy raiding party might set upon them.

War shaped children from their earliest memories. Boys' education and play involved mimicking male elders waging war and staging raids. Toys were small bows with arrows made from bamboo or long stalks of grass. Grass arrows routinely found their way into boys' eyes, leaving them half-blind but no less eager to grow into warriors. For girls, war meant having the upper halves of one or more fingers chopped off each time a close relative was killed, to satisfy the dead person's ghost. By the time a girl reached marrying age, her hands might be all thumbs. An anthropologist who followed the survivors into the valley years later described the process:

> Several girls are brought to the funeral compound early on the second day. One man, the specialist in this practice, is waiting for them. First he ties off a girl's arm with a tight string above the elbow. Then he smashes her elbow down on a rock or board, hitting the olecranon process, the 'funny bone', in order to numb the nerves in the fingers. Someone holds the girl's hand on a board, and the man takes a stone adze and with one blow he cuts off one or two fingers at the first joint.

Making war and appeasing spirits was not all the native people did. They built huts and watchtowers, grew sweet potatoes and other vegetables, tended pigs, raised families, and cooked meals. Most of the hard work fell to the women. Men built homes and watchtowers, and tilled gardens, which left plenty of time to spare. They devoted that time and energy to war – planning it, fighting it, celebrating its victories, mourning its losses, and planning it anew. In between, they talked about it, sharpened their weapons, pierced their noses so pig tusks would fit into the holes and make them look fierce, and wrapped greasy orchid fibres around their arrows to cause infections if the wounds were not immediately fatal. They also spent time scanning for enemy movements from the watchtowers on the edge of the vast no-man's land that separated their homes and gardens from their enemies' identical homes and gardens.

When the anthropologist Margaret Mead learned about the people of the Baliem Valley, she saw a connection between 'the distant past and the future towards which men are moving'. She wrote: 'These are clearly human beings, like ourselves, entrapped in a terrible way of life in which the enemy cannot be annihilated, conquered, or absorbed, because an enemy is needed to provide the exchange of victims, whose only possible end is another victim. Men have involved themselves in many vicious circles, and kingdoms and empires have collapsed because they could find no way out but to fall before invaders who were not so trapped. Here in the highlands of New Guinea there has been no way out for thousands of years, only the careful tending of the gardens and rearing of children to be slain.'

By evoking the name of the peaceful paradise in *Lost Horizon*, war correspondents George Lait and Harry E. Patterson had indulged in a calculated fantasy. Their readers longed for a Shangri-La after a daily diet of war news. The irony of the reporters' choice of name, however, was bitter. The Baliem Valley was a beautiful and extraordinary place, but it was no heaven on earth.

Colonel Elsmore's speculation about earthquakes notwithstanding, no one knew how people had come to live in the valley or how long they had been there. One possibility was that they were descendants of people who had lived on the island's coast but been driven inland by subsequent arrivals. Equally mysterious was the source of their beliefs and customs.

Yet clues to the past could be found in oral myths told around their fires. The first lines of a Dani creation myth, translated by an outsider, were: 'In the beginning was The Hole. Out of The Hole came the Dani men. They settled in the fertile lands around The Hole. Then came pigs. The

Dani took the pigs and domesticated them. Next came women, and the Dani took the women.' People who lived near the agreed-upon location of The Hole called themselves *iniatek*, the originals.

Another myth described how, after leaving The Hole, humans became separate from other creatures of the valley. At first, the myth explained, humans came out of The Hole with birds, bats, insects, reptiles and forest mammals. The assembled creatures asked the first man, called Nakmatugi, to differentiate among them. He organized them by type and gave them individual identities. At first he placed the birds and men together. But the birds thought otherwise, so they flew off and left their brothers on the ground.

The natives' belief in an ancient link between man and birds was a recurring theme. The myth of Bird and Snake describes the two creatures arguing about death, immortality, and the fate of mankind. Snake insisted that men should return from the dead, just as snakes could shed their skins and be reborn. But Bird said men should stay dead, like fallen birds, and other birds would smear mud on themselves to mourn. To decide which belief would prevail, Bird and Snake had a race. Bird won, so men, like birds, must die. People took the fable to heart. Women smeared their bodies with mud when mourning, and the weapons, ornaments, and other trophies taken from enemies killed in battle were called 'dead birds'.

In the natives' myths, mankind's early existence in the valley never featured an earthly paradise or a Garden of Eden. Violent death and hostile alliances dated to the beginning of time. When people emerged from The Hole, one myth claimed, a fight broke out and killings occurred. The victims' families joined forces and said, 'Let us take revenge on our enemy together.' They did, and when the enemy retaliated, the cycle of war never stopped.

The people of the valley also had a prophecy called 'Uluayek'. It told of spirits that lived in the sky over the valley, and of a vine that hung down to the ground. Long ago, according to the Uluayek prophecy, the valley people and the sky spirits climbed up and down the vine to visit one another. Some said the sky spirits had long hair, and light skin and eyes. Some said they had hairy arms they kept covered. No one knew for sure, because the spirits had stolen pigs and women, and the people of the valley had cut the vine, ending contact. The Uluayek legend claimed that one day the sky spirits would replace the vine and climb down again.

The spirits' return would herald the End of Days.

The cluster of huts the *Gremlin Special* passengers saw shortly before the crash was a village the natives called Uwambo. When the plane first roared through overhead, the villagers – members of the Yali tribe – were busy with their daily chores. The sound of the low-flying plane sent them ducking for cover in their sweet potato fields or running to hide in the surrounding jungle, which is why Margaret had not seen any natives near the huts.

The people of Uwambo had seen planes before, especially during the previous year, as Colonel Elsmore and other pilots made regular flights over their homes. Still, the natives did not know what to make of them. Westerners speculated that the natives thought the planes were giant birds, but the people of Uwambo knew how birds soared and turned and rushed through the sky, silent except for song or cry. These planes did not look, move or sound like birds. Some native children thought they might be large men with their arms spread. Few if any imagined that they carried people inside.

One thing the natives knew for certain was the sound the planes made. They used their word for noise, *ane*, pronounced ah-nay, and attached suffixes – *woo* or *kuku* – that approximated the engines' drone. Planes entered the native language as *anewoo* or *anekuku.*

As the passengers aboard the *Gremlin Special* looked through the windows searching for natives, a Yali boy named Helenma Wandik watched the *anewoo* from his hiding place in the jungle. He would always remember that this particular *anewoo* seemed to be flying especially low to the ground. His cousin, a teenage girl named Yunggukwe Wandik, who had recently been given her first pig, was working in the sweet potato gardens when she saw it. Fearful, she fell to the ground and grabbed the legs of a woman working alongside her.

Both Helenma and Yunggukwe thought the *anewoo* circled twice in the little valley, then pointed its nose towards a place they called the Ogi ridge, near a mountain stream they called the Mundi. Neither saw it crash into the trees, but Helenma wondered why he heard thunder on such a clear day.

When it grew dark the night of the crash, the people of Uwambo saw flames coming from the place on the Ogi ridge where the *anewoo* disappeared. A village leader named Yaralok Wandik sneaked through the jungle along the spine of the ridge to see what was happening. As he approached, he caught wind of a strange smell. When he reached the edge of the crash site, he watched unseen from the jungle. He saw creatures that resembled people, but the skin on their faces was light and they had straight hair. The skin on their bodies was strange. They had feet but no toes. Only later would he learn that coverings called clothing shielded their skin and that shoes encased their toes.

Yaralok left without being spotted. When he returned to Uwambo, he told no one what he had seen. Several other men did the same. Among them were Nalarik Wandik, whose first name meant 'Getting lost', and Ingimaruk Mabel, whose name meant 'Nothing in his hands'. Another man, Pugulik Sambom, went up, too, and among the natives he was perhaps the most disturbed by what he had seen. Yet at first none of them spread the news.

Their silence was the mark of a cultural idiosyncrasy among the Yali: the bearer of bad news risked being blamed for it. Rather than spread word about what they knew, the men kept silent. They joined the rest of their hamlet as the frightened people gathered half-ripe sweet potatoes and fled into the jungle.

The next day, Yaralok returned to the crash site and saw what he thought were three men and one woman, though in their odd coverings he could not be sure. One man – likely Decker – had a covering on his head that reminded Yaralok of the light-coloured markings on the head of a bird. He thought he saw them carrying a body away from what remained of the *anewoo*. He heard popping noises and the sound of small explosions. After watching awhile he sank back into the jungle, certain they were spirits from the sky.

To a Yali farmer-warrior from Uwambo, this was the most likely explanation. Since boyhood, he had heard the Uluayek legend, which anticipated the return of spirits whose rope to the valley floor had been cut. The legend described these creatures from the *anewoo* perfectly – light skin, long hair, light eyes, arms covered. The *anewoo* made sense, too. In the absence of a rope, the sky spirits had found another way down to the valley. Still, Yaralok was in no rush to share his conclusions.

As his nephew Helenma explained, 'Something cataclysmic was happening. He did not want to create panic or be blamed. These were spirits. The legend said long-haired people would come down from the sky. They were horrified. This could be the End Times. It was something they had been talking about and hearing about for generations.'

After other villagers began talking about the flames they had seen in the jungle, Yaralok broke his silence. To his relief, no one blamed him. They were too busy worrying what the visitors' arrival might portend. One village leader, Wimayuk Wandik, listened especially closely to Yaralok's story.

One option for the people of Uwambo was to welcome the spirits, even if their arrival meant the end of their world as they knew it.

The other option, more natural to a warlike people, was to kill them.

Twelve

'Chief Pete'

THE NATIVE MEN APPROACHING THE SURVIVORS, residents of Uwambo and nearby villages, had all danced to celebrate the deaths of foes. They had grieved the loss of family and friends as casualties of war. Some had shed blood in battle and drawn the blood of their enemies. Some had taken a life, or several. All could recount where those deaths had occurred and the names of their fallen foes. Some of the men emerging from the jungle might have butchered dead enemies and tasted human flesh as a spoil of victory.

'When we killed somebody we'd have a victory dance,' said Helenma Wandik. He accused his enemies, a clan called the Landikma, of eating the entire bodies of battle victims. He considered that barbaric. By contrast, Helenma Wandik said, his people only ate the hands of their enemies, severed after death and cooked in a pit with hot rocks.

The bad news, then, was that at least some of the bogeyman stories that Margaret, McCollom and Decker had heard about the natives eating the flesh of their enemies were true. The nearly naked, adze-wielding men who emerged from the jungle had no qualms about killing. And they had every reason to consider it wise to strike first at strangers.

The natives sorted the world into three useful categories of people: themselves, their allies, and their enemies. They lived or cooperated with the first two. They routinely tried to kill, and avoid being killed by, the third. Margaret, McCollom and Decker obviously did not belong to the first two categories. But they also did not resemble the natives' usual enemies. Although they did not know it, the survivors' best hope would be if the people of Uwambo continued to think they were spirits.

One piece of good fortune for the three survivors was that the Yali people of Uwambo were not among the natives who had come into contact with the Archbold expedition. They owed no payback to appease the spirit of the man killed by gunshot seven years earlier.

Standing in the native sweet potato garden, separated by a gully and ten thousand years of what might commonly be termed 'progress', the survivors and the natives waited for someone to make the first move.

In every immediate way, the natives had the upper hand. They outnumbered the survivors by more than ten to one. They were healthy and well fed. None suffered burns, head injuries, or gangrene. None had lived for three sleep-deprived days on sips of water and boiled sweets. Their sharpened stone adzes made a joke of McCollom's Boy Scout knife.

Beyond Shangri-La, of course, the situation was different.

By most conventional measures of wealth, education, medicine, and technological achievement, the world represented by Margaret, McCollom and Decker surpassed the natives' Shangri-La. Yet the crash survivors were parts of a military machine engaged in the largest and deadliest war in history, one that was about to become far deadlier.

As the survivors faced the natives, Allied leaders were considering the use of a new super weapon, a bomb that could level a city and plunge any survivors into a primitive existence. The bomb's makers were still uncertain whether it would work, but if it did, it would eerily fulfil the warning in *Lost Horizon* of a future in which 'a single-weaponed man might have matched a whole army'.

Albert Einstein once said: 'I do not know with what weapons World War III will be fought, but World War IV will be fought with sticks and stones.' Viewed in that light, the people of Shangri-La were the most advanced warriors on earth.

At the moment, though, Margaret wasn't thinking about the moral and practical relativity of modern and traditional warfare. She stared at the men with the stone-and-wood axes, their dark skin glistening with pig grease. As she waited for orders from McCollom, a thought ran through her mind: How awful to have survived a plane crash only to end up in a native stew.

After the B-17 stopped wagging its wings and flew off, McCollom had allowed himself a brief moment of respite and relaxed for the first time since the crash. Now, as the natives approached, he leapt back into action, barking orders at his companions.

'We haven't any weapon,' he told Margaret and Decker, wisely discounting the value of his little knife. 'There is nothing we can do but act friendly. Smile as you've never smiled before, and pray to God it works.'

McCollom told them to hold out their hands with their remaining Charms – they were sick of the sweets by then, anyway. He added his knife to the paltry peace offerings.

'Stand up – and smile,' McCollom said.

For the previous hour, since their discovery by the search plane, Margaret and Decker had been sitting in the dirt of the garden clearing. Exhausted and in pain, Margaret was unsure she could stand again. But with McCollom commanding her to rise, she struggled up from the ground, as did Decker.

McCollom watched as the natives began to line up behind a fallen tree, perhaps twenty-five metres from where the survivors stood. All he could see was their heads. By McCollom's count there were about forty of them, all adult males. Margaret, possibly exaggerating in her fright, put the number at more like one hundred. Over their shoulders they carried what she called 'wicked-looking stone axes'. At least one carried a long spear.

Margaret felt her hand shaking, rattling the sweets like dice. As she put it, 'The bottom had long since dropped out of my stomach.' She wrote in her diary: 'Black heads began to pop out from behind jungle trees. "Smile, damn it!" rasped McCollom. We smiled. Oh, we smiled to high heaven. We smiled for our lives. We smiled and held out the candy and the jackknife and then we waited as the black men advanced.'

McCollom heard one of his companions darkly muse: 'Well, maybe they'll feed us before they kill us.' He didn't recall who said it, but it sounded like Decker.

The noises the survivors had thought resembled dogs yapping stopped. After a brief pause, the silence was replaced with what Margaret called 'an excited and frantic jabbering, accompanied by much gesturing. We couldn't tell whether that was a good sign or bad. We could only fasten the smiles on more securely.'

A gully separated the survivors' clearing and a knoll at the edge of the jungle where the natives emerged. A long, fallen tree served as a bridge across the gully. An older man stepped forward. He was wiry and alert, naked except for a necklace with a narrow piece of shell that hung over his sternum, and a long, straight penis gourd more than thirty centimetres long that pointed towards the sky. McCollom and the others took him to be the chief.

He beckoned the survivors forward towards the log bridge. No one moved. He waved them towards him again, more forcefully this time.

'I think we ought to go,' McCollom said. 'We'd better humor them.'

Margaret didn't move. Her feet and legs hurt so badly that she could barely stand. She was sure she would fall off the slippery log. But that wasn't her only hesitation. She despaired at the thought that, having survived the crash and the march down the mountain, and having just been spotted by a rescue plane, she was being asked to deliver herself to men she thought were savages and, worse, cannibals.

'Honest, McCollom, I can't walk it,' she said. 'Truly, I can't.'

'I know, Maggie,' he replied. He considered the situation briefly then decided: 'Let 'em come to us.'

The survivors used their candy-filled hands to motion the natives towards them. After a brief discussion with his troops, the native leader stepped alone on to the log. McCollom thought it wise to meet him halfway, man to man. As he inched forward on the log, he called back to Margaret and Decker, demanding that they keep smiling.

The natives on the other side of the gully continued talking and staring at the survivors, until they again fell quiet. 'Their silence seemed a thousand times more sinister and threatening than their yapping or their chatter,' Margaret wrote. She and Decker stretched their arms forward more submissively to offer their gifts.

The two leaders edged closer on the log bridge. When they met in the middle, McCollom reached out and grasped the native's hand. He pumped it like a cross between a politician, a car salesman, and a long-lost relative.

'How are you? Nice to meet you!' McCollom said repeatedly.

In Margaret's recollection, the native was the one who held out his hand first, and McCollom, 'weak with relief, grabbed it and wrung it'.

Either way, McCollom turned the leader's attention to his small band of smiling survivors: 'Here! Meet Corporal Hastings and Sergeant Decker.'

Regardless of who extended his hand first, the tension broke and now both groups were smiling at each other. The native leader shook hands with Margaret and Decker, and in no time the rest of the natives followed suit. Margaret described the moment in her diary: 'There on the knoll we held as fine a reception as any ever given by Mrs. Vanderbilt,' she wrote. 'The black man who never had seen a white man and the white man who never before had met a savage on his own ground understood each other. The smiles had done it.'

As her fear ebbed, Margaret sensed that the natives were not fierce. They seemed shy, perhaps even afraid of the three bedraggled intruders. When she asked Decker if he thought the same thing, he shot back: 'Shh, don't tell 'em so!'

McCollom nicknamed his handshake partner 'Pete', after a college classmate. The survivors didn't know that 'Pete' and his fellow villagers thought they were spirits from the sky. And they never learned 'Pete's' real name.

'Pete' was Wimayuk Wandik, a leader though not a 'chief' in Uwambo.

Wimayuk had listened closely to his clansman Yaralok Wandik describe what he saw at the crash site. Although his name meant 'Fearful of war', Wimayuk was more cautious than afraid. He had been in many battles and he knew the cost of war – his younger brother Sinangke Wandik had been mortally wounded in battle. He and Yaralok Wandik shared the responsibility of calling the men of Uwambo to fight. It was a role he did not take lightly.

He told his son Helenma Wandik, the second of his five children, that he had acted warmly to the creatures he thought were sky spirits because of the way he had learned the Uluayek legend. Although the spirits' return meant the end of an era, Wimayuk Wandik believed that something good could come of it. He hoped the new era might be better for their people.

John McCollom shakes hands with Wimayuk Wandik, the tribal leader McCollom called 'Pete', weeks after the crash.

Also, Wimayuk Wandik was a man willing to be flexible when an opportunity presented itself. He and his fellow villagers were traders, regularly walking thirty or so kilometres from their homes to the Baliem Valley lands of the Dani tribe, the heart of what the outsiders called Shangri-La. They exchanged feathers from birds of paradise, string, and bows and arrows, for cowrie shells, pigs and tobacco. If a battle happened to break out while they were trading, they would join the fight on the side of their trading partners, even if they had no beef with the enemy. It was good for business, and good fun, too. When he found the survivors smiling and offering gifts in the clearing he called Mundima – the place of the Mundi River – Wimayuk saw an opportunity to befriend the spirits.

Although Margaret continued to refer to the natives as 'savages' in her diary, she realized how little substance many of the rumours that had circulated around Hollandia about the natives really had:

> Far from being seven feet tall, they averaged from five feet four inches to five feet seven inches in height. And certainly, only on close observation, they didn't look very fierce. They were black as the ace of spades and naked as birds in feathering time. Their clothing consisted of a thong around their waists, from which a gourd was suspended in front and a huge triple leaf hung tail-like in back. Some wore bracelets above their elbows. There were two kinds of bracelets. Those woven of fine twigs and those made of fur ... All but Pete, the chief, wore snoods suspended from their heads and hanging far down their backs. At least they looked like snoods. They seemed to be made of heavy string, like a shopping bag, and they were certainly the New Guinea counterpart of a shopping catch-all. In these snoods, the natives tucked anything they had to carry. After all, they didn't have any pockets.

Margaret wrinkled her nose at the powerful, musky scent of sweat mixed with the ash-blackened pig grease the natives smeared on their bodies: 'Pete and his boys certainly needed baths and a lot of rosewater,' she wrote. 'The breeze was coming from the wrong direction, and I prayed they would get tired of staring soon and go home.'

The feeling was mutual, at least about the odour. Wimayuk and Yaralok told their children that the spirits carried a terrible smell. Considering the gangrenous sores on Margaret and Decker, combined with their unwashed days in the jungle, all three survivors almost certainly reeked.

Margaret recoiled at the swarms of flies that hovered around the natives' cuts and scratches. She marvelled at the 'biggest, flattest feet any of us had ever seen'. The survivors thought all the natives at the edge of the jungle were adults, but during the handshakes and greetings Margaret noticed that a group of boys had followed the men – they had hung back until friendly relations were established.

As the greetings continued, a native started a fire – splitting open a stick and quickly rubbing a rattan vine to make a spark – to cook sweet potatoes, which the natives called *hiperi*. McCollom bent down and pulled up a plant he thought looked like the rhubarb he had grown in a garden back home in Missouri. He wiped off the dirt, bit into the stalk, and felt smoke shoot from his ears.

'That's the hottest damn stuff I ever tasted!' McCollom said later. He spit it out – sending the natives into peals of laughter. All except one.

The disgruntled native began protesting to 'Pete' in a way that the survivors interpreted to mean that they had trampled through his personal garden. Margaret felt afraid of the man, whom she called 'Trouble Maker'. But 'Pete' stepped in.

'The native who had the garden,' McCollom recalled, 'he apparently started griping to the chief, and the chief, in effect turned around and said, "Shut up." And from then on we were friends.'

The unhappy man was almost certainly Pugulik Sambom. His objections, according to Yaralok's daughter Yunggukwe, had not been about the ruined crops but about the survivors themselves.

'Pugulik was yelling at everyone that something bad would happen because of the spirits,' she said through an interpreter. 'He said, "They're spirits! They're spirits! They're ghosts! Don't go in there with them."'

She watched as Pugulik paced back and forth on a fallen log, more scared than angry, repeating his warning that the strangers were *mogat*, spirits or ghosts, and certain to bring bad tidings. The woman whose legs Yunggukwe had grabbed in the field when the *Gremlin Special* flew overhead was Pugulik's wife, Maruk, whose name meant 'Bad'. Maruk echoed her husband's warnings. Fortunately for the survivors, the Wandiks outnumbered the Samboms and welcomed them, spirits or not.

The survivors tried to get the natives to take McCollom's knife as a gift. They encouraged them to try the sweets.

'They handled the jackknife curiously,' Margaret wrote. 'We tried to show them that the candy was to eat. We would open our mouths, pop in a piece of hard candy, smack our lips and look rapturous – though we had come to hate it like poison. Apparently they didn't understand us. So we thought we would give the candy to some boys of ten or twelve who had accompanied Pete and his men. But when we started to feed the kids, "Trouble Maker" danced up and down and shrieked until we backed off in a hurry.'

Alarmed, Margaret dug into her pocket for her compact. She popped it open and showed 'Pete' his image. Delighted, Wimayuk Wandik passed the mirror from man to man. 'If ever anything was calculated to make friends and influence savages, it was that cheap red enamel compact from an Army PX,' she wrote. 'These naked strangers beamed and gurgled and chattered like magpies over a sight of their own faces.'

'Maggie,' Decker told her, 'you ought to write home to the missionaries to stock up on compacts.'

Physically and emotionally exhausted, her burned legs and feet throbbing, Margaret dropped back down to the ground. A group of natives circled around her, squatting on their haunches and staring. Using her compact, Margaret took stock of herself and understood their curiosity.

She wrote in her diary that not only was she the first white woman the natives had seen, she was 'the first black-and-white person they had ever seen'. Burns from the crash had darkened the left side of her face, while the right side was unmarked. Her eyebrows and eyelashes had been singed, and her nose seemed swollen. McCollom's jungle salon treatment had not helped her appearance – short

Margaret Hastings with a native child.

tufts of Margaret's once-lustrous hair stood at attention all over her head. She didn't know it, but even more interesting to the natives were her bright blue eyes.

As she stared at the natives and the natives stared back, Margaret felt relief. Soon it spread into affection. 'At the moment, I could not have loved Pete and his followers more dearly if they had been blood brothers,' she wrote. 'They had turned out to be a race of Caspar Milquetoasts' – the name of a mild-mannered comic book character – 'in black face instead of head hunters or cannibals. I was duly grateful.'

McCollom brought 'Pete' to Margaret and Decker to show him their injuries. The native leader nodded solemnly. Margaret detected sympathy in his reaction.

'He looked again and muttered, "Unh, unh, unh," over and over again. We knew he was trying to tell us he was sorry and wanted to help. The only native word we ever picked up was "Unh, unh, unh" repeated over and over,' Margaret wrote. In fact, 'unh' wasn't a word in the Yali or Dani language. It was a murmur, a local equivalent of a polite listener in English saying 'hmmm' to express interest.

'Pete' examined the gash in Decker's scalp. He stepped in close and blew into the cut. Margaret made light of it: 'For the first and only time, I thought Decker was going to faint. Old Pete then came over to me and blew on my legs and hand. And I thought I would faint. Pete undoubtedly had the world's worst case of halitosis.'

'Decker and McCollom and I came to the conclusion,' Margaret continued, 'that the blowing of the chieftain's breath on a wound was probably some native cure-all custom, like laying on of hands in other parts of the world. But Decker and I didn't appreciate the honor.'

The survivors' conclusion about the practice was close, but it failed to capture the full significance of the moment.

Margaret and Decker had just received a remarkable gift, one that signified that the people who had found them hurt and hungry in a sweet potato patch wanted nothing but for them to survive.

When a Yali or Dani man is wounded in battle, the physical damage is almost a secondary concern. More worrisome is the possibility that the injury might dislodge the essence of his being, his *etai-eken*, or 'seeds of singing'. A better translation: his soul.

Among people of the valley who enjoy good physical and spiritual health, the *etai-eken* are believed to reside in the upper part of the solar plexus, just below the front arch of the ribs. The native leader's shell necklace, hanging as it did at just that spot, might well have been placed there to protect his *etai-eken*. Under pain or duress – personal, such as a war wound, or communal, such as the death of a family member or ally – the *etai-eken* are believed to retreat from the front part of the chest to a person's back. Such a move is a spiritual calamity, a threat to an individual's well-being that demands urgent action.

First, a specialist removes any remnants of the arrow or spear that caused the wound. Then he makes several incisions in the victim's stomach to drain what the natives call *mep mili*, or 'dark blood', which is believed to cause pain and sickness. Next comes the more essential treatment. A person who is either close to the wounded warrior or especially skilled in the healing arts speaks directly to the man's *etai-eken*. He coaxes the soul matter back to its proper place, blowing and whispering special pleadings in the victim's ear. He also blows directly on the wounds.

A short time earlier, the survivors feared that they would be killed and eaten by Wimayuk Wandik, the native they called 'Pete'. Now he was tending to their souls.

By mid-afternoon the survivors were exhausted, but the natives were so fascinated by the sky spirits they showed no sign of leaving. Then, at about four o'clock, the cold nightly rains arrived. The natives gathered up the cooked sweet potatoes – 'They took the chow with them!' Decker complained – but left the knife, the compact, and the sweets behind. It would be another starving night for the survivors.

The trio found a smooth spot of cleared ground, laid out one tarpaulin, used the other as a cover, and went to sleep, 'too weak to do much and too happy to care,' Margaret wrote. They had scratched their way through the mountain jungle to a clearing, been spotted by a search plane, and made friends with the natives. Margaret summed it up with understatement: 'It had been a big day.'

When she awoke in the middle of the night, she sensed that someone was hovering over her. Before she could scream, she recognized a man's face: 'Pete'.

'It was as plain as day that he was worried about us and had come back to see how we were. He hovered over us like a mother hen. I woke up McCollom. He took a good look at Pete and said, "Holy smoke! We've got a guardian."'

Later, when she compared notes with McCollom and Decker, Margaret learned that whenever one or the other woke that night, he saw Chief Pete/Wimayuk Wandik watching over them.

Thirteen

Come What May

By November 1944, Earl Walter and sixty-six jump-qualified members of the 5217th Reconnaissance Battalion were sweating out the war in 'strategic reserve', stuck in steamy but peaceful Hollandia, Dutch New Guinea. The closest thing to excitement came when their battalion was renamed the 1st Reconnaissance Battalion (Special), known as the 1st Recon. The new name did nothing to change their idle fate. Neither did Walter's promotion from lieutenant to captain.

As months passed, Allied forces under General MacArthur were kept busy retaking the islands of the Philippines – one after another, from Leyte to Luzon, Palawan to Mindanao. As the fight progressed, paratroopers from the 503rd and 511th regiments carried out their dangerous and heroic missions on Corregidor and Luzon.

All the while, Walter and his men yearned to get out of the heat of Hollandia and into the fire of war. Their battalion's devil-may-care motto was 'Bahala Na!' a phrase from the Tagalog dialect of the Philippines that translated as 'Come What May!' The more time that passed without a mission, the more it seemed like a taunt. The problem, as Walter and his men saw it, was that nothing came their way.

While awaiting orders in Hollandia – some 3000 kilometres southeast of Manila – Walter's men pressed him for news. With families and roots in the Philippines, they wanted both the honour and the satisfaction of driving the enemy from their homeland. They craved payback for more than two years of Japanese occupation. They wanted revenge for the Bataan Death March of 1942, during which Japanese troops killed or brutalized thousands of captured Filipino and American soldiers along a forced 160-kilometre march to a prison camp. Newspapers had detailed the atrocities, fuelling a combustible mix of fear and hatred of the Japanese, perhaps nowhere more so than among the men in Walter's unit. One of them, Corporal Camilo 'Rammy' Ramirez, had experienced the horrors at Bataan firsthand before making a daring escape.

Walter tried to boost morale and conditioning, leading gruelling runs around Hollandia to keep their legs strong for parachute landings. Yet privately, Walter feared it was a waste of time. He worried that he would spend the rest of his life saying 'nothing much' when asked what he had done in the war.

'My men would come to me and say – I was a lieutenant then – "Lieutenant, when in hell are we going to get to the Philippines?"' Walter recalled. 'And I'd say, "As soon as I can get us there."' One hindrance, at least from Walter's perspective, was that the Japanese were retreating faster than expected, potentially making unnecessary his unit's unique language, intelligence and parachute skills.

Walter proposed one combat task after another to his superiors, to no avail. Showing some gumption, he tried to cut through the Army bureaucracy by drawing up plans for a behind-enemy-lines parachute drop. He shared the plans with an acquaintance – a lieutenant who happened to be the son of General Courtney Whitney, who oversaw guerrilla resistance in the Philippines and was MacArthur's closest confidant.

When that gambit failed to spark a response, on 13 March 1945, Walter took the next step and wrote a blunt letter to General Whitney. In it, Walter complained about being idle and fairly pleaded for combat duty in the Philippines. If that wasn't possible, he wrote, he wanted to be reassigned to a fighting unit in Europe or anywhere at all before it was too late and the war was already won.

'As you know, Sir,' Walter wrote to the general, 'I came to this theater at my own request, in fact I worked hard for the assignment, but now I find that my efforts were in vain.' After making his case, he acknowledged that he had violated protocol and jumped multiple levels in the chain of command by sending the letter. 'In closing may I add that I admit I have stepped over the line but I am afraid this is a trait I inherited from my father.'

Whitney seemed to admire Walter's pluck. He responded two weeks later with a letter filled with praise and encouragement. The brigadier general gently explained to the young officer that matters more pressing than personal ambition – however courageous or well-intended – took priority in the effort to reclaim the Philippines. Whitney urged Walter to keep his men ready to invade Japan, and offered flattery and morale-building suggestions. 'The work of the Battalion and the preparation of your parachutists for active service has been brilliant,' the general wrote. 'Your leadership in this latter field has been cause for much satisfaction on the part of every staff officer of this Headquarters ... My advice to you is to do all possible to keep your men in trim and keep patient a little longer. I am sure that your desire for an opportunity to employ these men in the manner for which they have been trained will be fully satisfied in the campaigns which yet lie ahead.'

Whitney's letter cheered Walter. He wrote to the general in response: 'I took the liberty of reading it to my parachutists, and to the man they were overjoyed, and their morale has climbed to a new high. They are all very anxious to do their part, and the work given us, no matter how difficult, I can guarantee will be a complete success. The men will be kept in trim and when our turn comes we will be ready. Thank you for giving the hopes of my officers and men a new foundation and I can easily say for all, you can count on us for anything.'

General Whitney returned his attention to the war. Weeks passed with no further word on a role for the 1st Recon, and Walter's excitement ebbed. He grew frustrated to the point of distraction. He became convinced that his father had followed through with the threat he had made at the submarine landing site, and that his concerns about his son's safety had sidelined the paratroopers of the 1st Recon.

'I was an only son, an only child, and I think my dad worried,' Walter explained. 'My dad was strong enough in the guerrilla movement, and known well enough by people in the Army, that when he said "I don't want you using my son overtly," they listened.'

Whether his father had such power is unclear. No records exist to confirm that the elder Walter had raised objections to his son's participation in risky duty. But the fact remained that in May 1945, as Captain C. Earl Walter Jr approached his twenty-fourth birthday, the war seemed to be winding down, and he and his unit were men without a mission.

A few weeks before the crash of the *Gremlin Special*, Walter was invited to lunch by his former military school teacher, Lieutenant Colonel John Babcock. In the officers' mess hall, Babcock listened as Walter told him about the Filipino paratroopers he had trained for behind-enemy-lines missions. Walter poured out his exasperation at being stuck in New Guinea, unable to find a way into action.

Babcock had taught classes at Black-Foxe Military Institute for six years before joining the Army Air Forces, so he knew when a boy became a man. Walter's transformation could not have escaped his notice. Walter still had the slim-hipped, broad-shouldered build of the All-American swimmer he had been at school. But the class-cutting, undisciplined boy who sold half-price notebooks to classmates to finance visits to strip clubs had become a sober, determined captain in the airborne infantry. If he listened closely, Babcock also must have recognized that Walter was determined to prove to his father, and to himself, that he could lead troops into danger and back out again.

Babcock and Walter left the lunch with a promise to meet again. But before they had the chance, Babcock became involved in planning the rescue of survivors from the *Gremlin Special* crash. He learned that Colonel Elsmore believed that no paratroopers were available in Hollandia.

'When Babcock heard that,' Walter recalled, 'he said, "I've got just the people to go in there and get them out."'

A parachute drop into Shangri-La was not a combat posting or an intelligence assignment, at least not in a conventional sense. But compared to endless, apparently pointless, physical training in Hollandia, it was a welcome adventure. When Babcock told him what was happening, Walter leapt at the opportunity. A series of hastily arranged meetings followed, during which Walter met Elsmore and other senior officers coordinating the search and rescue effort. The meetings were straightforward enough, devoted largely to making certain that Walter understood the situation and the dangers that he and his men would face.

When he had absorbed the warnings, Walter returned to the tents occupied by his unit. His men gathered around him, the tallest among them a full head shorter than their captain. Even before he began to speak they bustled with excitement, sensing that – at least for some – their months of waiting were over.

When they settled down, Walter explained the situation. Word of the crash had spread throughout the sprawling base, but news of survivors was still trickling through the unreliable pipeline of fact, rumour and gossip. Walter announced that the paratroopers of the 1st Recon had been chosen for a special mission – to protect survivors of the *Gremlin Special* crash on the ground and eventually lead them to safety. He needed ten volunteers to join him, including two medics. But before taking names, he delivered a four-part warning:

Captain Earl Walter (back row, centre) and the members of the 1st Reconnaissance Battalion outside their 'Club Bahala Na' in Hollandia.

First, Walter told them, the area they would be jumping into was marked 'unknown' on maps, so they would have nothing but their wits and their compasses to guide them.

Second, the two medics would parachute as close as possible to the survivors, into a jungle so thick it would be what Walter called 'the worst possible drop zone'. He and the eight other volunteers would drop on to the floor of the valley some forty to fifty kilometres away. There, they would establish a base camp with the goal of eventually leading the medics and any survivors from the crash site down to the valley.

Third, if they survived the jumps, their band of eleven men would confront what Walter described as 'a very good possibility that the natives would prove hostile'. They would have the advantage in terms of weapons, but they could expect to be outnumbered by hundreds to one in any confrontation.

Walter saved the worst for last: fourth, no one had a plan, even a rough one, to get them out of the valley. They might have to trek 240 kilometres either to the north or south coast of New Guinea, through some of the most inhospitable terrain on earth, with crash survivors who might be hurt and unable to walk on their own. Complicating matters, if they travelled north they would go through an area 'known to be the domain of headhunters and cannibals'. If they went south, they would pass through jungles and swamps occupied by perhaps ten thousand Japanese troops who had been hiding since the Allies captured New Guinea's coastal areas.

Walter did not mention it, but if they did have to trek their way to the coast, he would choose to face the Japanese rather than the headhunters. Death seemed a strong possibility either way, but at least they would go into the fight with a clear idea how Japanese soldiers would react to a group of American paratroopers. Also, unlike the natives, the Japanese would not have home-field advantage. Maybe best of all, being horribly outnumbered by Japanese troops while leading his men in jungle warfare would mean that Walter had followed in his father's footsteps.

As Walter stood before his men, he recognized that each one had his own reasons for being there, whether revenge, patriotism, opportunity, or all three. One quality he knew they had in common was desire. All had volunteered for military service, after which they had all volunteered for reconnaissance work and parachute training. Now Walter was testing them again.

When Walter finished his litany of warnings, he waited a beat then asked for volunteers. As Walter recalled it, every member of the parachute unit raised his hand. Then each one took a step forward. Walter swelled with pride.

'Bahala Na,' several said, voicing the battalion's motto. Come what may.

Fourteen

Five-by-Five

AFTER ANOTHER FITFUL NIGHT, THE SURVIVORS awoke at dawn – Thursday, 17 May – still weary, cold, wet and hungry. Knowing that more search planes would return to the spot where Captain Baker tossed out the life rafts as markers, they ate some of their remaining sweets and talked about being rescued. Unaware of the technical limits, McCollom predicted that the Army Air Forces would use a helicopter to pluck them from the jungle and whisk them back to Hollandia in no time. The only obstacles he anticipated were the trees, but he considered that a minor inconvenience. 'We can clear enough space for it to land,' he told the others.

They spotted the first plane around nine that morning – a C-47. For the first time, Margaret, McCollom and Decker could see what the *Gremlin Special* must have looked like from the natives' perspective before it crashed.

When the plane was over the clearing, a cargo door opened to deliver its payload: wooden supply crates attached to big red cargo parachutes. Margaret watched as the first chute blossomed in the sky like a huge, upside-down tulip. The crates swayed in the breeze before landing about a hundred metres from the clearing. McCollom and Decker plunged into the jungle to retrieve it, while Margaret stayed behind on the relative high ground of the little knoll. She kept busy by taking note of where subsequent chutes and boxes landed.

The two men took a while to drag it out, but when Decker and McCollom returned they bore a prize more precious than food: a portable FM radio that could be used to transmit and receive messages. It was almost certainly a rugged, waterproof, thirty-five-pound, two-way radio the size of a small suitcase. Developed by Motorola for the Army Signal Corps, the device could be carried on a soldier's back, hence its immortal nickname, the 'walkie-talkie'. Its design was a milestone that contributed to a revolution in portable wireless communication, but to the survivors its value was immediate and immense.

'McCollom swiftly set it up,' Margaret told her diary. 'The plane was still circling overhead, and Decker and I were in a true fever as we watched it and then McCollom.'

Holding the radio's telephone-like mouthpiece near his lips, McCollom felt emotions welling up that he had suppressed since crawling out of the burning plane. For the first time since the death of his brother, he found himself too choked up to speak. He had to swallow hard, twice, before his voice returned. 'This is Lieutenant McCollom,' he croaked finally. 'Give me a call. Give me a call. Do you read me? Over.'

The answer came back swiftly and clearly. 'This is *three-one-one*,' said the plane's radio operator, an affable New Yorker named Sergeant Jack Gutzeit, following Army Air Forces protocol by identifying himself by his plane's last three serial numbers. '*Three-one-one* calling *nine-five-two*' – the final serial numbers of the *Gremlin Special*.

Using radio lingo to describe the strength and clarity of a signal, Gutzeit said: 'I read you five-by-five' – a perfect connection.

Tears flowing, Margaret looked at her two comrades. Her companions. Her friends. She saw that McCollom and Decker were crying, too. They were still marooned in the jungle, but now they had a lifeline to home.

Regaining his composure, McCollom briefly described the *Gremlin Special* flight, the crash, and the aftermath. In doing so, he delivered the heartrending news that Gutzeit would need to relay to his superiors, for dispersal through the Army ranks and beyond: no other survivors.

The first hopes dashed would be in Hollandia, among the friends and comrades of the twenty-one lost passengers and crew, including Ruth Coster, awaiting word about Helen Kent, and James Lutgring, praying for the safety of his pal Melvin Mollberg. From there, word would spread via Western Union telegrams to blue-star families throughout the United States. Formal letters of sympathy would follow.

An Army flight surgeon aboard the *three-one-one* named Captain Frank Riley asked McCollom to report their condition. Margaret and Decker knew that their burns had turned gangrenous and their other injuries were infected or nearly so. Margaret described herself and Decker in her diary as 'almost too weak to move'.

McCollom was not sure what to say, so he looked to them for an answer.

'Tell 'em we're fine,' Margaret said.

Decker agreed: 'Tell 'em we're in good shape. There's nothing they can do, anyway.'

McCollom followed their orders.

The plane continued to circle overhead. Radioman Jack Gutzeit told the survivors that a plan was being drawn up to rescue them, but nothing was firmly in place. First, though, they intended to drop medics by parachute as soon as possible. In the meantime, he assured them, 'We're dropping plenty of food. Everything from shrimp cocktails to nuts.'

When the plane flew off, the survivors saw that the natives had returned.

'There on the knoll across from us were Pete and his chums,' Margaret wrote. 'They were squatted on their haunches, grinning and watching us like an audience at a Broadway play.' She counted her blessings, with a touch of condescension: 'The natives, who might easily have been head-hunters, stood about and watched us with childish pleasure.'

The natives made a small fire to warm themselves in the morning chill, and they sat around it contentedly smoking stubby green cigars. Margaret, McCollom and Decker looked on with envy. They had cigarettes in their pockets, but McCollom's lighter was spent and their matches were wet. His spirits lifted by the conversation with the men on board the C-47, McCollom told the others: 'I think I'm going over and borrow a cup of sugar from the neighbors.' He cadged a light, then shared the flame with Margaret and Decker.

'The natives smoked on their knoll and we smoked on ours,' Margaret wrote. 'No peace pipe ever tasted better.'

Margaret began to fantasize about 'the luscious Spam and K-rations probably awaiting us within a stone's throw'. Despite her hunger, she told her friends, there were certain foods she wouldn't savour: 'One is canned tomatoes and the other is raisins,' she said. 'When I was little I ate myself sick on both, and now I can't stand the sight of either.'

McCollom answered: 'I could eat the tomatoes, can and all, if I could get 'em.'

He rose and marched off in search of the supplies. Margaret appreciated McCollom's endurance and leadership. She was even more impressed by the man shadowing him through the jungle.

'Decker was emaciated, his eyes like burnt holes in a blanket,' she wrote. 'We knew he was hurt, but just how gravely we were not to discover for a few more hours. How Decker got to his feet I shall never know. But he did, and staggered uncomplainingly after McCollom, determined to do his share of the work.'

Although McCollom explained during the radio conversation that there were only three survivors, the C-47 had been packed optimistically, with supplies for two dozen. Their orders were to drop the supplies, and Captain Mengel and his crew had no intention of disobeying. The sky over Shangri-La filled with cargo parachutes.

While Decker and McCollom went off in search of supplies, Margaret worried that the natives might collect boxes of rations she saw falling on the other side of a nearby hill. 'I decided to scout that situation,' she wrote. 'It was excruciating to stand on my burned, infected legs. So part of the way I crawled on my hands and knees. When my infected hand hurt too much, I would sit down and bounce along on the ground.'

When she reached the other side of the hill, Margaret was stunned to see a split-rail fence that she thought looked straight out of the Old West. Just beyond it was a native compound. She wrote:

> It was an odd and fascinating New Guinea housing project, with one large section and several smaller ones mushroomed around it. The huts were round, with bamboo sides and thatched roofs, and seemed to be at least semi-attached to each other. As for the roofs, they were alive with natives, all craning their jet-black necks for a better look at me. I

> could see a large-sized hole in one thatched roof. A hunch and a sinking feeling hit me simultaneously. I knew that one of our packages of supplies had gone through one roof. I was right, too, McCollom discovered later. I wondered if the natives were angry about this, or if they might go on the warpath because one of their houses was damaged. But they just stood and stared, entranced by the free show I made. So I decided to leave well-enough alone and go back to my own knoll.

The crate that crashed through the roof did no harm beyond requiring new thatch. But another crate, dropped without a parachute, permanently embittered one resident of Uwambo towards the sky spirits in her midst.

Yaralok's daughter Yunggukwe, a girl on the cusp of womanhood, had recently become the owner of her first pig. This milestone, and the possession itself, was of immense importance to a Yali girl. So great was the pig's value to Yunggukwe – emotionally as well as, eventually, gustatorily – that its worth could only be exceeded by two pigs.

That morning, she tied her pig to a stake outside her hut, thinking it would be safe there. But when the supply plane roared over Uwambo, the pig had nowhere to run. To save parachute cloth, some of the boxes containing unbreakable items such as tents were pushed freefall out the C-47's cargo door, and such was the case with a crate dropped this day.

There was no evidence of intent, but no pinpoint-bombing raid during the war found a mark more squarely. It landed on Yunggukwe's pig, killing it instantly and striking with such force that the animal shattered into pieces. Yunggukwe never received an apology or compensation, and she neither forgot nor forgave.

'That was my own pig that died,' she said angrily sixty-five years later.

Margaret crawled back to the clearing just as McCollom and Decker returned from the jungle, 'grinning like apes'. In their arms were half a dozen cans of the only food they could find: tomatoes and tomato juice.

'Come on, Maggie,' Decker said. 'Be a big girl now and eat some tomatoes.'

She forced down four mouthfuls before quitting. Watching Decker and McCollom gorge themselves on the fleshy fruit, she grew so angry she demanded that they return to the jungle to find her something else to eat. They headed in the direction where they thought the parachutes landed, but turned up only a half-dozen 'jungle kits' filled with Atabrine pills for malaria, ointments for wounds, water purification tablets, and bags to collect water from streams or lakes. Also inside were jungle knives, mosquito nets, bandages, and gauze. The only food in the kits was chocolate bars. Margaret felt only slightly better about the chocolate than the tomatoes. 'By this time I was almost as sick of candy as I was of tomatoes,' she wrote.

Again Margaret marvelled at Decker's fortitude. Determined to do his part, he gathered the water bags and went to fill them in the icy stream. 'He was gone so long I began to worry about him,' Margaret wrote. 'It took every ounce of his strength to get back to our knoll, and when he reached us he just sagged gently onto the hard earth.'

McCollom, meanwhile, was worried about his companions. He decided the time was overdue to tend more thoroughly to their wounds. On McCollom's orders, Margaret rolled up her pants to expose the wide rings of burns around her calves. Left untended for four days, they oozed pus and reeked of dying flesh. The burns and cuts on both her feet had turned gangrenous, as had part of her hand.

'Decker and McCollom looked at me, and I knew they were alarmed. Suddenly I was in terror, lest I lose my legs,' she told her diary. She fought to remain in control, fearing

Crew members aboard a C-47 prepare to drop supplies to the survivors of the *Gremlin Special* crash.

that letting down her guard might trigger a spiral into panic. She helped McCollom to apply an ointment they had found in the jungle kits, after which he wrapped her wounds in gauze.

Even without looking in her little mirror, Margaret knew that she was filthy and unkempt, almost unrecognizable from the eager, take-charge WAC who cared about her appearance and spent nights tailoring her khakis so they would fit her petite figure. Decker, in what was becoming his usual blunt way, didn't hold back.

'Maggie, you are certainly a sad sack,' he said.

McCollom wisely kept his mouth shut, but even that wasn't enough to spare him her wrath. Margaret looked at the two of them – equally dirty, with four days' growth of beard on their hollowed cheeks. She shot back: 'Neither one of you are exactly Van Johnsons,' she said, referring to the actor whose all-American good looks landed him heroic roles in MGM war movies.

After Margaret it was Decker's turn for triage. The gash on his forehead was deep and oozing. Wimayuk Wandik's breath might have salved his soul, but it did nothing to heal the wound. Margaret and McCollom worried that any attempt to treat it without sterile tools and proper medicine might only make matters worse, so they left it alone. They took the same approach with what appeared to be a broken right elbow, focusing instead on Decker's one seemingly less-urgent complaint. Several times during the previous days, Decker had mentioned discomfort caused by his pants sticking to his backside. They thought the cause might be burns from the crash, but the fabric was neither torn nor scorched, so they didn't believe the burns to be serious. Now McCollom ordered Decker to drop his trousers and lie face-down on the ground.

'What we saw horrified us both,' Margaret wrote, 'and made us realize for the first time what pain Decker had been suffering in silence.'

His buttocks and the back of his legs were laced with angry burns that had turned horribly gangrenous. Margaret found the sight sickening. Frightening, too. From the look on his face, so did McCollom. They didn't want to upset Decker, so they said nothing and went to work trying to gently wipe away ruined skin. They cleaned the area as much as they could and applied a generous coating of ointment.

Decker had no idea how he had been burned. One possibility was that he fell against a piece of scalding metal during the crash. The result would have been the same as ironing pants while still wearing them: the trousers would be fine but the skin underneath would be destroyed.

Decker accepted the treatment with stoicism until McCollom covered the burns on his bottom with a large, triangular bandage that resembled a diaper. 'That momentarily broke Decker's spirit,' Margaret wrote. As much as possible, they had all maintained a gallows humour since the crash, ribbing each other and themselves to boost morale and seal their camaraderie. Decker's bandage could have been an easy source of jokes, but the others knew better. 'We were all silently worried and trying not to let the other fellow know it,' Margaret wrote. Fearing that her legs would have to be amputated, and that Decker's infections would fatally poison his blood, she wrote: 'We were all wondering if the medics would reach us in time.'

After the infirmary session, McCollom ordered both patients to lie down and remain still. All three stayed close together, listening for the planes they hoped would drop the promised medics before nightfall. But clouds rolled in and by two o'clock that afternoon the weather had turned foul. A heavy mist settled on the valley and on the survivors' hopes. They knew no paratrooper medics would dare to jump into such soup, especially because hidden beneath it was a thick jungle in which to get tangled or impaled. They could do nothing but spread out the tarps and try to keep warm.

By nightfall, only McCollom could get around on his feet. Decker could barely move, worn out from his injuries, his exertions and his embarrassment. Margaret felt equally bad. She told her diary that, despite his obvious exhaustion, McCollom patiently ministered to her 'as if I were a baby'.

She felt helpless, too sick and too weak to walk. All she could do was pray. She told her diary that she had never prayed so hard in her life.

Fifteen

No Supper Tonight

After every paratrooper in the 1st Recon volunteered to jump into Shangri-La despite the dire warnings, Captain Walter assembled a ten-man squad. He chose as his right-hand man, Master Sergeant Santiago 'Sandy' Abrenica, whom Walter considered a good friend and the best soldier he had ever met. Abrenica was thirty-six, whippet-thin, with dark, deep-set eyes and a wary expression. Born on Luzon in the Philippines, Abrenica emigrated alone to the United States in 1926, when he was seventeen, declaring that his intended address was a YMCA in Seattle. As a civilian he'd worked as a gardener, and as a hobby he raced model airplanes.

Next Walter needed two medics who he thought might have the toughest job of all. They would be parachuting into a dense jungle to treat the survivors, while the rest of the unit jumped into a flat, mostly treeless area of the Shangri-La Valley some forty-eight kilometres away to establish a base camp. After talking to his men and leafing through their service records, he picked Sergeant Benjamin 'Doc' Bulatao and Corporal Camilo 'Rammy' Ramirez.

Both Doc and Rammy were good-natured, with easy smiles – Rammy's was more distinctive, as it revealed two front teeth made of gold. Otherwise they were entirely different. Doc Bulatao was quiet, shy almost, while Rammy Ramirez had the gift of the gab and an outsized personality for a man who stood just 1.54 metres.

Like Abrenica and most other enlisted men in the 1st Recon, the thirty-one-year-old Bulatao was single and had emigrated to the United States as a young man. A farm worker before the war, Bulatao joined the 1st Filipino Regiment in California before being assigned to Walter's unit.

Rammy Ramirez's route to Hollandia was both more circuitous and perilous. Born in the city of Ormoc on the island of Leyte, Ramirez enlisted ten months before the war. He was assigned to the Philippine Scouts, a unit of the US Army consisting of native Filipinos who served in the islands under American command. When the Japanese invaded the Philippines after Pearl Harbor, Ramirez was part of the overmatched, undersupplied force that held out against the enemy, hunger, and dysentery for more than four months on the Bataan Peninsula. After Filipino and American troops surrendered in April 1942, Ramirez endured the Bataan Death March, suffering not only from his captors' brutality and a lack of food and water, but also from malaria and dengue fever. Only a daring gambit spared him from a prisoner-of-war camp.

At a temporary holding area, Ramirez noticed a hole at a corner of a fence that had been patched with barbed wire. 'I said to myself, "I will get through there,"' he recalled. The next night, he waited until a Japanese guard set down his rifle and appeared to doze off at his post. 'So I roll, little by little, towards the gap in the barbed wire.' He tried to pry apart the patch to enlarge the opening but couldn't find the strength – 'It's kind of hard, because I am small, you know.' As he crawled through, his shirt snagged; razor wire ripped a gash in his side.

'About ten feet from the barbed wire were bushes, lots of bushes and trees. So I went toward the bushes when I got out. I didn't even notice that I cut myself.' He was about 150 metres from the fence, running through the woods, when he heard gunfire behind him – 'boom, boom, boom, boom, boom!' Later Ramirez learned that Japanese guards had opened fire when other prisoners tried to follow him through the hole. 'I kept running, and my head was really pounding – the fever, malaria fever and dengue fever mixed.'

Ramirez dragged himself to a nearby house, where sympathetic residents gave him clothes to replace his uniform. He hid his dog tags in his shoe, avoided main roads, and headed towards Manila, an 'open city', supposedly safe from bombing by either side. He saw an ambulance and hitched a ride to a hospital, but everyone there was evacuating to a medical ship bound for Australia. Manila was blacked out, but he found his way to the pier and saw the ship silhouetted in the moonlight. He talked his way on board and curled up in a warm spot on the deck amid scores of sick and wounded.

After a month recovering in a Sydney hospital, Ramirez regained his strength just as the 1st Filipino Regiment was arriving in Australia. He was still officially attached to the US military, so it seemed a natural fit. 'They discharged me from the hospital and put me with them.'

In time, he was assigned to medical, commando, and paratrooper training in Brisbane as part of the 5217th Reconnaissance Battalion, the predecessor to the 1st Recon, under the command of Captain Walter. Now twenty-six, with a scar for life from his escape, Rammy Ramirez wanted to help Margaret, McCollom and Decker to make their own getaway.

Walter was especially glad to have Ramirez on the team. 'I just liked his gung-ho attitude. He was happy.' Other medics, including Bulatao, were more experienced treating patients, 'But they weren't as free and easygoing as Rammy was. I felt the two survivors that were badly injured ... needed someone that was kind of happy and a good talker, and was not the least bit hesitant about talking back and forth.'

'That's how I picked those two for the jump,' Walter said. 'I picked 'em mainly because Ben was the most qualified and Rammy had the most guts.'

After Abrenica, Bulatao and Ramirez, Walter filled out his parachute infantry team with seven of his most senior and capable enlisted men: six sergeants – Alfred Baylon,

Captain Earl Walter with Corporal Camilo 'Rammy' Ramirez (left) and Sergeant Benjamin 'Doc' Bulatao.

Hermenegildo Caoili, Fernando Dongallo, Juan 'Johnny' Javonillo, Don Ruiz and Roque Velasco – and a corporal, Custodio Alerta.

In civilian life, they had been gardeners and kitchen workers, farm hands and labourers, familiar with the slights and discrimination routinely experienced by Filipinos in America. Now they were US soldiers, volunteering to parachute into uncharted territory to protect and rescue three Army comrades. When Walter was choosing his team, neither he nor his men knew that the first natives who made contact with the survivors were friendly. All they knew were Walter's warnings: no maps, no safe drop zone, no predicting the natives' response, and no exit plan. Yet all they wanted to know was how soon they could jump into Shangri-La.

After a further meeting with senior brass, Walter joined a flight crew for several reconnaissance passes over the valley, the crash site, and the survivors' clearing. Then he spoke again with his superiors. 'I was very concerned because I knew we had to parachute in there,' Walter recalled. 'It was the only way. The territory north of the valley was inhabited by headhunters, we figured, and south of the valley were Japanese troops. So there's no way to get in there by foot unless you wanted to get into a firefight, and I wasn't the least bit interested in exposing us to that.'

Walter instructed his men to pack supplies and parachutes. None of them had jumped since leaving their training base in Brisbane months earlier, so he arranged for each to make one or two practice jumps in Hollandia. 'That was a mess because the only place they found that we could use was kind of a swampy area,' Walter said. 'The men and I laughed about it afterward, but we sure as hell didn't at the time. We were in what they called kunai grass' – with sharp edges, each blade a couple of metres high. 'It was very thick and almost one hundred percent coverage. We'd take two or three steps and then purposely fall forward to make an indent in the grass, and then we'd take two or three steps and fall again. A mess.'

Walter went back to his medics and asked, 'Do you really want to do this?'

'I remember both of them saying, "Yes, sir. We want to do this because they need us."'

Walter noted in a journal that it was his twenty-fourth birthday, Friday, 18 May 1945. Having finally found himself engaged in a real mission, he was too busy and too distracted to celebrate. After his last practice jump, he returned to camp, packed parachutes and went to bed.

On their sixth day in Shangri-La, the survivors spent the morning waiting for the comforting sound of the approaching supply plane. When the *three-one-one* appeared, the sky filled with parachutes slowing the descent of wooden crates. When the survivors made contact with the plane's crew by walkie-talkie, they warned that however bad the terrain looked from the sky, it was even worse on the ground.

In her diary, Margaret wrote that she told the crew: 'Don't let anyone jump in here if it means he'll be killed. I'd rather die right here than have anyone killed trying to get me out.' McCollom and Decker felt the same. 'We had seen enough of death and tragedy,' she wrote. 'God knows we wanted to live, but not at the expense of someone else.'

Their fears for the paratroopers would remain with them for at least another day. The mist rolled in early, shrouding the jungle and the surrounding ridges. That made it impossible to fly safely over them, much less jump into the cloudy mess.

When the plane was out of sight, McCollom traipsed into the jungle in search of cargo. 'I could no longer move at all,' Margaret wrote, 'and Decker was so white and feverish that McCollom sternly ordered him to stay in camp. Flesh had melted away from all of us, even McCollom.'

On successive trips, McCollom brought back a package filled with clean trousers and shirts, but only in a size small enough to fit Margaret. She was grateful, though she wished he had also found pants and bras to replace the underwear she had removed five days earlier to make bandages. On another outing, he found enough thick blankets to fashion two makeshift beds in their jungle infirmary. He made one for Margaret and the other for him and Decker to share. That night, fleas in the blankets tormented Decker but ignored McCollom, which annoyed Decker even more.

Returning to their knoll after another trip, McCollom shouted, 'Eureka! We eat!' In his arms were boxes of ten-in-one rations.

'Food, real food, at last, after almost six days,' Margaret wrote. She confessed that her stomach ached from hunger, and the men admitted the same despite having gorged on the tomatoes without her. As McCollom pried open the packages, Margaret's spirit soared: 'It was such a beautiful sight: sliced bacon in cans, canned ham and eggs, canned bacon and eggs, canned meat, canned hash and stews, the makings of coffee, tea, cocoa, lemonade and orangeade, butter, sugar, salt, canned milk, cigarettes, matches and even candy bars for dessert.'

All three chose cans of bacon and ham, and each hastily worked little key openers to reveal the tasty-under-the-circumstances innards. As they dug into their cold breakfasts, the survivors gave no thought to making a fire. For one thing, all the nearby wood was saturated from the relentless rains. 'Even more important,' Margaret wrote, 'even McCollom was too far gone physically to do anything that took an extra, added effort.'

Despite how hungry she had been, Margaret felt stuffed after only a few bites. She stopped eating before she had finished one small can, realizing that a steady diet of boiled sweets, water and a few mouthfuls of tomatoes had shrunk her already small stomach.

As they waited for the medics, the survivors' anxiety grew about Margaret's and Decker's injuries. The ointments and gauze they had found in the supply crates had done nothing to slow the spread or the flesh-killing power of gangrene. After they ate, McCollom did what he could to tend to their wounds. He removed the dressings on Margaret's legs, releasing the nauseating stench of infection. McCollom tried to ease off the bandages, but they were stuck to the burned skin. He closed his eyes, knowing the pain he would have to cause Margaret by ripping them off.

'Honest, Maggie, this hurts me worse than it does you,' he told her.

Within an hour the fresh bandages he had applied were drenched with foul-smelling pus. They repeated the excruciating process. Margaret wrote: 'I tried not to show my growing terror that I would lose both legs, but it was mounting in me like a tide, and sometimes I thought I would pass out with fear.'

Margaret's fears deepened when she tried to help McCollom treat Decker. The gangrene on his legs and backside had grown worse during the previous twelve hours. 'He was in great pain and we knew it, although he had never said a word,' she wrote. 'He lay on his stomach all day with a kind of exhausted patience and pain.'

In the afternoon, the native leader they called Pete returned with his greatest show of trust yet: a woman whom Margaret took to be his wife. The couple stood on the knoll across from the survivors' camp and beckoned them over. Neither Margaret nor Decker could walk, so McCollom went alone. The two leaders shook hands and tried to communicate, with little success. At breaks where a response seemed appropriate, McCollom murmured

'Uhn, uhn, uhn,' just as he had heard the natives do when the two groups met. The conversation did not progress much beyond that.

Elsewhere in her diary, Margaret wrote of the natives: 'They would chatter like magpies to us. We would always listen carefully, from time to time muttering, "Uhn, uhn, uhn." They would be delighted, like the bore to whom you keep saying, "Yes, yes, yes" during long-winded conversation. "Uhn, uhn, uhn," we would say as the natives chattered. They would beam at us and then talk twice as fast.'

As McCollom spoke with his counterpart, Margaret sized up the native woman. Margaret was pleased to find that the first woman she had seen up close in Shangri-La was 'shorter than my five-feet, one-and-one-half inches'. A woven bag hung down her back, suspended from a string handle draped over her head. She stood 'mother naked', other than what Margaret described as 'a queer New Guinea g-string woven of supple twigs' that somehow remained in place on her hips.

Unknown to Margaret, the woman's name was Gilelek. Despite the practice of polygamy that would have allowed Wimayuk Wandik to take more than one wife, she was his one and only.

'She and all her jungle sisters under the skin were the most graceful, fleet creatures any of us have ever seen,' Margaret wrote. 'And they were shy as does.'

The couple left, and in the late afternoon the survivors settled into their blanket beds. Less than an hour later, Wimayuk and a large group of his followers returned. It appeared as though his wife had approved of the strangers, and had reminded him that his obligation to guests went beyond kindness.

'They held out a pig, sweet potatoes and some little green bananas, the only fruit we ever saw,' Margaret wrote.

A native couple in a Dani village, photographed in 1945.

'They want to give us a banquet,' McCollom said. 'Maggie, if our lives depend upon it, I cannot get up and make merry with the natives.'

'Amen,' said Decker.

If the feast had been offered a day earlier, the survivors would have leapt at it. 'But tonight,' Margaret wrote, 'for the first time in days, our stomachs were full of Army rations, and we were bushed.' They used sign language to explain as politely as possible that they were too tired, too sick and too full to appreciate another meal.

By declining the dinner, Margaret, McCollom and Decker had unknowingly missed a chance to become bonded to the natives through one of their most significant community rituals: a pig feast. As an anthropologist later explained: 'It is the remembrance of pigs which holds ... [this] society together. At every major ceremony pigs are given from one person to another, and then killed and eaten. But they leave behind memory traces of obligations which will be paid back later; when this happens, the people will create new obligations. And so the network of the society is constantly refurbished by the passage of pigs. A single man in his lifetime is bound to his fellows by the ties of hundreds and perhaps thousands of pigs which he and his people have exchanged with others and their people.'

Despite the deep symbolism of their offer, the natives took no apparent offence at the survivors' refusal to share a pig.

'Pete, who must have had a wonderfully understanding heart in that wiry black body, comprehended at once,' Margaret wrote. 'He tucked the pig more firmly under his arm. He ordered his men, who had started a fire by some magic known only to them, to put it out. Then he clucked over us reassuringly and herded his followers home.'

The survivors burrowed into their beds and went to sleep, feeling sated and relatively warm and comfortable for the first time since leaving Hollandia. In what Margaret called 'the irony of an evil fate', they were awakened several hours later by a sudden cloudburst. Margaret's nest of blankets, arranged on low ground, became a woolly swamp. The bed on higher ground shared by McCollom and Decker was wet, but not soaked. Margaret ordered them to make room, and she crawled in alongside them.

'Lord,' said McCollom in mock protest, 'are we never to get rid of this woman?'

They huddled together against the cold and wet through the night, talking now and again under the blankets about helicopters, medics and being rescued.

Sixteen

Rammy and Doc

FLYING IN A C-47 OVER THE SURVIVORS' CLEARING, Earl Walter was sweating.

The plane carrying him and the medics Rammy Ramirez and Doc Bulatao took off from Sentani Airfield around eight a.m., Saturday, 19 May. During several passes over the intended drop zone, it looked more treacherous than Walter remembered from his first view, two days earlier. Adding to his concern was the unpredictability of the mountain winds. He had already dropped five wind dummies – weighted bundles used to assess turbulence – without any benefit. 'The reason I dropped five,' he explained, 'is because every one of them changed direction, so I had no idea' which way the winds would blow the medics.

Walter pushed their equipment out of the cargo door over the jungle near the survivors' campsite, so the two medics would not have to carry the supplies the entire way from the landing area. The cargo drops provided no more useful information about the wind conditions. As he watched the dummies and the equipment crates spin and twist in the shifting currents, Walter kept his fears to himself.

'I never told Ben or Rammy because, well, it wouldn't have done any good,' Walter said. 'I mean, it didn't make any difference. We knew we had to put two people in there, no matter what.'

The young captain knew that the two men were about to become what paratroopers call 'human wind dummies'. If they had been officers like Walter rather than enlisted men, they would have earned the more formal moniker 'turbulence testers'. Either way, the swirling winds added another danger to an already frightening jump.

Walter's biggest worry was the drop zone itself, an area of metre-high brush, jagged rocks and sharp-topped tree stumps that looked as though it had been the scene of a recent lightning fire. 'I can remember flying over there at roughly a couple of hundred feet because I wanted to get down and see what it looked like,' he said. 'And it looked like hell. Pardon the expression, but it did. I mean, there'd been fires, there were rock formations, stumps, trees that had been broken or whatever. I don't remember ever hearing about a drop zone like that.' An ideal landing area was flat and soft, wide open, with little or no breeze; this was the opposite.

Reluctantly, Walter chose the area because it was within three kilometres of the survivors' campsite, and it was better, though not much, than parachuting into a full-fledged jungle. Jumping into the campsite itself wasn't an option because it was too small a target.

Walter's plan called for the medics to exit the plane only a hundred metres above the ground, to reduce the chance of drifting miles from where the survivors desperately needed their help. But improving the odds for the survivors meant increasing the risks for Bulatao and Ramirez.

Cords called static lines ran from their parachute packs to an anchor cable inside the plane. If everything went as intended, the lines would ensure that their chutes would deploy automatically after the men stepped out the door and were clear of the plane. But jumping so close to the ground meant that they would have no time to deploy a reserve parachute if their main chutes failed. The mountain altitude added to the peril. They were more than 2500 metres above sea level, which meant the air would be thin and they would fall faster. They would have little opportunity to steer themselves away from trees or other hazards by pulling on the nylon straps that linked their harnesses to the cords leading to the parachutes' umbrella-like canopies.

A light man in thin air with an 8.5-metre-diameter Army parachute might descend at a rate of 4.5 metres per second. If that rate held true, from the time they left the plane, Ramirez and Bulatao would be on the ground – or stuck in a tree, or impaled on a jagged stump, or lost in a rocky gorge – in less than thirty seconds. That is, if the winds did not spin them around, tangle their lines, and turn their parachutes into narrow 'streamers'. Without a reserve chute, a streamer meant almost certain death.

Walter and the pilot conferred about wind speed and direction, then agreed on what they thought would be the best approach. Both knew their calculations were only slightly more useful than expert guesses.

Ramirez and Bulatao rose from their seats and did the paratrooper shuffle to the jump door to keep from losing their balance with their heavy loads. Walter 'stood them in the door' – paratrooper lingo for preparing to jump – and again checked their resolve.

He shouted over the engines and the wind: 'Are you ready?'

In unison, Ramirez and Bulatao answered: 'Yes, sir!'

Describing the scene more than sixty years later, Walter's eyes misted with pride.

The medics leapt into the void, one after the other, their parachutes opening as intended and filling with air. At first, they seemed to be headed towards an area below the clearing where Walter thought they could make a relatively safe landing. Then the winds shifted again, blowing them off course.

Margaret, McCollom and Decker awoke that morning anticipating the medics' arrival. 'It was patent to all of us now – though we never once mentioned it – that Decker might die and I would surely lose my legs unless the medical paratroopers reached us immediately,' she wrote.

All three were 'wet, miserable and aching' from the rainstorm the night before as McCollom served her and Decker cold breakfast rations. Their ears pricked up at the sound of the plane, and McCollom manned the radio. 'They told us the two medical paratroopers were aboard,' she wrote, 'and would jump two miles down the valley as soon as the plane had discharged its 'chute cargo of pup tents, ponchos, blankets, more medical supplies and food.'

A radio operator on the plane assured them the medics would be taking care of them within forty-five minutes. When McCollom relayed the message, Margaret rattled her lips in a sardonic cheer. McCollom and Decker joined in. 'We had some intimate knowledge of the jungle by this time,' Margaret wrote, 'and we knew that even over a native trail it would take hours for the medics to make the two-mile hike.'

The survivors watched as two small figures left the plane and their parachutes mushroomed in the sky.

A single thought crossed Decker's mind: 'God bless you.' He considered the medics to be 'the difference between life and death for us'.

When they lost sight of the paratroopers, Margaret wrote, they knew there was nothing they could do but wait and pray. 'I said more "Our Fathers" and "Hail Marys" in the next two hours than ever before in my life.'

Watching from the plane's open jump door, Walter did the same.

On the way down, struggling against the wind in a futile effort to get back on course, Ramirez gained a more complete understanding of the challenges he faced. 'We were about a hundred feet above the jump zone,' he recalled. 'I could see the stumps and the rocks. I said to myself, "There's all this – it's dangerous." So I tried to face away from the wind. I tried to pilot the parachute toward the woods, where I could see no rocks in there. I missed the stumps, but I did not miss the rock.'

He stumbled as he landed, painfully wrenching his left ankle. After discarding his parachute, Ramirez examined his ankle and was relieved to find that the bone was not broken and he was not bleeding. Doc Bulatao landed safely nearby. That was the good news.

Immediately upon the medics' landing, they were surrounded by natives. Ramirez reached for his rifle, a semi-automatic M-1 carbine with an eighteen-inch barrel and a fifteen-round clip. 'The natives have spears, and bow and arrows,' Ramirez said. 'And I had my carbine cocked, in case somebody acted to throw the spear, or bow and arrow.'

Out stepped a native man Ramirez called 'the chief of that village' – Wimayuk Wandik, whom the medics would soon also know as Pete. They didn't understand each other's language, but using hand signs and body English, Ramirez explained himself. 'I expressed my mission. That an airplane crashed. Catch on fire. I'm here to help.'

Wimayuk nodded. He called over a group of boys and instructed them to lead the two medics to Mundima, the place by the river Mundi where the survivors were camped. 'We followed them, just like rabbits, through the jungle,' Ramirez said. Hobbled by his twisted ankle, Ramirez found it hard to keep up with the nimble, barefoot boys, who leapt from stump to stump, scampered across fallen logs wet with moss, and saw paths where anyone else would have seen none. Bulatao hung back with his friend. After several hours of losing and regaining sight of the boys, trekking through, over and around the ferns and vines and trees, they arrived at the clearing.

Margaret, McCollom and Decker rose to shake hands with the medics. 'When I got close to them,' Ramirez said, 'Margaret was crying. She hugged me, and I kept smiling.' Margaret recorded the scene in her diary:

> When I spotted them down the native trail, I couldn't keep the tears back any longer. They spilled out of their own volition and poured down my one blistered cheek and my one good cheek. Leading the way and limping slightly was Corporal Rammy Ramirez, medical technician. Rammy had a heart of gold, we came to know, and a smile of the same hue. Even as he came limping up the trail, his face was split in a wide, warm smile, and his two gold front teeth shone resplendently. Rammy was better for morale than a thousand-dollar bill. I felt better just looking at him through my tears. Sergeant Ben Bulatao, medical technician, brought up the rear. When the sergeant walked into camp, there arrived to take care of us one of the most kind and gentle men God ever put on earth ... I want to say right now that when better men are born, they will undoubtedly be Filipinos. If ever they or their islands need aid or a champion, they only have to send a wire to enlist me in the cause.

Rammy rummaged through the jungle, gathering the supplies Walter had tossed from the plane. Favouring his bad ankle, he 'hopped around on one foot like a cheerful sparrow', Margaret wrote. He built a fire, pulled up a dozen or so sweet potatoes to roast, and boiled water. He shaved pieces of chocolate into a canteen cup and made hot chocolate – the survivors' first warm drink in nearly a week.

'It was heavenly,' Margaret wrote. 'We gulped down the first cup like ravenous animals, and then held them out for more.' By the next morning, Rammy and Doc would be waking them with the rich aromas of hot coffee and fried bacon.

They wolfed the hot potatoes, too, amusing Rammy with their excitement about a vegetable that had been under their feet the whole time. Then the two medics turned their attention to the injuries. Starting with Decker, they poured peroxide and an antibacterial powder called sulphanilamide into his wounds and on to the gangrenous burns on his buttocks. The gash on Decker's head was spread too wide to stitch. Doc Bulatao – who took the lead on medical matters, with Rammy assisting – gently massaged the skin around the wound, pushing the two sides closer so they could eventually be knit together. Rammy worked on Decker's broken elbow. He fashioned a splint from tree bark and held it against Decker's arm as he wrapped it in bandages, immobilizing it. The medics decided not to set the break, fearing that without X-rays they might do more harm than good.

Then it was Margaret's turn. The two men spent the next two hours working on her legs. The bandages McCollom had applied were stuck fast to her burns. Doc Bulatao knew that removing them would be torture.

'He would try to work the bandages off without hurting me too much,' Margaret wrote. 'But he winced as much in the process as I did. "You ought to see the way I rip them off!" McCollom encouraged him. "But I'm afraid I'll hurt her," Doc would reply.'

Margaret was more worried about losing her legs. 'If I were back at Fee-Ask,' she told Bulatao, 'the G.I. medic would yank the bandages off and then scrub my legs with a brush. Go ahead, yank.' So he did. 'Not long afterward did he tell me how shocked he was at the sight of me,' Margaret wrote. 'I was skin and bones. I doubt if I weighed ninety pounds at that time.'

Bulatao knew there was little he could do that first night to treat the gangrene on Margaret or Decker. It would be a slow, painful fight. He and Rammy would cut away the rotten skin, wash what remained with peroxide, daub it with ointment, dress the wound, then repeat the process day after day. If it was not too late, eventually the gangrene would retreat and healing could begin. Otherwise, they would have to consider more drastic steps, including amputation.

'Doc must have read the fear in my heart,' Margaret wrote. 'In the middle of bandaging up my sorry-looking gams, he smiled at me and said, "You'll be jitter-bugging in three months." But I knew he wasn't sure, and neither was I.'

Seventeen

Custer and Company

AS MARGARET HASTINGS WAS ENDURING THE REMOVAL of her bandages in the mountainous jungle, Earl Walter finally got a chance to experience danger serving his country. It wasn't a combat assignment or a spy patrol in the Philippines, but it was the next best thing: a rescue mission in Shangri-La.

Colonel Elsmore and the planners at Fee-Ask still were not sure how they'd attempt to get everyone *out* of Shangri-La, but in the meantime they were certain they needed more soldiers *in* the valley. They wanted Walter and five members of his paratrooper team to set up a base camp in the main valley, trek through the jungle to the survivors' clearing, collect them and the two medics, and return with everyone to the base camp to await pick up or further instructions. While Walter and his group were en route to the survivors' campsite, the other three paratroopers would stay in the main valley to maintain the base camp and to level and create a makeshift runway by clearing brush, trees, mud, quicksand and other obstacles.

The runway idea emerged as planners continued to narrow their options for rescue. A helicopter had already been ruled out because of its inability to fly in the thin air at altitude. Elsmore's team also rejected a suggestion that they use an amphibious plane; unaware that Richard Archbold had landed on a lake near the valley with *Guba* seven years earlier, they mistakenly believed such a plane was unsuitable for the mission. Marching the 240 kilometres to Hollandia was among the last resorts, along with the idea of piloting a Navy Patrol Torpedo or PT boat up a river from New Guinea's south coast to within eighty or so kilometres of the valley. Among a half-dozen remaining options, some more outlandish than others, were landing a C-47 in the valley – a dubious prospect because of the conditions – and the equally implausible idea of dropping motorless gliders into the valley, loading them with passengers, and using low-flying planes to snatch them back into the sky.

In the meantime, at ten o'clock on the morning of Sunday, 20 May, Walter and eight of his men, weighed down and clanking with parachute packs, guns, ammunition, bolo knives and sundry supplies, climbed aboard a C-47 at the Sentani Airstrip destined for Shangri-La.

Walter told the pilot, Colonel Edward T. Imparato, to take the plane in low – a hundred metres above the valley floor. Walter, about to make his forty-ninth jump, did not want the swirling winds to turn their parachutes into kites and spread him and his men miles apart. He also hoped that a low jump might escape the natives' notice, as opposed to a long, slow descent that would be seen by every tribesman for miles.

For a drop zone, Walter and Imparato chose an area with no huts or sweet potato gardens in the immediate vicinity, a relatively flat stretch of land in the shadow of a soaring rock wall, with only a few trees and shrubs and small knolls between hundreds of otherwise uninterrupted acres of kunai grass. Shortly before noon, with Imparato flying only a hundred metres above the valley floor, the paratroopers tumbled from the plane like dominoes off a table. Their parachutes deployed as designed, and all nine men reached the ground without incident.

They gathered in a defensive formation they had planned beforehand – in close proximity to one another but not bunched together. Walter had heard radio reports from the survivors and the two medics that the natives near the crash site were welcoming, but his landing site was thirty to fifty kilometres away from that happy scene. The natives in the main valley of Shangri-La could be different altogether, and far less hospitable.

'When we first landed,' Walter said, 'everybody was spread around different places. Not far apart, but I wanted them to be spread out a little bit so we didn't all get speared or whatever to start with.'

His wish for a stealth landing proved a pipe dream. Even before the parachutes reached the ground, scores of men with spears and bows and arrows came running from all directions into the landing field. Walter estimated that more than two hundred Stone Age warriors surrounded him and his men. Master Sergeant Abrenica put the number at three hundred.

Walter tensed. He grabbed his carbine. Abrenica was at his side, equally ready for combat.

'Captain,' Abrenica said, 'you know what this reminds me of?'

'No, not really, Sandy. What?'

'Custer's last stand.'

Stifling laughter, Walter held the carbine under one arm, his hand near the trigger. In his other hand he held a .45 calibre pistol – a gift from his father. He sensed that the natives were hostile but hesitant to attack. Walter shouted to his men to stay ready but to hold their fire until he gave the command.

'For God's sake,' Walter called, 'don't get itchy fingers and pull the trigger just to scare someone. I don't want anything like that to happen. If we hurt any of them or kill any of them, then we'd really have a problem.'

Abrenica did not like the way the natives rubbed their spears together, a practice that made a 'frightening, weird sound like the call of the Australian kookaburra'.

Although they were outnumbered more than twenty to one, Walter believed the superiority of their firepower put them squarely in control. 'Of course we had a lot of weapons,' he said. 'No mortars or anything like that, but we had machine guns and submachine guns and our own carbines.'

Abrenica agreed: 'We had jumped fully equipped for a combat mission, so we hastily erected a barricade and set up our machine guns behind it. We thought we'd have to shoot our way out.'

In the middle of Shangri-La, the modern and prehistoric warriors stood their ground, locked in a standoff.

Walter and his men had landed in the northwest part of the valley, in an area known to the natives as Wosi. Specifically, they were in part of Wosi called Abumpuk, not far from a village called Koloima. No huts were nearby because the paratroopers' drop zone was smack in the middle of a no-man's land – a designated battlefield – that separated the territories of two warring groups of Dani tribesmen, the Logo-Mabel clans on one side and the Kurelu on the other.

The Dani people in this part of the valley were separated by distance, heritage and politics from the Yali people of Uwambo and the clans that lived near the survivors' clearing in the jungle. They had not seen or heard anything about the *Gremlin Special* crash. With enemies all around them, an event that took place thirty kilometres away might as well have happened on the other side of the world.

Like the Yali people near the crash site, the Dani people around Wosi had grown accustomed to seeing planes, which they called *anekuku*. But they had not made the connection between the noisemakers that flew over their valley and the nine strange-looking creatures in their battlefield. Instead, like the people of Uwambo, at least some of them thought the strangers were embodiments of an ancient legend.

'When we saw them, we thought they were coming down on a vine from the sky,' said Lisaniak Mabel, who witnessed the paratroopers' arrival as a boy.

Although some natives thought the visitors were spirits, others believed that they were warriors like themselves who had escaped a massacre of their people. The coverings on the strangers' bodies reinforced that impression. When Dani people mourn, they cover their shoulders or their entire bodies in light-coloured mud. Surely, they believed, the strangers' khaki-coloured coverings must be made of mud.

The men and boys surrounding the paratroopers were from the Logo-Mabel clans, and their leader was a powerful warrior with many kills in battle and a large collection of 'dead birds' captured from fallen enemies. He was a Dani, but his name was Yali, and he was from the Logo clan.

As Yali Logo and his clansmen studied Walter and his men, they felt certain of one thing: the strangers were not their Kurelu enemies, so they had no immediate need to kill them.

Walter had no idea what thoughts passed through the minds of the spear-carrying men surrounding him and his troops. But he sensed that the eyes upon him were filled more with curiosity than hostility. None of the local people moved to throw a spear or notch an arrow. In turn, none of the soldiers used a firearm. This museum-like diorama of first contact continued for three hours.

Before the jump, Walter and his men had been told by the rescue planners that a universal sign of friendship among New Guinea natives was to wave leaves over one's head. As the face-off lingered on, Walter tried it.

'I waved those damned leaves for hours,' Walter said, 'and then when I got no response I began to realize how foolish I must look, and I quit.'

Finally, after what Walter described as energetic 'motioning and beckoning', both sides relaxed and lowered their weapons. The paratroopers made a fire to gather around, and the natives followed suit nearby.

'When we first started to get acquainted with them, I think they realized almost as soon as we did that they had nothing to fear from us.'

Writing that night in the journal he updated daily throughout the mission, Walter recorded his first impression of the locals: 'Natives wear nothing but hollow gourds over the penis and tie their testicles up with string, suspending the whole works from a string which goes around their midsection. Seem very healthy, teeth are in excellent shape, feet are badly misshapen from constant barefoot walking. Some have long, matted hair and look like French poodles, some short and are all kinky. So far no malformity of the body. Believe each family has different markings and hair-dos. Some, doglike features; others, slightly anthropoid in appearance, and still others are as finely featured as the average white race. We are the first in this valley from the outside world.' Walter noted that the natives, redolent of pig grease and sweat, seemed to be people who 'never bathed'.

When both sides were at ease, the natives studied the soldiers' appearance, too. In a journal entry, Walter described a particularly flamboyant inspection by the men and boys of the Logo-Mabel clans that bloomed into a classic cultural misunderstanding.

As the two groups came close for a good look at one another, the natives gently stroked the soldiers' arms and legs, backs and chests. They also engaged in what Walter described as 'a lot of hugging. It drove my men wild, because they couldn't figure out what the hell.' The natives murmured as they massaged Walter and his men up and down.

Uncomfortable with the apparent shows of affection, Walter and his men concluded that the natives had somehow arrived at the mistaken conclusion that the visitors were women. What other explanation could there be for nearly naked men to rub their hands over the bodies of other men?

This touching scene went on awhile, until Walter and his paratroopers had had enough. The tall Army captain, towering over the natives as well as his own men, tried to forcefully communicate that they were male. No luck. The rubbing resumed. It reached a point that Walter described as 'making love'.

When the tribesmen showed no sign of ending their laying on of hands, Walter devised a strategy of decidedly unconventional warfare, unknown to any military handbook. First, he unbuckled his belt and pulled down his trousers to show that he had the necessary equipment to wear a gourd of his own, if he so chose. After revealing himself several times, Walter realized it wasn't working. He ordered his entire detachment of the 1st Recon to join him in what has to be one of the Second World War's most unusual show of force.

'God damn it, let's take our pants down,' Walter told his men, 'and show them that we're men, not women. I'm tired of this.'

Walter stripped off his shirt, trousers and underwear. His men followed suit. They walked around nude for the next several hours while the natives wandered among them, more modestly attired in penis gourds.

'First time I ever had to do that to prove I was a man,' Walter said.

Bringing out the heavy artillery, Walter pulled from his wallet a photo of his wife, 'and they went wild with interest'.

As far as Walter was concerned, this two-pronged display of his manhood and his mate did the trick. No longer did the natives 'make love' to the paratroopers.

In fact, the Dani people of the valley were not at all confused about the soldiers' gender. If they were confused about anything, it was the paratroopers' sudden nakedness.

When the men of the Logo-Mabel clans came in close after the standoff, they learned to their surprise that the strangers were not covered in mud for mourning, after all. Narekesok Logo, who witnessed the scene as a boy, explained that he and the other men and boys were intrigued by the coverings on the men's bodies. Having never before seen clothes – he said the Archbold expedition had not passed through their territory – they were fascinated by this soft, apparently removable second skin.

Another witness, Ai Baga, said: 'We came close and felt the clothes and said, "That's not mud!"'

Equally perplexing to the Dani people was the soldiers' response. From the time a male Dani is about four years old, he never fully exposes himself in public. Even if the gourd does not fit, he wears it. What seemed like near-nudity to outsiders like Walter and his men was quite the opposite to the Dani men who surrounded them. Penis gourds, or *horim*, are worn at work, at play, at war, and even while sleeping. They only come off in private: for urination or sex, or when a man inside his hut exchanges one *horim* for another. A man wearing a *horim* is modestly attired in Dani culture. A man without a *horim* is caught in an embarrassing state of undress.

To the native men and boys in the battlefield that day, Walter and his men were making spectacles of themselves.

Word spread quickly about the soldiers' 'show', said Lisaniak Mabel. More people flowed into the area from distant villages the next day. But after that first display Walter and his men kept their clothes on, and the latecomers returned home disappointed. Those natives who did see the naked soldiers told the story, laughing, for the rest of their lives.

After dressing, the paratroopers set up camp, scouted the area, collected equipment and supplies dropped from the plane. They also searched for a source of fresh water. By gulping from their canteens and pouring out a few drops, the soldiers expressed their need to the locals, who led them to a freshwater spring nearby. Walter and Don Ruiz, a handsome sergeant, walked near one of the villages, but the Dani people shooed them away, making it clear that the strangers were not welcome inside the fence that ringed the huts and courtyard.

After dinner and a few cigarettes around the campfire, Walter fended off swarms of dive-bombing mosquitoes. He organized his men into guard shifts that rotated every two hours. 'No evidence of any hostility, but still do not want to take any chances,' he wrote in his journal. Feeling better than he had in months, Walter could have stood the night-long watch himself. 'Too excited,' he wrote. 'Having a hell of a time getting to sleep.'

That same day at the survivors' camp, Doc Bulatao followed breakfast by getting back to work on Decker's wounds. Margaret described the scene in her diary: 'For six hours, he peeled the encrusted gangrene from the sergeant's infected burns. It was a very tedious and painful process. All of Doc's gentleness could not lessen Decker's ordeal. The sergeant lay rigid on his pallet. Decker was a very sick man, but never by a flinch or a whimper did he reveal the torment he was enduring ... There wasn't any anesthetic nor even a stiff drink of whisky available to ease Decker's pain.' Margaret noted with surprise, and perhaps a little disappointment, that they found no evidence the natives had learned how to distil their crops into alcoholic drinks.

Decker's agony was difficult for McCollom to bear. Only half-joking, he suggested they 'hit him in the head and put him out of his misery for a few hours'. Margaret noticed that the lieutenant was as drenched in sweat as Decker and Doc, just from witnessing the excruciating procedure.

Also interested was Wimayuk Wandik, who watched in rapt attention from nearby along with 'his mob of natives', as Margaret described them.

The people of Uwambo were growing ever more relaxed about the survivors and the medics in their midst. With each passing day, they also became less afraid of the low-altitude supply drops that initially had sent them running into the jungle for cover. They scoured the jungle for crates and parachutes, then hauled the supplies back to the survivors' camp.

One young man became much too comfortable with what he had seen.

'A native came running into our camp,' Margaret told her diary. 'He was terribly excited and upset. He motioned for the men to follow him with such urgency that we knew some crisis had arisen. Our men hurried after him to the edge of the jungle. The native, in great distress, pointed up to the top of a fifteen-metre tree. There was another native, with an open parachute preparing to make a free jump!'

The fall might have killed him, and the survivors and the medics feared that the people of Uwambo would blame them. Only after a great deal of yelling and pantomime negotiation would the young man relent. He gave up his dreams of flight and climbed down from the tree.

When the supply plane passed over that day, the radio operator informed the survivors and medics that Walter and eight enlisted paratroopers had landed in the main valley. The pilot underestimated their distance, saying they were about 16 kilometres away. McCollom later estimated that the base camp was more like 55 kilometres away, while Walter put it at 37 kilometres. The pilot told them that Walter and five of the paratroopers would soon start their trek to the jungle camp.

'They will be with you by nightfall,' the radioman said.

Margaret, McCollom and Decker dismissed the promise as cockeyed Army optimism.

Margaret felt more energized from another message relayed by the radioman, this one about Walter Fleming, the sergeant with whom she had planned a swimming date for the evening after her day trip to Shangri-La. She told her diary: 'My beau, Wally ... had been too frantic to talk coherently about the accident, even after he learned that I had survived by a miracle. Up to that moment, I had worried constantly for fear Wally would be terribly upset by first, the accident, and then my present predicament.'

The radioman's message changed her tune. 'As soon as I knew he was worried half to death, I was pleased as punch!'

As she was reflecting on Walter Fleming's concern for her well-being, other minds turned to more basic requirements. Menstrual cycles were notoriously out of whack among WACs in Hollandia, a byproduct of tropical climate, weight loss, stress, and any number of other factors. Sometimes WACs would have their periods twice or more in a single month, and other times they'd skip several months. When WAC officers at the base learned that one of the survivors was a woman, they ordered the supply plane to have McCollom ask Margaret the dates of her last period. When she reported that it had been a couple of months, McCollom told the supply plane to drop a box of sanitary towels, just in case. An act worthy of Laurel and Hardy ensued.

When he returned to the base, radio operator Jack Gutzeit went to the WAC commander's office like a husband sent to the drug store on an awkward mission.

'Maggie wants a couple boxes of Kotex,' he told the top WAC.

She brushed him off, telling Gutzeit that medical supplies for the rescue were the responsibility of the hospital commander. He trudged to the base hospital, where the hospital commander said, 'Go see the WAC commander. They're supposed to take care of all the women's stuff.'

After more back-and-forth, Gutzeit got fed up with the pass-the-napkin game. He returned to the Sentani Airstrip and asked a telephone operator to place calls to the WAC commander and the hospital commander. With all the moxie of his native Brooklyn, the sergeant told them both:

'This plane is leaving in one hour, and if I don't have Kotex from you folks, I'm calling General Clement at Far East Air Service Command Headquarters!'

That day, the cargo drop included a half-dozen boxes of sanitary napkins. In the days that followed, the supplies doubled then tripled.

'I bet we had twenty boxes of Kotex down there every day!' McCollom said.

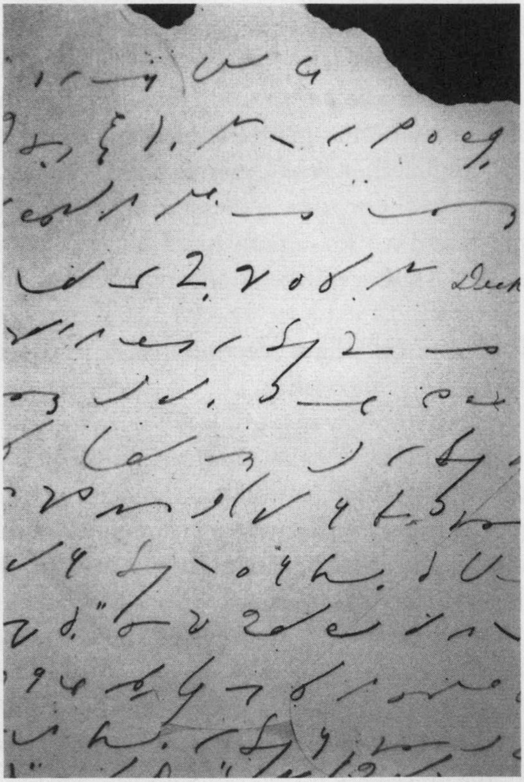

A page from Margaret Hastings' diary. It reads in part: 'Doc is the most gentle person I have ever seen, especially for a doctor. The day he arrived he didn't get around to dressing my legs till late in the evening, after he had done Decker. He then started to remove the bandages from my legs, and what a mess they were. They had bled considerably and the bandages had stuck so that you couldn't tell what was burned skin and what was bandage. He was pulling very gently and kept saying "I am so afraid I will hurt you."'

Care for the survivors' spiritual needs also came with that morning's supply drop. Major Cornelius Waldo, the Catholic chaplain from Indianapolis who had been on the B-17 search plane that spotted the survivors, assembled a package with a Bible, prayer books, and Margaret's Rosary beads. The religious supplies came in handy when Doc and Rammy went to work on Margaret.

'It was the same peeling process, and after five minutes I clutched my Rosary and gritted my teeth,' she wrote. 'My pride was involved! I was determined to be as good a soldier as Decker. For four endless hours, Doc peeled my legs, my feet, and worked on my hand. I didn't cry or make a sound. But I was yelling bloody murder inside all the time.'

Rammy remembered her reaction differently. 'We had to slice, little by little, slice, slice, until it bleeds ... She always cried. Cry, cry, cry. It was painful when I cut, but I think she tried to hide it. It was painful. To me it was very painful.'

The treatments left the medics exhausted and Decker and Margaret bed-ridden. Margaret was in such pain she had to lie on her back with her knees bent, to keep her clothes from chafing against her leg wounds. Despite her agony, she began to believe that Doc would save her legs.

As she settled in for the night, she called out to the four men nearby: 'It's wonderful to go to bed and know you're on the road to recovery instead of ruin.'

Eighteen

Bathtime for Yugwe

MARGARET AWOKE THE NEXT MORNING, EAGER TO rid herself of a hard week of sweat, blood, gangrenous shavings, and jungle grime.

She gratefully accepted a toothbrush Doc Bulatao had tucked in his pocket before the jump. Then she asked Rammy Ramirez to help her with a bath. He was happy to oblige, but the question was where. McCollom and the medics bathed in the cold creek, about a hundred metres from the knoll where Rammy and Doc had set up a little Army village: a cook tent and a shelter for supplies made from draped parachutes, and pup tents for them to sleep. They dug a latrine and tented that, too. But the idea of Margaret bathing alone at the creek worried them, and they did not want to intrude on her privacy by hovering close by.

Rammy solved the problem with the universal soldier's bathtub: his helmet. Hobbling on crutches he made from branches to ease his sore ankle, he found a semi-private area on the far side of the knoll and filled the helmet with fire-warmed water. He gathered soap, towels, a washcloth,

From left, Corporal 'Rammy' Ramirez, Corporal Margaret Hastings, and Sergeant Benjamin 'Doc' Bulatao.

and a small khaki uniform earmarked for Margaret in one of the cargo drops.

With McCollom's help, the medics carried Margaret to her makeshift bath area and left her to wash in what they expected would be complete privacy. She stripped off her soiled shirt and tattered pants. Naked, she lathered the washcloth and began to scrub. Almost immediately, she felt eyes upon her.

'I looked around and there on a neighboring knoll were the natives,' she told her diary. 'I never could figure out whether they were goggle-eyed at the queer rite I was performing, or at a skin so different from their own.'

McCollom spotted them, too: 'Big smiles on their faces.'

When she had failed to shoo them away, Margaret gamely finished her bath. She dried off, pulled on her new clothes, and called for her bearers to return her to her tent. The bath routine became a daily event for Margaret, and a highlight for the men and boys of Uwambo.

When they first met the visitors, the natives had been fascinated by McCollom's straight blond hair. Margaret's bath had that beat. One of the smiling regulars at the show was young Helenma Wandik.

'We saw she had breasts, so we knew she was a woman,' he said. 'She would wave us away, but we thought it was interesting so we stayed until she finished.'

Once they were certain that Margaret was a woman, the tribespeople jumped to a conclusion. Although they still believed them to be spirits, they assumed that the three survivors were 'a man, a woman, and the woman's husband', Helenma Wandik said. The 'husband' was the man the natives called 'Meakale', their attempted pronunciation of McCollom.

Although the survivors and medics did not learn the names of the natives, the people of Uwambo tried to make sense of what to call their visitors. They heard McCollom calling Margaret 'Maggie', but to their ears it sounded like 'Yugwe', so this is what they called her. In her diary, Margaret wrote that she 'always heartily detested' the nickname Maggie, 'but I loved it the way the natives pronounced it'. She said they softly slurred the syllables. She heard the result not as Yugwe, but as 'Mah-gy'.

The natives never witnessed sexual relations or intimate affection between 'Meakale' and 'Yugwe/Mah-gy'. The basis for assuming the two were married, Helenma Wandik said, was their own culture. In male-dominated Yali and Dani society, a healthy woman who reached sexual maturity wasn't single long. The people of Uwambo did not know that Margaret was thirty, but one look at her naked body told them she was past thirteen. They identified Meakale/McCollom as the group's leader, so they thought she must be his wife.

———

On their first full day in the valley, Earl Walter and the eight enlisted paratroopers of the 1st Recon enjoyed ten-in-one rations for breakfast. Afterward, Walter took Master Sergeant Abrenica and two sergeants, Hermenegildo Caoili and Juan Javonillo, on what he described in his journal as 'a short recon' of twelve kilometres round-trip through the valley. Along with native tracks and a deserted village, they came upon 'one skeleton near [the] trail, with rotten flesh' and a broken spear nearby. Walter wrote in his journal that the 'cause of death [was] undetermined'. But he suspected the body was evidence of the native battles and enemy raids. During the march, Walter got his first look at a native woman. Writing in his journal, he judged her looks with a harsh Western eye: 'Very unattractive hairdo, not fancy hair, and ... much less hair than the men. She wore a loose cloth draped around the crotch and private parts (very skimpy). No other clothing. Looked like she was pregnant.'

Upon their return to camp, Walter found that the men who had stayed behind had rigged a parachute as a tent to cover their equipment from the rains. As he put it, 'The circus has come to Hidden Valley.' In mid-afternoon, a C-47 dropped water, supplies and best of all, a stack of letters from home. Walter remained excited by the adventure, writing in his journal: 'Everyone is in fine spirits ... This promises to be one of the most interesting parts of our lives.'

As the paratroopers arranged their camp, people from the Wosi area crowded around to watch. Walter's men grew edgy from the proximity, the incessant touching, and the body odour. Walter pointed a carbine in the air.

'Fired a few shots to see effect on natives and most of them didn't stop running till they were out of sight,' he wrote. His men followed suit, including one who fired a burst from a Thompson submachine gun, the famous

'Tommy Gun'. As the natives fled, 'ass over tea kettle', as Walter put it, the men trampled the smaller boys. Some of his paratroopers got a kick out of it, but Walter ordered a cease-fire. 'The men were doing it just for the hell of it, to make the natives run and yell and whatnot,' he said.

The guns' noise frightened the natives, but Walter wrote in his journal that 'they do not understand the killing power of the modern firearm'. They seemed more afraid when the soldiers held up sticks or branches to resemble spears.

Later that day, Alfred Baylon, a stocky, cigar-smoking sergeant who was qualified as a medic, walked to the Baliem River followed by a group of natives. When a flock of ducks flew overhead, he used his carbine to shoot one. The natives retrieved it, and Baylon brought it back to camp. In his journal that night, Walter praised the 'excellent dinner with barbecued duck'. Of the natives, he wrote: 'Imagine they now know our weapons can kill.'

More than six decades later, the warning shots fired by the paratroopers and the duck hunt by Baylon – whom the natives called 'Weylon' – still reverberated in the minds of old men who were boys when they witnessed the displays.

'One man, named Mageam, came in to the white men's camp,' said Lisaniak Mabel. 'He was getting too close, and the white people got irritated and fired shots to keep him away. We didn't know the sound, and we ran ... Then Weylon shot the duck. We understood he did it with the gun.'

Several also remembered the walks Walter took through the Wosi area. On one of his treks, Walter stopped at an area called 'Pika', near the edge of the no-man's land, almost in enemy territory. Tribespeople believed that he was purposely standing guard at Pika. They viewed this as an act of bravery and a warning to their enemies. They called Walter 'Pika', as a tribute to his apparent courage.

'Pika was shooting the gun a lot, to show the enemies not to come,' said Ai Baga. 'We liked when Pika went there. We told Pika to stay there, so our enemies wouldn't attack.'

Narekesok Logo, his wiry body marked with long-healed arrow scars, remembered the paratroopers' visit as a time of peace: 'Pika and Weylon were standing there with their guns, so our enemies didn't come.'

Equally memorable to the tribespeople was the soldiers' practice of digging a single hole covered by a tent where all

Sergeant Ken Decker in a makeshift latrine in the jungle.

of them went to defecate. Native practice called for bodily waste to pass in private, in the jungle or the high grasses. However revolting the soldiers found the natives' hygiene, it could not exceed the natives' disgust at the soldiers' use of a house for *inalugu* – a pile of faeces.

The next day was Tuesday, 22 May 1945. Walter ate a hearty breakfast of ham and eggs, biscuits and marmalade, washed down with hot chocolate. He and five men – Corporal Custodio Alerta and sergeants Hermenegildo Caoili, Fernando Dongallo, Juan Javonillo and Don Ruiz – were ready to begin the trek to the survivors' campsite. That left his first sergeant, Sandy Abrenica, in charge of the base camp along with the two sergeants, Alfred Baylon and Roque Velasco.

Walter enlisted a group of Dani men as carriers and 'native guides'. After convincing himself that they understood his intended destination, they marched boldly out of base camp.

After three hours of steady uphill climbing, they broke for lunch. Walter pulled out his journal. 'God only knows why mountains are this high,' he wrote. 'Now we are going down again. Passed by a few native villages and had to stop near each one so that the people could gather around and satisfy their curiosity.' Along the way, the six soldiers gained and lost several groups of guides, 'as they do not seem to go far beyond their own villages'.

With no maps, Walter and his men estimated that they travelled eleven kilometres before stopping to pitch camp for the night. His gut told him that the natives were no threat – he made a casual reference in his journal to their spears and arrows, and wrote that their 'only means of cutting are stone axes'. The paratroopers needed rest for the next day's march, so Walter told his relieved men that they would not post guards that night.

Walter's decision to skip guard duty proved uneventful, but not solely because his judgement that the natives 'seem very friendly', as he wrote in his journal, proved correct. Unbeknownst to Walter, tribal leaders along the route from the Wosi area base camp towards the Ogi ridge where the plane crashed had set aside their traditional enmities. They had granted the strangers safe passage.

'A declaration, called a *maga*, was made that no one would attack them,' said Yunggukwe Wandik, daughter of the Uwambo leader Yaralok Wandik. 'It was said, "Do not kill them. These are spirits. Don't kill them. They are not human."' If not for the *maga*, the six sleeping soldiers might have been ambushed and slaughtered by hundreds of spear-carrying warriors summoned at short notice by a regional leader.

Not everyone agreed with the *maga*. Clearly defined territorial boundaries were deeply ingrained in the people of the valley, and the idea of strangers traipsing through their land was not welcome with some. 'There were people who thought killing them was a good idea,' Yunggukwe Wandik said. If not for the soldiers' skin colour – Walter's whiteness more than the Filipino-Americans' toffee colouring – the *maga* might not have held. 'Do you think we had ever seen white skin before?' she said. 'That made people afraid.'

Despite the *maga*, more than once en route to the survivors' camp Walter and his men were met by antagonism when they came close to villages. 'In a couple of cases they actually came out on a path and stopped us,' he said. 'They didn't want us going into their village.' Walter attributed the defensiveness to a shortage of available wives. 'Sandy Abrenica and I figured out later that they were afraid that we would steal their women. This happened over there. There was some thievery of women between tribes.'

Walter's description of natives blocking his path echoed the confrontation that led to the killing of a native during

Richard Archbold's expedition seven years earlier. It is not clear whether Walter and his men passed the same villages, but the paratroopers never found it necessary to use – in Archbold's euphemistic phrase for the shooting – 'more than a show of force'. At the same time, the natives the paratroopers encountered either were unaware of the shooting or chose not to avenge it for reasons lost to time.

Walter did not know anything about the Archbold expedition or the Uluayek legend about the sky spirits and their rope to the valley, so he was unaware that the native men had good reason to suspect them of violence, pig theft and wife stealing.

For his part, Walter said he wanted to avoid violence if at all possible. As for pigs, they had no time for a roast. And the last thing they wanted were native women. 'Well, they didn't ever mingle,' he said later. 'And I told the men, absolutely not. I don't think any of them were good-looking enough for the men, anyway.'

Spent from his exertions, Walter fell into a deep sleep and the night passed without incident. The next morning, he and his men ate breakfast and waited for the supply plane, as much to get a fix on their location as to collect fresh provisions. Believing that they were on their last lap to the survivors' camp, they began the day in high spirits. But the plane never came and the latest group of native bearers proved unhelpful. 'So far the natives are more bother than good,' he wrote, 'as they will not carry.'

They broke camp and started out, believing that they had communicated to their latest guides where they were headed. But after an arduous twenty-kilometre march, Walter and his men found themselves right back where they had started. The previously buoyant tone in Walter's journal disappeared: 'Did not understand that we want to go up to the wreck, not back to our camp. We are slightly discouraged to say the least. Hiked too long before setting up camp and were caught in the rain, thus getting everything soaking wet. Made camp and ate supper. What a rotten life.'

On the third morning of their trek, they awoke chilled, water-logged and tired. Having planned a one- to two-day hike, Walter and his men were out of food. Still unsure of their location, they moved on, guided by Walter's innate sense of where they were going and 'dead reckoning' – navigating in a fixed direction based on a previous known location, in this case their base camp. They headed towards a dip between two ridges that Walter called 'the saddle'.

'Things look bad,' he wrote. 'Our last rations are gone and we are still a long way from our objective. Broke camp and kept on going up and up toward the saddle, which is somewhere at the top of this canyon.' Late in the morning he finally made contact with the supply plane to request rations. In the meantime, they continued marching without lunch. Much of the way they cut a fresh trail as they went, slogging through brush and high grass. A quick bath in a cold creek refreshed them, but the feeling did not last long. Soon they were exhausted, yet they 'just kept going on and on and up and up'.

In late afternoon the rains came. Soaked, hungry and cold, the would-be rescuers made camp around five o'clock in the afternoon. They laid out their bedrolls and went to sleep without dinner.

'God only knows where that last ridge is,' Walter wrote that night in his journal. 'We can last for a few more days at this rate, but sure as hell would like to know about where we are. Don't like this fooling around without maps.'

Nineteen

'Shoo, Shoo Baby'

THEIR STOMACHS EMPTY AND GROWLING, WALTER and his team awoke early to a breakfast of hot water and hope. His top priority was receiving a drop of ten-in-one rations. He tried hailing the C-47 supply plane by walkie-talkie as it flew somewhere in the vicinity overhead, even as he worried that his campsite at the edge of the jungle might not be visible from the air. Marching farther towards the survivors' campsite would only put them deeper under the canopy. So they stayed put, talked and waited.

'Finally they are over us and have us spotted,' he wrote in his journal on Friday, 25 May, his first upbeat entry in two days. 'Rations dropped. Best things I have seen in a long time. Men recovered the rations and I learned that we are two miles by air due west of the wreck.'

Ravenous, Walter stuffed himself. He paid the price when they broke camp: 'The first hour was terrible. Too much food.' But eager to reach their destination, they pressed on, slower than usual and taking more frequent breaks. After several hours, they reached the crest of a

Earl Walter speaking by walkie-talkie with a supply plane after parachuting into the valley.

ridge and began to hike on a downward slope. Walter hoped they were close.

At the survivors' camp, the radioman in the *three-one-one* supply plane passed on the news that the paratroopers were close by: 'Earl will get down there pretty soon, and you'll hear him.'

In late afternoon, Margaret heard what she called 'that yapping noise peculiar to the natives'. As the noise grew closer, it was replaced by an unmistakably American sound:

> 'Shoo, shoo my baby, Shoooo.
> Goodbye baby, don't you cry no more.
> Your big tall papa's off to the seven seas.'

Walter marched buoyantly towards the campsite, swinging his bolo knife to clear the trail and singing the Andrews Sisters' recent hit, 'Shoo, Shoo Baby'.

Writing about the paratroopers' arrival in her diary, Margaret's first impression of Walter bordered on starry-eyed: 'He looked like a giant as he came down the trail at the head of his Filipino boys and the ubiquitous escort of natives. The captain's arrival was like a strong, fresh breeze. He was not only a capable and efficient officer, but a one-man floor show. Two minutes after he arrived the camp started jumpin'.'

Doc and Rammy rushed from their tents to greet their comrades. Walter was happy to see the survivors, but he was overjoyed to see the two medics. 'I knew they were all right,' he said, 'but I wanted to see them and congratulate them again, first of all on the jump, and secondly on the good job they had done. And just to get back together with them. The rest of the men felt the same way. We were all quite concerned about them.'

Margaret watched as Walter and the medics exchanged embraces, handshakes and hearty pats on the back. She wrote in her diary: 'His men worshipped Walter, and the affection was patently mutual.'

Walter, meanwhile, could not help but notice that Margaret, despite her jungle haircut, her weight loss, and her injuries, 'was a pretty good-looking gal'.

With the survivors' camp now expanded to ten men and one woman, Walter set his troops to work putting up more pup tents as sleeping quarters. They also erected a large pyramidal tent with a peaked roof and walls about five metres long on each side, to serve as a combined headquarters, mess hall, and jungle social club for the two officers, Walter and McCollom; one WAC; and eight enlisted men.

Soon an American flag waved from a makeshift flagpole outside the big tent, making the camp a quasi-official US Army Base. In one journal entry, Walter called it 'The Lost Outpost of Shangri-La'. He wrote: 'The Stars and Stripes now fly over the Oranje Mountain Range. Being the first white people here, we can claim this territory for Uncle Sam, but doubt if the Aussies would appreciate it.'

After a bath in the creek and dinner served up by McCollom, Walter pulled out a deck of cards and organized the first of what became daily games of poker and gin rummy. Margaret was no poker player, preferring Bridge, but she kept herself amused as they 'won and lost thousands of dollars' in every session. Lacking chips, they bet with Raleigh and Chelsea brand cigarettes, along with wooden matches to light their winnings. She modelled her gambling style on the freewheeling ways of Sergeant Caoili, who would bluff like mad on a pair of threes. Caoili was relentless in everything he did; when he was not focused on winning and losing matchsticks, he earned the nicknames 'Superman' and 'Iron Man' for his powerful build and tireless work habits.

The 'headquarters' tent at the jungle clearing, with (from left) John McCollom, Ken Decker, Ben Bulatao and Camilo Ramirez.

Sitting around their improvised card table in the big tent, Walter smouldered at Margaret's card-playing style. He stewed over what he viewed as her stubborn refusal to learn the rules of the game.

'There ought to be a law against women playing poker!' he shouted.

Neither was he impressed when she invented a poker-like game she called 'Deuces wild, roll your own, and fiery cross'. Incomprehensible to everyone but Margaret, the game involved a muddle of wild cards and an opportunity for players to form the best possible hand using fifteen cards.

Walter declared: 'Maggie, you don't know how to play cards.'

'I do too!' Margaret answered.

'Well, you probably know how to play Bridge, but I don't know how to play Bridge. This is poker we're playing, and there are: a pair; three of a kind; a straight; a flush; and so on.'

In Walter's view, Margaret could never remember the ranking of the best to worst poker hands. 'We'd always get into an argument because I knew what I was drawing to, and she didn't,' he said.

Margaret thought Walter's anger could be traced to another source: his machismo. 'The captain played just as earnestly as if it were for real money,' she told her diary, 'and when I would bluff him out of a big pot he would be livid.'

After cards, the paratroopers, the survivors and some of the natives passed the evening hours by entertaining each other. Margaret sang WAC tunes, and several paratroopers showed off their vocal stylings with Visayan love songs from the Philippines. The natives played the only musical instrument the survivors and paratroopers ever heard in Shangri-La: a simple mouth harp whose tune sounded to the outsiders like a monotonic funeral dirge.

But there was only one star: Camp Shangri-La's commanding officer.

'Walter was a personality kid,' Margaret wrote. 'Often, after supper, he would put on a one-man floor show. He could give a wonderful imitation of a nightclub singer or a radio crooner ... "Shoo, Shoo Baby" was always his favourite. Walter was wonderful for morale. No one could be downhearted for long in his presence.'

As they spent more time together, Walter got the strong impression that Margaret found him sexually attractive. He picked up signals that she expected him to make a pass at her, and she looked for opportunities to spend time with him. Walter may have been tempted, but he insisted that he never made a move. As Walter explained, he took seriously his marriage and his role as the mission's commanding officer. He never explained his behaviour to Margaret, but she apparently got the message.

When Walter didn't rise to the bait, he said, Margaret turned her attentions to one of his men, Sergeant Don Ruiz.

Walter was no prude – only a few years earlier, he had played truant from school to visit LA strip clubs – and he did not care what enlisted personnel did in private, on their own time. But he felt responsible for everything that happened on his watch in Shangri-La. He knew there was no birth control in the valley, and he did not want unexpected consequences.

Not certain how best to proceed, Walter approached McCollom for help.

'I wanted him to tell Maggie to leave the men alone,' Walter said. Don Ruiz 'was one of my best noncoms, and also one of the handsomest men around. Maggie sort of had her eyes on him and tried to seduce him a couple of times.'

Torn between interest in Margaret and respect for his captain, Ruiz found a private moment to speak with Walter.

'Captain,' he said, 'what am I going to do?'

'Just leave her the hell alone,' Walter answered. 'Walk away, just walk away.'

A flirtation between the two continued, but as far as Walter knew, it remained unconsummated.

After speaking with Ruiz, Walter gathered his troops and laid down the law to the entire squad: 'If anybody lays a hand on her, so help me God, you're busted to private the next minute.'

Walter explained: 'I had to remind my men a couple of times that I sure as hell didn't want a pregnant WAC flying out of there ... That would have given me a pretty bad reputation. So I had to be adamant about that.'

The day after arriving at the survivors' camp, Walter watched Doc and Rammy slice and peel the gangrenous skin from Margaret's and Decker's wounds. He took admiring note of the medics' work in his journal, writing that 'both men deserved all the credit in the world'. But one look at the injuries convinced Walter that his hope of a quick return to the base camp in the big valley had been overly optimistic. He wrote in his journal that they would be stuck at the jungle campsite for at least a week, maybe longer. Even then, he thought that he and his men would have to carry Margaret and Decker at least some of the way through the jungle and down the slippery mountain slope.

That day, just before lunchtime, the supply plane dropped its usual load of provisions, as well as books and magazines to help pass the time. When they gathered the cargo, the paratroopers found supplies for their difficult next task: burial duty. The *three-one-one* dropped twenty-one freshly pressed silver dog tags, along with twenty wooden crosses and one wooden Star of David. The Army believed that the crash victims included sixteen Protestants, four Catholics, and one Jewish WAC. Only much later would the military learn that a second Star of David should have been dropped, for Private Mary Landau of Brooklyn.

Aboard the plane that day, helping to toss the funerary supplies out the cargo door, was Sergeant Ruth Coster, whose workload had kept her from flying aboard the *Gremlin Special*, but whose best friend, Sergeant Helen Kent, died in the crash. Other than keeping Helen's memory alive, it was the last thing Ruth could do for her.

On Sunday, 27 May, two weeks after the crash, Walter awoke at seven in the morning, ate a hearty breakfast, and set out for the wreck with five sergeants: Bulatao, Caoili, Dongallo, Javonillo and Ruiz. Following detailed directions from McCollom, they tried to retrace the survivors' trail in reverse, using the stream to guide them up the mountain. But they became confused about which of its tributaries to follow. The paratroopers left their equipment and the grave markers at an easy-to-find spot and split up – Walter and Ruiz went one way, and the other four men went another. Trekking through the jungle proved impossible, especially since they were not sure where they were headed. After several hours, both groups returned to the campsite, exhausted. To make matters worse, Walter strained his groin on the trek.

The following day, Walter sent Caoili and Javonillo on another search mission for the crash site, but they had no better luck. Walter knew what he needed: someone who had been there before. Finally, McCollom led a group back up the mountain towards the wreck, navigating by the river and a few landmarks he remembered. McCollom knew they were close when he spotted wispy strands of light-brown hair tangled in vines and shrubs. He recalled how Margaret's long hair had snagged in the brush when they had left the crash site for the clearing, and how he had used his pocketknife to give her a jungle cut. McCollom and the paratroopers followed the trail of Margaret's hair directly to the burned, broken remains of the *Gremlin Special.*

As they entered the area where the plane had mowed down trees and carved a hole through the canopy, McCollom hung back. 'There it is,' he told the paratroopers, pointing the way. He had already seen enough. He did not need to see the remains of his brother; his commander, Colonel Peter Prossen; and his friends, colleagues and fellow passengers.

Later that night, McCollom relied on reports from the paratroopers who had walked with him to describe the situation to Walter. 'Lieutenant Mac's report on the wreck is very disheartening,' Walter wrote that night in his journal. 'Only three bodies are identifiable – Captain Good, Sergeant Besley and Private Hanna. The last two are both WACs. The rest of the bodies are in a cremated jumble. Still not decided on disposition.' Several days later, Walter received his orders via walkie-talkie: Return to the crash site with the grave markers and shovels.

They started out just after dawn and reached what was left of the *Gremlin Special* in late morning. Joining Walter were the five paratroopers who had accompanied him from the big valley. McCollom had refused to join the burial patrol, and Margaret and Decker were too hurt to help. Even with McCollom's instructions, the jungle was so thick that at one point they came within twenty metres of the *Gremlin Special* without knowing it.

When the paratroopers reached the wreck, they buried Laura Besley and Eleanor Hanna, side by side in an area they called the cemetery. 'After that,' Walter wrote in his journal, 'we buried Captain Good and made a common grave for the eighteen unidentifiable persons.'

As he recounted the day's events, the tone of Walter's journal shifted. He and his men had jumped into the valley for the adventure of a rescue mission. Now they were on grave duty, and the tragic reality hit home:

> Those eighteen were all mixed up, and most of the bodies had been completely cremated by the intense heat of the fire. It was the best burial we could give them under the circumstances. All of us had to use gas masks, as the odor was terrific. I don't mind dead women, but dead women in the nude is something different. Also the bodies were almost a month old. After the burials were completed, I took some camera shots of the wreck and the graves. God only knows how anyone got out of the plane alive. It is without a doubt the most thoroughly destroyed aircraft I have ever seen.

After covering the graves, Walter and his men pounded the crosses and the Star of David into the damp earth, draping each one with a dog tag. Their labours took until late afternoon, and by then the sun was setting, its last rays reflecting off mountain walls. The nightly mist slithered into the jungle.

As Walter and his men worked, circling overhead was an Army plane with two chaplains.

'Out of the depth I have cried unto thee, O Lord,' prayed Father Gearhard, as the service was broadcast over the walkie-talkie to the cemetery area and the survivors' campsite. Chaplain Cornelius Waldo, who had earlier dropped Bibles and prayer books to the survivors, later told a reporter that the scene 'seemed to whisper a peace more living and beautiful than any spot I've ever seen'.

Margaret wrote in her diary: 'From that plane, over the radio, came the saddest and most impressive funeral service I have ever heard. We sat around the camp radio, silent and very humble as a Catholic, a Protestant and a Jewish chaplain in the plane read burial services for the dead on the

One of the crosses erected by the burial crew near the wreckage of the *Gremlin Special*.

mountaintop. We were very humble because we have been saved where so many had perished. Lieutenant McCollom sat with his head bowed, his usual controlled self. But Sergeant Decker's and my hearts ached for him. On one of those white crosses up that cruel mountain hung the dog tag of his twin brother, Lieutenant Robert E. McCollom, from whom only death could separate him.'

The burial team hiked back towards the campsite, stopping along the way to bathe in the creek. They cleansed themselves, but without heavy-duty soap and hot water, they couldn't wash the stench of death out of their uniforms. Later, Walter asked the supply plane for replacements, so they could throw away the clothes they had worn for the burials. After their baths, the enlisted men had a late lunch, but Walter settled into a contemplative mood and skipped the meal.

That night at the campsite, McCollom kept to himself. Walter, Margaret and Decker fell into what Walter called 'a long discussion on the world at war'. Decker gave up after a while and went to his tent, but Walter and Margaret kept arguing deep into the night about politics and the military. 'She seems to have it in for the Army, will not listen to any logical reasoning,' Walter wrote. 'Man, but she is really stubborn.'

Still, he respected her. 'Margaret had a lot of gumption and a lot of guts,' Walter said later. 'It might have been that she was the only woman surrounded by a lot of men, and she had to hold her own. But she would never listen to anyone trying to tell her anything!'

The bickering kept the camp from sleep. Rammy called to them that it was past midnight, and the debate ended. Walter wrote: 'Off to bed we went with nothing at all settled.'

The people of Uwambo watched as the creatures they thought were spirits made repeated trips to the top of the Ogi ridge. The natives, who cremated their dead, did not comprehend the burial rites. With no religious symbols of their own, they also did not understand the meaning of the crosses and the Star of David.

'When they climbed the mountain,' said Yunggukwe Wandik, 'we all thought they wanted to know if they could see their homes from there.'

By the time the funeral was complete, the US War Department had sent two dozen telegrams to the next-of-kin of the crew and passengers of the *Gremlin Special*. All but three began with some variation of the standard military death notice: 'The Secretary of War deeply regrets to inform you ...'

Margaret Nicholson of Medford, Massachusetts, the mother of Major George Nicholson, received condolence letters from three of America's top generals: Douglas MacArthur, Clements McMullen, and H.H. 'Hap' Arnold. Although pilot error might have been suspected, Nicholson's full role in the crash was not known; even after it emerged that he was alone at the controls, the Army Air Forces never fixed blame for the wreck of the *Gremlin Special*. Talk of an investigation fizzled, and vague suppositions about sudden downdraughts remained the presumptive cause in the official record.

Hap Arnold, commanding general of the Army Air Forces, described Nicholson to his mother as having died 'while he was flying in the service of his Country'. McMullen, Fee-Ask's commanding general, wrote: 'You may well be proud of the important part which your son took in forwarding the mission of this command.' MacArthur wrote: 'Your consolation for his loss may be that he died in the service of our country in a just cause which, with Victory, will give freedom from oppression to all peoples.'

For the McCollom family, the official notices highlighted the twins' permanent separation. A condolence telegram went to the young wife of Robert McCollom. Her in-laws, who were listed as John McCollom's next-of-kin, received a different letter altogether. Theirs was the embodiment of answered prayers. It echoed the letters received by the parents of Ken Decker in Kelso, Washington, and Margaret Hastings' widowed father, Patrick Hastings, in Owego, New York.

On 27 May 1945, three long days after he received the initial 'missing' telegram, Patrick Hastings opened a letter from the Army saying that 'a corrected report has now been received which indicates that your daughter was injured in a plane crash ... and that she is safe instead of missing in action as you were previously advised'. The letter promised updates on rescue operations and Margaret's condition.

A follow-up came twelve days later, in more human terms, from the Hollandia chaplain, Cornelius Waldo: 'Notice has reached you by now that your dear daughter Margaret has had a very miraculous escape in a plane crash. Due to the fact that the survivors are in a rather inaccessible spot, it will be some time before she will be back at the base to write you herself. I talked to her on the radio the day we dropped supplies and paratroopers. She is quite all right in spite of her harrowing experience.'

Waldo didn't mention her burns, her gangrene or her other wounds, or the fact that the Army still didn't know how to get Margaret, her fellow survivors, and their rescuers back to Hollandia.

Twenty

Hold the Front Page

AFTER THE BURIALS, THE JUNGLE RECUPERATION camp fell into a routine of medical treatments, meals, reading, card games and bull sessions, punctuated by near-daily supply drops and encounters with the natives. Eager to get moving, Walter radioed Major George Gardner, who oversaw the supply runs from aboard the *three-one-one*, to request a helicopter transport from the jungle campsite to the valley. That way, Walter figured, they wouldn't need to carry Margaret and Decker or wait until they were well enough to travel by foot.

Walter's request for a helicopter could be chalked up to wishful thinking, lack of aviation expertise, fatigue or all three. If a helicopter could fly over the surrounding mountains to ferry them from the jungle campsite, it presumably could fly them out of the valley altogether, even if only one or two at a time. And if a helicopter had been a viable alternative, Colonel Elsmore and the other rescue planners in Hollandia might not have needed Walter, the medics and the other paratroopers in the first place.

The most likely explanation for Walter's wish for a helicopter – expressed several times in his daily journal entries

– was his desire to hasten his return to Hollandia. He thought he could parlay success in Shangri-La into a combat posting, and he was keen to play that card with the Army brass.

While Walter waited for answers from Gardner on a helicopter, and from the medics on the survivors' ability to move out, the young captain's growing impatience seeped into his journal:

> May 29, 1945: Decided to straighten up our kitchen, so Don [Ruiz] and I went to work on it, then waited around for the plane. Finally it came, a new plane and new crew ... They dropped one bundle two miles from us and it fell apart. They must think this is a tea party we are on. I blew my top and the plane took off for Hollandia ... All clothes for Hastings. She has enough now for a trousseau. No medical supplies. What a snafu [screwball] bunch is running this show ... Here's hoping on the helicopter.
>
> May 30, 1945: Waited for the plane but it did not come. We have plenty of food but our medical supplies are very low ... Spent the afternoon in the sack reading and shooting the breeze. What a life. Certainly wish the answer on the helicopter would come through. Or at least that the patients would get well enough to travel ... Rain came early so we are all in the sack and most of the boys are reading. Spirits are fine and we are only wishing for some excitement ... God only knows what is going on in the outside world.
>
> May 31, 1945: Up a little later this morning as there was nothing in particular to do. After breakfast I sent Caoili and Alerta out on a recon for a shorter route to the valley ... The plane came over early this morning ... and the helicopter is out, so that is that and we hike out. I certainly hope the three survivors can take it.

June 1, 1945: This is really going to be hell, just sitting around, waiting to get out of here ... Patients' recovery is all I am waiting for.

June 2, 1945: The plane came over at ten-thirty with our supplies and mail. We certainly needed the medical supplies and I received eight letters, which certainly helped the old morale. They gave us a brief resumé of the world news, and it is certainly encouraging. After lunch I read *Bedside Esquire* and then we got ready for dinner ... Certainly hope the recovery of the patients speeds up a bit.

June 3, 1945: What a morning. Slept till eleven-thirty. First time that has ever happened to me without a hangover involved, at least on Sunday anyway. Had some cereal and then waited for lunch ... This is quite a life and getting damn tiresome, but can't do anything till I am sure that the trip to my base camp will not hurt the patients. Oh well – it's a good rest.

June 4, 1945: In the morning, I fired a few rounds with the carbine. That is an excellent way to waste time. After you are through, you have to clean the weapon so it takes up a little time. Dinner tonight was really something. Prepared by Dongallo and Bulatao. Casserole of bacon, corned beef, sweet potatoes and peas, with rice on the side. Last but not least peaches for dessert. Weather still bad and no plane today. Morale is excellent.

June 7, 1945: ... Sat around and talked about home.

June 8, 1945: Well, one year ago today I said goodbye to my wife Sal. It certainly seems a hell of a lot longer than that. I miss her more than ever up in this place, and that is going some. Don [Ruiz] woke me up this morning telling me that the plane was overhead ... Two war correspondents were in the plane, so I imagine this damn show is

> getting plenty of publicity back in the States. I hope so, as the men have worked plenty hard on this show, and maybe it will open a few people's eyes to the possibilities of my future plans. The two were Mr. Simmons of *The Chicago Tribune* and Mr. Morton of AP.

The 'show' – the crash, the survivors, the natives, and the rescue mission in Shangri-La – had indeed reached the United States and beyond. After a nearly three-week news blackout, Colonel Elsmore let out word to the press that something remarkable was happening in the heart of New Guinea. Several reporters took the bait, but none more avidly than the two reporters Walter mentioned in his journal.

Walter Simmons of the *Chicago Tribune* was thirty-seven, a native of Fargo, North Dakota, whose father sold patent medicine. After two years of college, Simmons signed on as reporter for the *Daily Argus-Leader* in Sioux Falls, South Dakota. Ten years later, in 1942, he moved to the big time with a job covering the war in the South Pacific for the *Tribune*. Beneath the gruff exterior of a grizzled war correspondent, Simmons showed a flair for rich images and tight, well-turned phrases. 'The dawn comes up like thunder every morning and this is how it goes,' he began a story about the daily life of American troops on Leyte Island. 'Suddenly there is a sound like a giant hand beating a carpet. "Whomp, whomp, whomp" it goes. It is a 40 mm gun battery signalling a raid alert. Soldiers and civilians leave their beds.'

In the weeks before Simmons hopped aboard the supply plane over Shangri-La, he had kept busy feeding such stories to *Tribune* readers. Reporting in May 1945 from the Philippines while travelling with a division of the Illinois National Guard, Simmons wrote stories whose persistent theme was reflected in their headlines: 'Midwest Yanks

Fight Way Out of Jap Ambush', 'Chicago Yank's Penknife Ends Fight With Jap', 'Yanks Harvest Crop of 19 Japs in Rice Garden', and 'Midwest Yanks' "Banzai" Charge Wins a Jap Hill'. In addition to appearing in the *Tribune*, Simmons' stories were distributed by the Chicago Tribune News Service, which had more than sixty newspapers as subscribers, and also by Reuters, the British news service.

Simmons' colleague and competitor, Ralph Morton of the Associated Press, reached an even wider audience. Like Simmons, Morton was thirty-seven and a reporter who had reached the big leagues after years in obscurity. A native of Nova Scotia, Morton had worked as a reporter for the *Halifax Herald*, the Canadian Press news service, and *Protestant Digest*. He joined the AP in 1943 in New York, and early in 1945 was promoted to war correspondent and the wire service's Australia bureau chief. The AP served more than fourteen hundred newspapers during the Second World War, and the wire service also provided news to radio stations across the country. With the wire service's enormous reach, Morton's voice was amplified many thousand times over.

After flying over the survivors' campsite, Simmons and Morton filed stories that lit up newsrooms around the world.

The guts of the stories written by Walter Simmons and Ralph Morton were basically the same: an Army plane had crashed near a lost valley in Dutch New Guinea inhabited by a tribe of Stone Age cannibals. Three of the twenty-four people aboard survived. One was a beautiful WAC. Another survivor lost his twin brother in the crash. The third suffered a terrible head injury. A crack team of paratroopers jumped into treacherous terrain to help and protect them. Tense confrontations with tribe members evolved into cross-cultural understanding. Friendship, even. No rescue plan was yet in place.

Simmons' story began: 'In a hidden valley, one-hundred-thirty miles southwest of Hollandia, a WAC and two airmen are awaiting rescue following one of the most fantastic tragedies of the war. No white man had ever set foot in this isolated paradise before a C-47 transport plane circled over it at 3:15 p.m., May 13.' In the next paragraph, Simmons disclosed that the flight's purpose was for the passengers and crew 'to see the queer, unclad people who threw spears at planes'.

Simmons' story created suspense by focusing on the Army's uncertainty about how the outsiders might exit the secluded valley: 'For three weeks the tiny WAC secretary and the two men have been cheerfully awaiting rescue, but no plan has been definitely worked out. Several ideas have been suggested – an autogiro [forerunner to the helicopter], a seaplane which might land on a lake thirty miles away, a glider snatch, and tiny liaison planes which could bring out one passenger each trip.' Simmons pointed out obstacles to each approach, and that 'an overland trek is possible but it would require weeks'.

An Associated Press story, relying on Morton's dispatches, focused more squarely on the natives: 'The crash of an Army transport plane in the wilds of Dutch New Guinea has unlocked the secrets of a mountain-bound "Shangri-La" where six-foot tribesmen live in a state of barbaric feudalism inside walled towns.' Ratcheting up both the height of the mountains, and presumably the drama, the AP story claimed that the plane crashed into a 5200-metre peak. That would have made it some 600 metres higher than New Guinea's tallest mountain.

Newspaper editors across the country, including those at the *New York Times*, ran the stories on the front page. News of the war still occupied the hearts and minds of Americans – the savage, two-month Battle of Okinawa remained under way, with many thousands of dead on both sides. But a dramatic story about a military plane crash in a 'real' Shangri-La, with a WAC and two male survivors, living among Stone Age tribesmen and a team of brave paratroopers, with no certain rescue plan, was war news with a new and exciting twist.

The widespread, enthusiastic response to the initial stories confirmed what Simmons, Morton and their bosses no doubt suspected: the story of Shangri-La was hot. Even better, the *Gremlin Special* crash had what reporters call 'legs'.

A flood of interest followed the dispatches by Simmons and Morton. Other war correspondents clamoured for seats in the supply plane, all eager to write their own version of a story that, in journalistic shorthand, became known as 'A WAC in Shangri-La'. Colonel Elsmore, always enamoured of press coverage, happily obliged. He even arranged for a WAC stenographer, Corporal Marie Gallagher, to fly aboard the *three-one-one* to transcribe walkie-talkie conversations between the plane and the survivors' camp.

In one transcript, one of Margaret's tent mates, Private Esther 'Ack Ack' Aquilio, relayed a message through the radio operator. The message described Esther's fears for Margaret's safety and enquired about how Margaret was feeling. Margaret shot back: 'Tell her to stop worrying and start praying!' The reporters ate it up.

In another transcript, Walter described Margaret as 'the queen of the valley'. He told the reporters how he and his men had limited success trading with the locals, but Margaret had collected woven rattan bracelets and 'just about anything she wants from the natives'. Again the reporters pounced. Their stories called her 'The queen of Shangri-La'. Major Gardner got in on the act on his daily talks with Walter via walkie-talkie, asking: 'How's the queen this morning?' The major tried to goad Margaret into speaking directly to him and the reporters. She declined.

Walter and McCollom alternated on the ground end of the conversations, with Gardner, radio operator Sergeant Jack Gutzeit, and the AP's Ralph Morton taking turns manning the radio on the plane. Morton could not have been happier with his participation in the story. He even began taking supply orders from the ground crew. In one story – headlined 'Shangri-La Gets Latest News From Associated Press' – Morton breathlessly described how he read a summary of the world and the war to the survivors.

To avoid being left behind, Walter Simmons started to file his stories with the dateline, 'Aboard Transport Plane Over Hidden Valley'. Within days, the *Tribune* offered Margaret, McCollom and Decker one thousand dollars each for their 'exclusive' stories upon their return. While the survivors considered the offer, Walter admitted to his journal he suffered a pang of jealousy.

On one flight, Decker's cousin, WAC Private Thelma Decker, came along to offer encouragement. But when she stood from her seat to approach the radio compartment, she was overcome with airsickness and felt too ill to speak.

Another time, radioman Jack Gutzeit brought a phonograph to play Benny Goodman and Harry James records. Walter joked about jitterbugging in Shangri-La, but the music came through garbled.

Meanwhile, Gutzeit developed an air-to-ground crush on Margaret. On his day off, he hitched a flight to Brisbane, Australia, where he bought a box of chocolates and dropped them to her by parachute. A few days later, Gutzeit got cheeky when Walter relayed a request from Margaret for 'one complete outfit – shirt, t-shirt, trousers and a bra'.

'Tell her she doesn't need that down there,' Gutzeit said. 'She can go native.'

The supply drops became routine and the supply plane began treating them like milk runs. But one flight through the valley nearly ended with the deaths of two supply crew members. When the crew chief, Sergeant Peter Dobransky, and the cargo supervisor, Sergeant James Kirchanski, opened the rear cargo bay, the wind caught hold of a door and ripped it off its hinges. Dobransky and Kirchanski were sucked towards the opening. As Walter Simmons reported in the *Tribune*, the two men 'clawed at the aluminum door frame and managed to keep each other from falling out of the plane'. The wayward door slammed against the plane's tail section, but the *three-one-one* remained airworthy. The two sergeants suffered only scratches and bruises, and were back aboard the next flight.

During one supply run, the AP's Ralph Morton wondered if Shangri-La might contain hidden riches. He asked Walter if the paratroopers had tried panning for gold in the Baliem River. Walter delivered the disappointing news: not only were there no fish in the river, there were no precious metals, either.

Much of the radio conversation was devoted to Walter and McCollom making small talk with the reporters, Major Gardner, Jack Gutzeit and a new pilot, Captain Hugh Arthur. Now and then they placed orders for supplies and sea shells, for trading with the natives. As days passed, those orders included cases of beer, which meant that alcohol had entered Shangri-La for the first time in recorded history.

The flights also brought regular mail from home. For Margaret that meant letters from her two sisters, 'who said my father was too overcome to write'. McCollom and Decker heard from their parents, Walter from his wife, and the paratroopers from friends, sweethearts, and family. The mail drops gave editors at the *Chicago Tribune* an idea: they offered to have Walter Simmons deliver personal messages from the survivors' families. Although the families could just as easily have done so themselves in letters, they took up the newspaper's offer.

'We are all fine at home and will be looking for you just as soon as you can get here,' said the message from Patrick Hastings. 'Hope and pray you are well and unhurt. Your sisters want to say hello. It really is something to have a famous daughter. Wait till you see the papers. Thank the *Chicago Tribune* for getting this message through to you. It is a real thrill to send it. We will be seeing you soon, we hope. Love, Dad.'

Bert Decker's message to his son read: 'We hope you are recovering satisfactorily and will soon be back at your post. Mother and I are fine, but anxious. Dad.'

Rolla and Eva McCollom sent a message tinged with controlled Midwestern sadness: 'We are happy that you survived. Anxiously awaiting direct word from you. So sorry about Robert. Our love to you. Dad and Mom.' Later, McCollom responded privately in a letter in which he tried to allay his parents' and sister-in-law's fears that Robert had suffered or had wandered, hurt and alone, into the jungle. He wrote: 'Robert was killed instantly and the body was burned completely. I was up to the wreck fifteen days after the accident and could find none of his personal belongings. Even if I could have identified him it would be impossible to get his body out.'

Morton and Simmons filed daily stories, and soon they began straining for news. Simmons seemed to get a kick out of reporting Margaret's one persistent supply request: 'How about dropping me some panties? Any kind will do.' But when other reporters repeated the story, the request got mangled.

'A few days later,' Margaret wrote in her diary, 'Major Gardner told me with great glee that a story had been published saying I was begging for a pair of pants. That was one of the few incidents that ever worried me. I knew if my father read the story and thought I was running around in the jungle without enough clothing, he'd have a fit.' No matter how many times Margaret asked, no panties ever arrived.

Other times, the walkie-talkie transcripts read like letters home from summer camp:

> Lieutenant John McCollom: We're listening to the beautiful morning breakfast club. Over.
>
> Major George Gardner: So this is the breakfast club. What are you guys eating this morning? How about a little chatter?
>
> McCollom: We had a pretty good breakfast. Rice pudding, ham and eggs, bacon, coffee, cocoa, pineapple – anything you want to eat. Drop in and see us some morning, boys. The best mess hall in the Southwest Pacific.

As Margaret and Decker healed, Doc Bulatao found himself with hours of free time. Every morning, after checking on his American patients, Bulatao visited with the people of Uwambo. 'Tropic skin diseases and festering sores yielded to Doc and to modern drugs like magic,' Margaret wrote. The native wars remained on hiatus while the survivors and paratroopers were at the area the natives called Mundima, but the natives enjoyed demonstrating their bow-and-arrow skills nonetheless. Once, however, a native man became the victim of friendly fire, and Doc patched an arrow wound in the man's side.

The medical care provided by Bulatao and Ramirez endeared them to the natives, who called them 'Mumu' and 'Mua'. Walter and the other paratroopers also received local names from the people of Uwambo, including Pingkong and Babikama, but which name belonged to which man was lost to time.

While waiting to move out, Walter recorded lengthy thoughts about the natives in his journal. He was generally respectful, and some of his conclusions showed anthropological insight. He admired their gardens as 'excellent examples of hard work and common sense', and credited their homes as 'well constructed and weatherproof'.

Other observations, however, relied on incomplete data and mistaken assumptions. Because few women joined the men who visited the campsite, Walter believed there was a shortage of native women. And because he did not see the natives eat pig, he assumed they were strict vegetarians. Elsewhere in his journal, Walter repeated cultural stereotypes of the natives as 'childish in everything they do or say'. He was keen to comment on the men's gourds:

> Today we showed one of the natives some pictures of pinup girls. Immediately he seemed to understand that they were women and he tapped the gourd around his private parts in a knowing manner. Some of the boys goaded him on a bit, and soon the gourd could no longer contain his excitement. It appears that sexual pleasure is an uncommon occurrence amongst these natives due to the shortage of the female sex. He finally beat a hasty retreat when he found that the gourd could no longer contain or act as a covering for his state of mind. It appeared as though he was thoroughly embarrassed, to say the least.

Walter also enjoyed a laugh at the sight of a little boy, perhaps six years old, who couldn't quite fill his gourd. The dried shell hung to one side, exposing the boy's not-yet-proud manhood.

His curiosity about the tribe went deeper than this schoolboy humour. As part of his bid to attempt to understand something of their customs, Walter conducted an experiment in which he drew simple pencil drawings on blank paper. He showed them to the same man involved in the pinup incident, then gave him paper and a pencil. 'He then proceeded to draw many curving lines on the paper much like a baby would do when first meeting crayon and paper. He was very proud of his achievement and showed his efforts to me with a big smile.' Walter concluded: 'It seems to me that these natives could be educated easily with the proper methods.'

Interviewed by walkie-talkie by the *Tribune*'s Walter Simmons, Walter described the natives' physical features, the 'excellent condition' of their teeth, and their villages in great detail. Despite his impression of them as 'an agile and strong race', Walter expressed surprise that they didn't make better bearers. He chalked it up to 'the fact that they are so used to going around naked and carrying nothing'. In another interview, he said the natives 'treat us like white gods dropped out of the sky'. Then he gushed: 'These are possibly the happiest people I've ever seen. They are always enjoying themselves.'

Two native tribesmen photographed in 1945.

Later, he elaborated: 'They lived well, had all they needed to eat, they had a place to stay, and they were a happy bunch,' he said. 'It was a garden paradise all by itself, and nobody bothered them. They had clashes amongst themselves, but no trouble with the outside world ... The whole outside world was at war and here we had complete peace and happiness in this little valley.'

In one important respect, the natives did not acquiesce to the outsiders. Walter wrote in his journal that 'they still don't want us in their villages and this feeling persisted during our entire stay ... Also, we are warned constantly about being around in the same area as their women and also they try to keep us away from their camote [sweet potato] patches as much as they can.' When he happened upon a young woman, Walter appraised her more generously than he had the first woman he described: 'This one was lighter than the others and quite attractive for a native girl. Her busts were large and well formed, but not out of proportion. She was without a doubt the best-looking girl we saw during our stay in the valley.'

Walter's journal observations reflected what he thought and experienced. But they were limited by a lack of knowledge of the tribe's language or perspective. He had no idea that the people of Uwambo regarded him and his companions as spirits from the sky, or that their appearance had fulfilled the prophecy of the Uluayek legend.

Their return having been foretold, the survivors and paratroopers were welcomed by the otherwise warlike natives. But there were limits. In the long-ago times recounted by the legend, the spirits climbed down the rope from the sky and stole women and pigs.

Had he known about Uluayek, Walter might have been less surprised by how the native men behaved when he came within range of the native women.

Twenty-one

Promised Land

As days passed, Walter began to court the reporters' attention. 'Both W.C. [war correspondent] men were along again today, and it appears that this little job is making headlines all over the world,' he wrote in his journal. 'All I hope is that out of this possibility we might get a combat mission.' Another day he wrote: 'If this deal is getting all the publicity it appears to be, I am sure that my prayers on the future will be answered.'

Within days of writing those words, Walter learned that his prayers had indeed come true, up to a point. It is unclear whether the press coverage played any role, but Walter learned via walkie-talkie that he and his men had received orders to ship out for the Philippines, if and when they returned to Hollandia. The Japanese had almost given up the fight in the islands – resistance on Mindanao was nearing an end, and General MacArthur was on the verge of declaring the Philippines 'secure'. Still, Walter was as eager as ever to join his guerrilla leader father in action. 'My last news of Dad said that he was okay, but still out on patrol,' he wrote after learning about his orders.

When the excitement faded, Walter despaired that the survivors' slow recuperation seemed to be conspiring against him. Twice Walter pushed back his target date for the return march to the valley base camp, after Doc Bulatao declared that Margaret and Decker were not ready for the arduous trek. In his journal, Walter described the conflict he felt between responsibility and desire: 'I will not risk any further infections of the patients' wounds, possibly resulting in amputation.' Immediately afterward, he added: 'The whole party is a little discouraged by this delay, especially my boys and myself, who are on orders to leave for the P.I. [Philippines Islands]. There is a war going on, and we are tired of being left behind.'

On Friday, 15 June, thirty-three days after the crash, Doc Bulatao gave Margaret and Decker a thorough going-over to be sure their wounds had sufficiently healed. After the exams, he pronounced his two patients fit enough to travel. They would need more medical treatment – Decker, in particular – but he believed that they were out of immediate danger and capable of a hike, with help, to the big valley.

Walter couldn't wait to strike camp and hit the trail, but he delayed their departure until noon, so the supply plane could drop extra flares and a spare walkie-talkie, in case of problems en route to the base camp.

With the AP's Ralph Morton doing double duty as reporter and radio operator, the supply plane made the cargo drop and checked in with the jungle campsite. After exchanging small talk and details about Walter's planned route to the valley, it became clear that Margaret was the reporters' primary interest. No matter how hard John McCollom tried to distract him, Morton kept after his journalistic prey:

Ralph Morton: How's Corporal Hastings this morning?

Lieutenant McCollom: She's feeling pretty good. In fact, everybody is feeling good. We're pretty anxious to get out of here. The three of us have been sitting here for better than a month, and we're kind of anxious to get back to work in Hollandia. And the paratroopers have been here for three weeks or so.

Ralph Morton: Is Margaret able to carry anything for you?

Lieutenant McCollom: Corporal Hastings is carrying a small pack – probably weighs about fifteen pounds. The rest of us have packs weighing from fifty pounds to seventy-five pounds. It will be rough going until we pick up some natives [as bearers].

Ralph Morton: That sounds like a pretty good load for a ninety-eight-pound girl to carry …

Even when far back from enemy lines, standard practice among reporters in war zones was painstakingly to record, and then publish, the names and hometowns of service men and women. That way, their families and friends back home could enjoy the acknowledgement of their loved ones' courage, as well as the reflected glory of knowing someone involved in the war effort. 'Names are news,' as the saying went. Publishers encouraged the practice for commercial reasons as much as journalistic ones: printing a local person's name in the newspaper generated loyalty among readers and encouraged the purchase of extra copies, for posterity.

With one glaring, categorical exception, the reporters covering the *Gremlin Special* crash faithfully followed this practice. They published the names and hometowns of the survivors and the crash victims, and also the chaplains who flew over the valley for the funeral rites, the planners in Hollandia, and the crew of the *three-one-one* supply plane.

They included not only the names of the pilot, co-pilot, and radio operator, but also the flight engineer, Sergeant Anson Macy of Jacksonville, Florida, and the cargo crew.

But as obvious as the reporters' obsession with Margaret was their tendency to overlook the 1st Recon paratroopers of Filipino descent. That oversight came despite the fact that all but Rammy Ramirez were natives or residents of the United States, and all were full-fledged members of the US Army. When speaking with the reporters by walkie-talkie, Walter and McCollom repeatedly tried to draw attention to the enlisted paratroopers, particularly the heroic jump by Bulatao and Ramirez into death-defying terrain, and their life-and-limb-saving ministrations to Margaret and Decker.

Yet in one story after another, the medics and paratroopers received little or no credit. Sometimes they appeared anonymously, as in one typical mention: 'Two Filipino medics laden with supplies also were dropped by parachute.'*

When the supply plane dropped news clippings about the events in Shangri-La, Walter reacted angrily in his journal to how little acclaim his men received: 'So few reporters have given my men the credit due them and are always bringing in outsiders for credit. I certainly hope that when I get out of here I can give the credit to those who deserve it and [to] my enlisted men, who made possible the rescue of these people. It has definitely been no cake party jumping into unexplored country and climbing mountains over the damnest trails ever seen. No complaining, but just slugging along, doing their job.'

As the paratroopers' leader, Walter received glowing mentions in the press reports. Reporters gave him the title of

* To his credit, Ralph Morton of the Associated Press eventually devoted some ink to the enlisted men of the 1st Recon, as did the *Tribune*'s Walter Simmons.

'rescue chief', as Ralph Morton put it, presumably to distinguish him from the native chiefs. But throughout the mission reporters used his unloved given name, 'Cecil'. And they routinely added an 's' to his last name, calling him 'Walters'.

Before setting off to the valley base camp, the survivors and paratroopers picked through their supplies to decide what to carry and what to leave behind. As he stuffed provisions in his backpack, McCollom noticed the unused boxes of sanitary towels that had been dropped by the supply plane for Margaret. Ever the engineer, an idea crossed his mind.

'Maggie,' he asked, 'you gonna use any of this?'

When she scoffed, McCollom tore open the boxes. He handed out the white sanitary towels to each of the men, who tucked them under the shoulder straps of their heavy backpacks. Reflecting later on his innovation in infantry padding technology, McCollom said: 'Man, those are good for that sort of thing.'

As she collected her belongings, Margaret focused on the natives. 'We tried to say our farewells to Pete and his men,' she wrote in her diary. 'The term "savages" hardly applied to such kind, friendly and hospitable men as these natives. We could never understand each other's language. But we could always understand each other's hearts and intentions. The greatest miracle that befell McCollom, Decker and me, aside from our escape from death in the crash, was the fact the natives were good and gentle people.'

Eager to return to the base camp, Walter wrote in his journal that he did not see the natives as he left camp. But before she started down the trail, Margaret searched for Wimayuk Wandik, the man she called Pete. She found him weeping at their departure along with his men.

'Some of us could have wept, too,' she wrote in her diary.

Unknown to Margaret and the other outsiders, the natives had given them a parting gift. When they understood that the visiting spirits intended to walk out of the jungle towards the valley, the people of Uwambo communicated with their allies. They bestowed another *maga* – a declaration of safe passage – along the intended route.

As she fell into line for the march, Margaret glanced back over her shoulder at the campsite. She took one last look at the sweet potato garden that had been her salvation after the crash; the place where she, McCollom and Decker were spotted by Captain Baker in his B-17; the jungle 'hospital' where her gangrene was treated and her legs were saved by Bulatao and Ramirez. Her final vision of the place: the pyramidal tent they left behind, with the American flag flying above it.

During the month they spent in the little camp near the Mundi River, the survivors and paratroopers repeatedly offered extra food to the natives. They found no takers, not even for a taste. McCollom tried everything: rice, canned beef, a chocolate bar. 'We'd break off a bite and eat it,' he said. 'They wouldn't touch it.'

When the visitors broke camp, the natives gathered the food left behind and placed it in a cave. 'Nobody knew what the food was,' said Tomas Wandik. 'The people were afraid of it, so they put it all in one place and it became sacred objects. Pigs were killed and their blood was sprinkled on it in a purification ceremony.' The natives planted a bamboo-like tree near the entrance to the cave, to mark it as a place of magic. They also conducted a blood-sprinkling ceremony along the path the spirits followed down the mountain.

Although he would not eat their food, Wimayuk Wandik accepted McCollom's offer of a machete with a rope tied through a hole in the handle. Chopping wood was daily, time-consuming work, and the blade – by all indications the natives' first exposure to a metal tool – was prized for slicing through trees faster than any stone axe or adze. At first, Wimayuk returned the gift every morning, only to be reassured on a daily basis that the knife was his to keep. When McCollom left, Wimayuk kept the machete for good.

Although Wimayuk, Yaralok and others were sorry to see the spirits leave, not everyone in Uwambo was unhappy. 'Some people were getting mad at Wimayuk because he was going in with the spirits too much,' said his son Helenma. 'They said, "Take that machete back!"' Some of the objectors' anger might have stemmed from the paratroopers erecting their tents in the middle of the community garden. 'They destroyed the sweet potato and taro,' he said.

Throughout the spirits' stay, a consistent pacification effort involved cigarettes. 'They loved them,' Margaret wrote, 'but they were always terrified by matches or cigarette lighters. So we used to light cigarettes from our own and hand them over to Pete and his men.' She noted that 'Pete' became a Raleigh man.

After the spirits left, Wimayuk climbed to the top of the Ogi ridge. He used the machete McCollom gave him to chop up pieces of the *Gremlin Special* wreck for tools and building supplies. One piece became part of a village fence. It remained in use for more than six decades after the crash.

In the months that followed the spirits' departure, the people of Uwambo returned to the rhythms and routines they had followed for untold centuries. They raised their pigs and sweet potatoes, they tended to their villages and their families, and they resumed their wars with their enemies. One difference was that when they told their children the Uluayek legend, now it included the tale of Yugwe, Meakale, Mumu, Mua, Pingkong, Babikama and the other spirits who came from the sky.

It would take a few years, but just as the legend had prophesied, the spirits' return indeed marked the beginning of the end of the lives they had always known.

With overloaded packs on their backs, sanitary pads on their shoulders, and no clear route to follow, the survivors and the paratroopers began the treacherous trek from the jungle campsite towards the base camp.

'It was up and down and crevice to crevice,' Walter recalled. 'We had to go across the creek that went down the mountainside for a long ways. We had to crisscross that a half-dozen times because it was the only way that we knew exactly how to keep our bearings as to where the hell we were going.'

Margaret set out feeling strong and brimming with confidence. Walking single-file through the rain-slicked jungle, she felt like one of the troops. She kept up as they crawled over fallen logs, edged along a precipice 'that fell away into a bottomless gorge', and hopped from one tree stump to another. But a half-hour into the trek, Margaret found herself struggling to catch her breath. Her thoughts flashed back to the nightmare journey after the crash, crawling and inching her way down the mountainside and through the stream.

'I thought I was well and strong, much stronger than Sergeant Decker, who still looked gaunt and ill,' she wrote in her diary. She discovered otherwise. 'The steady, rhythmic infantry pace set by the paratroopers was too much for me.'

'Please, stop!' she called to Walter. 'I've got to rest.'

'Me, too,' Decker said, much to Margaret's relief. She felt certain that if she had not called a halt, Decker would have continued silently and stoically until he dropped.

Walter noted in his journal that the lack of native bearers and the needs of the 'two patients' slowed his intended pace. But he added: 'Hats off to Sergeant Decker and Corporal Hastings. They are both showing great spirit.'

Three hours into the first day of their trek, they stopped to pitch camp for the night. The early hiatus gave the medics time to re-dress Margaret's and Decker's wounds before nightfall. It also spared them from being caught in the nightly rains. Quickly a little camp emerged: Margaret got a pup tent of her own, McCollom and Decker shared another, a few paratroopers crammed into a third, and the rest hung jungle hammocks from trees.

The next morning, they were up early and back on the trail shortly after eight o'clock. Walter described the day's route as 'plenty rugged, straight up and down'. Margaret's right thigh ached terribly from muscle cramps – 'Corporal Hastings was really hurting today, but she is game,' Walter wrote – so they slowed again.

When the supply plane passed overhead and they established a radio connection, Walter told Major Gardner about the absence of natives who could be put to work as bearers. He observed that the natives did not like the outsiders passing close to their villages.

'Are they hostile?' Gardner asked.

'I doubt it very much,' Walter answered. 'But we're all set on that score. Don't worry. We have plenty of ammunition, but we're not expecting anything. They are very peaceful and very friendly. As long as we stay away from their women and their camote patches, we'll be all right.'

Later that day, several natives from a village along the way proved willing to lug the trekkers' bedding and bedrolls. By the time they made camp in the mid-afternoon, Walter had achieved his goal of a sixteen-kilometre day. 'Our main trouble is water,' he wrote in his journal. 'There is plenty around, but God only knows where in this jungle.'

Walter didn't want anyone to know it, but he had wrenched his left ankle while hopscotching from rock to rock in the mountain stream. 'My main concern was Maggie and the other two survivors, Ken Decker and Mac,' Walter recalled. 'So I wasn't paying attention and I stepped on this rock, which was covered with moss. I slipped badly and got a pretty bad sprain out of it, which lasted a long time.' It swelled to nearly twice its normal size, so he asked Doc Bulatao to apply a tight wrapping. The pain continued, but at least Walter could stay on it. 'We are rolling too well to hold up the progress for me,' he wrote in his journal. 'So "Bahala Na." I'll go with it.'

Margaret's throbbing leg eased, and she grew stronger each day. By Sunday, 17 June, their third day on the trail, Walter proclaimed that she had the makings of a first-rate infantry soldier. He wrote in his journal: 'My hat's off to Corporal Hastings, Sergeant Decker and Lieutenant McCollom. Lots of spirit and great people. Corporal Hastings deserves plenty of credit and I don't mean maybe.'

Margaret noted the change in her diary, writing that she felt 'like a million dollars'. But now that her strength had returned, she had a new concern: unwanted suitors.

'One of the natives we instantly named "Bob Hope",' she wrote. 'He had a ski nose just like his namesake. Unfortunately, our Bob developed a terrific crush on me.

The survivors, paratroopers and tribesmen rest during their trek from the jungle to the village campsite.

His idea of courtship was to hang around and leer at me hour after hour.' Margaret's discomfort at the attention deepened into frustration when the paratroopers teased her about her new love interest. It only got worse.

'Suddenly Bob had a rival,' she wrote. 'A young native who must have been in his teens was smitten, too. His idea of wooing a girl was to pick up a stick and throw it at her. Obviously, I was expected to throw it back. He was like a pup.' Eventually the amorous natives backed off, and the march continued.

On the morning of Monday, 18 June, the ragged little band cleared the gap between two mountains that Walter called 'the saddle'. They followed a winding path alongside the muddy Pae River and broke for lunch. After two more hours of marching, the three paratroopers who had remained at the base camp – Sergeants Sandy Abrenica, Roque Velasco and Alfred Baylon – spotted them and came running up the trail. Walter beamed at the sight of men he called 'the best damn field soldiers in the world'.

As the supply plane flew overhead to herald their arrival in the valley, the three survivors jumped up and down and waved. At the controls was the chief planner himself, Colonel Elsmore, with the AP's Ralph Morton sitting beside him in the cockpit.

Five weeks after they left Hollandia, Margaret, McCollom and Decker finally got a firsthand look at Shangri-La.

'Surely the followers of Moses when they came upon the Promised Land saw a sight no more fair,' Margaret wrote in her diary. 'It was a beautiful, fertile land, ringed by the giant peaks of the Oranje Mountains. A copper-coloured river wound through the valley's green length. It was *our* Promised Land, too.'

When the survivors settled down, they learned that Elsmore had a surprise in store.

Twenty-two

Hollywood

WHEN MARGARET HEARD THAT THE SUPPLY PLANE carried a surprise, she was certain they would drop a few cases of beer for a base camp arrival party. She was right, in a way. The beer had, in fact, been dropped – back at the jungle campsite, after they had left. 'And there it lies today,' she wrote in her diary. 'Two fine cases of American beer to greet the lucky Robinson Crusoe or Trader Horn who stumbles on them. The natives will never touch it.'

The surprise did, however, have something to do with alcohol.

After briefly surveying the base camp, Walter heard one of his men calling him to the walkie-talkie. The radioman told him the plane carried a filmmaker who planned to make a documentary about life, death, the natives, and the rescue effort. The filmmaker had slipped into a parachute harness and was preparing to jump when Walter made contact with the plane.

'This guy ever make a jump before?' Walter asked.

'No.'

Worried, Walter learned that a fellow 1st Recon paratrooper back in Hollandia had given the filmmaker a half-hour verbal lesson on the basics of avoiding certain death.

'For Christ's sake,' Walter said, 'tie a rope on his ripcord!' At least then, if the man froze in fear in midair, the chute would open and he would have a fighting chance.

The survivors and paratroopers watched as the plane swooped through the valley with an open jump door, but no sign of the promised filmmaker. Another pass, and still no movement to the door. Finally, on a third pass over the base camp, a large figure appeared unsteadily in the opening, camera equipment strapped to his body. He lurched through the jump door, out into thin air. A puffy white canopy blossomed above him as he floated towards the valley floor.

As they watched, the paratroopers sensed a problem. The parachutist was oddly limp.

By her own admission, Margaret knew next to nothing about parachuting. Still, she knew enough to brand the jumper 'a rank amateur'.

'He swung in a vast arc from one edge of the chute to the other,' she wrote in her diary. 'We were terrified that he would swing all the way over, spill the air out of his 'chute and plummet to earth.'

Walter and his men yelled frantically to the human metronome dangling above them.

'Pull your legs together!'

'Check your oscillation!'

'Pull on your risers!'

No response.

Margaret joined the chorus, repeating the paratroopers' expert shouted advice, all of which went unheeded by the falling, swinging, apparently lifeless man.

Somehow, the parachute held its air. The parachutist landed, spread-eagle on his back, in a clump of tall briar bushes some distance from the base camp. Fearing that he was dead or seriously wounded, several paratroopers raced through the high valley grasses to his aid. First to reach him was Sergeant Javonillo.

After a momentary inspection, Javonillo popped up from the bushes – 'looking as if he'd seen a ghost,' Margaret wrote. He called to Walter.

'Captain, sir?' Javonillo said. 'This man is drunk!'

McCollom arrived in the bushes moments after Javonillo and confirmed the diagnosis: 'Drunker than a hoot owl.'

When they pulled the man out of the thicket, Walter took stock of the filmmaker in his midst. Walter radioed a wry message to the departing supply plane: 'The valley is going Hollywood – and fast.'

Walter had no idea how right he was.

The prone, besotted man in the shrubbery was Alexander Cann, a dashing forty-two-year-old adventurer who had taken an unlikely path from respectability to Shangri-La.

Born in Nova Scotia, Alex Cann was the eldest child of a prominent banker named H.V. Cann and his wife, Mabel Ross Cann, whose father was a member of the Canadian House of Commons. Mabel Cann died when Alex was young. When the boy was seven, H.V. Cann moved the family from Canada to Manhattan, where in 1914 he helped to launch the Federal Reserve Bank of New York. The family spent seven years in the United States before returning to Canada, when H.V. Cann became a top executive with the Bank of Ottawa.

Alex Cann attended the Royal Naval College of Canada, then returned to New York to study structural engineering at Columbia University. His timing could not have been worse: when the Great Depression struck, new building stopped, which made structural engineers as unnecessary as stockbrokers.

Alexander Cann.

Adding to his misfortune, he proceeded to gamble away his sizeable inheritance on poker. 'He was very roguish, my father, and hopeless about money,' said his daughter, Alexandra Cann.

But being broke did not mean he had no assets. Tall, dark and hazel-eyed; deep-voiced, handsome and powerfully built; funny, cultured and charming, the well-bred young Alex Cann drifted west to Hollywood, where those qualities retained great value despite the Great Depression. Worried about sullying his family's good name, he took the stage name Alexander Cross – literally a cross between his surname and his mother's maiden name, Ross.

In no time, Alexander Cross found his way into small movie roles. In 1936, he won parts in a half-dozen studio movies, including roles as a watchman in *Fury*, a Spencer

Tracy film directed by Fritz Lang; as a detective in *Smart Blonde* with Glenda Farrell; and as a crew member in *China Clipper*, starring his drinking buddy Humphrey Bogart. His acting run stretched into 1937, including a part playing a prison guard in the movie *San Quentin*, again starring Bogart. He moved up the Hollywood food chain by landing roles with more lines, playing named characters, such as Bull Clanton in the 1937 western *Law for Tombstone*. His star kept rising, as he won the role of bad guy Black Jack Carson in the *Hopalong Cassidy* series of films starring William Boyd and Gabby Hayes.

But just when the actor Alexander Cross began to hit his stride, his real-life alter ego Alexander Cann disproved the old Hollywood adage that 'any publicity is good publicity'.

On 28 March 1937, the *Los Angeles Times* featured a front-page story headlined 'Actor Confesses Theft of Gems at Palm Springs'. The story explained that a 'film character actor' whom police identified as Alexander Howard Cross Cann had confessed to stealing a diamond bracelet and a bejewelled ring from Alma Walker Hearst, the beautiful ex-wife of newspaper magnate William Randolph Hearst Jr. The story went on to describe possibly the worst-planned jewel heist in history.

Cann, a ladies' man who had met the former Mrs Hearst a month earlier, attended a small gathering at her Palm Springs home ten days before the *Times* story ran. Late in the evening, the party moved to downtown Palm Springs. Somewhere around one in the morning, Cann doubled back to Alma Hearst's home and pocketed her jewels. Later that day, Cann walked into a Hollywood pawnshop and sold the gems, which were valued at more than 6000 dollars. He negotiated a terrible deal, collecting just 350 dollars.

'In his confession,' the *Times* story said, 'Cann ... told the officers he had been losing heavily in horse race-betting, and was hard pressed financially when he took the jewelry. He also said he had been drinking at the time of the theft.'

When Alma Hearst noticed her jewellery missing, she provided police with a list of her servants and guests. Investigators focused quickly on Cann, and a deputy sheriff called his home. Cann admitted the crime over the phone and told the officer where to find the jewels, which were recovered from the pawnshop and returned to their owner. At the officer's insistence, Cann went to Palm Springs and turned himself in. He was charged with burglary and hauled off to jail.

With her jewels in hand, Alma Hearst decided that she had had enough of the attention and of Alex Cann. The following day, the *Times* ran a second story reporting that charges against Cann would be dropped if he made restitution. Netting only 350 dollars turned out to be a small bit of good luck; it was relatively easy for Cann to repay.

An officer quoted Alma Hearst as saying: 'Nobody likes to prosecute a friend. But when people do such things, they must expect to pay.'

Before the story – and Cann – disappeared, the wire services had a field day. Newspapers far from Hollywood ran headlines such as: 'Host's Jewels Are Stolen By Thespian'. Even the *New York Times* couldn't resist a story about a Hearst and a heist.

As Alexander Cross, Cann appeared in one more Depression-era film. In 1939, he played the title character – an unnamed bomber – in *The Human Bomb*. The role was a fitting coda to Alex Cann's Hollywood years; his arrest blew his movie career to smithereens.

Cann shrugged it off as best he could and kept moving. By the end of 1941 he had been married and divorced three times, though he had not yet fathered any children. With no spouse, no dependants, and no immediate prospects, he returned to his roots and joined the Royal Canadian Navy.

En route to the South Pacific, a Japanese torpedo struck Cann's troop ship and blew him into the water. He survived, but with a broken back that would pain him for the rest of his life. In 1943, while recuperating in Australia, Cann washed up regularly in local nightclubs. A convivial drinker and gifted storyteller, he would tell tales of his Hollywood days. 'He managed to convince several people that he knew a great deal more about filmmaking than he did,' said his daughter.

Through his nightclub connections, Cann learned that the Dutch government-in-exile in London needed correspondents and filmmakers for its newly created Netherlands Indies Government Information Service, an agency whose aim was to counter Nazi propaganda and keep Dutch concerns on the world stage.

Based on Cann's exaggerated claims of filmmaking expertise, and also, presumably, on the limited military use for a forty-year-old sailor with a broken back, the Canadian Navy 'loaned' Cann to the Melbourne-based Australia section of the Netherlands Information Service, as the agency was known. He gained the title 'War Correspondent and Cinematographer', acquired a 35 mm camera, and used his charm and Canadian accent to cadge hard-to-get film from the US Army Signal Corps.

Cann threw himself into his new role, fearlessly covering combat throughout the Philippines and the Borneo campaign. During the Allies' October 1944 invasion of Leyte, in the Philippines, Cann found himself aboard the heavy cruiser HMAS *Australia* when it came under fire from a Japanese dive-bomber. The Japanese plane, a model known to the Allies as a 'Betty', slammed full-speed into the *Australia*, mortally wounding the captain and the navigator, and killing or mortally wounding twenty-eight others. Numerous accounts declared it the first successful *kamikaze* attack of the war. But as an eyewitness and a survivor, Cann challenged that claim. A week after the attack, he told a reporter for the Associated Press that the pilot was already dead when the plane struck the ship: 'The Jap Betty came through a terrific barrage, out of control and with smoke already pouring out.'

By that point in his life, Cann had survived gambling away his inheritance, three divorces, an arrest as an actor-turned-jewel thief, a torpedo attack that broke his back, and a Japanese plane crashing into his ship. Under these circumstances, an uncontrolled, drunken sky dive into Shangri-La seemed an almost predictable next step.

When the news stories by Walter Simmons, Ralph Morton and other reporters spread word about the survivors, the paratroopers, and the Stone Age tribe in Shangri-La, Alex Cann decided to try his luck once more. He flew from Melbourne to Hollandia on 17 June. The next morning he hitched a plane ride over the crash site before returning to Sentani Airfield to request a parachute. He received a few pointers from a captain in the 1st Recon named Isaac Unciano, but Cann apparently spent his brief lesson joking around. Unciano best remembered Cann for promising 'six quarts of whisky and a party' if he returned safely.

'He knew it was obviously dangerous,' said Alexandra Cann, a London literary agent. 'But he wanted to go in, so my father volunteered. He had never parachuted in his life. They offered to train him but he said, "No thanks, I'll only do this once. If I don't jump, push me."'

Cann never personally confirmed his drunkenness whilst parachuting, but he came close. In an account distributed by the Associated Press, he wrote: 'I don't know whether I jumped or was pushed at the "go" signal, but I was busy shooting pictures on the descent after the chute opened. Then I landed unhurt, flat on my back in some bushes.'

After Javonillo and the others untangled him, Cann put a dent in the camp's aspirin supply then found himself propped up at a dinner of chow mein and fried potatoes. When Cann sobered up enough to talk, Walter enquired how he ended up in the valley anaesthetized.

'I drank a full fifth of Dutch gin before I jumped,' Cann said, according to Walter.

'Why'd you do that?' Walter asked.

'I didn't want to hesitate.'

Walter considered this before pronouncing his verdict: 'You ought to be a paratrooper.'

Later, Major Gardner asked Walter via walkie-talkie whether Cann was hung over. Walter answered: 'He says he'll never do that again – at least not until another story comes along.'

When Cann regained the ability to focus, he got his first good look at Margaret Hastings. His eye for a beautiful woman was unaffected by his crash landing. Cann asked Walter to relay a message to the AP's Ralph Morton: 'Corporal Hastings is the most magnificent survivor that I have ever seen.'

He added: 'To the boys in the rescue party, she is known as the Queen of Shangri-La.' Asked about the royal title, Margaret finally responded: 'I am ready to go, and will give up my crown at any time.'

Walter and Cann became fast friends. The captain soaked up the wisdom and the lessons that Cann had learned from what Walter called 'experience and hard knocks'. They spent hours talking, playing poker, swimming in the river, hiking around the valley, and arguing about sports figures and military policies. Cann believed that the military should not censor reporters' stories from war zones. Walter disagreed, vehemently. 'I like to get a man like that riled up,' Walter wrote in his journal, 'as I can then really learn something.' Walter paid his highest

Alexander Cann filming in 'Shangri-La'.

compliment to Cann, declaring him 'one hell of a swell egg'.

With Cann's arrival, the camp that Walter renamed 'United States Army Outpost at Shangri-La, D.N.G. [Dutch New Guinea]' – 'Camp Shangri-La' for short – reached its full and final complement of fifteen people: Commanding officer Captain Walter; ten enlisted paratroopers; three crash survivors; and one Canadian-born-engineer-turned-actor-turned-jewel-thief-turned-sailor-turned-war-correspondent.

They settled into a 'pretty little city', in Walter's phrase, spread out in the shadow of the mountain wall, on a mostly flat area of the valley floor. The three sergeants who had stayed behind organized the camp as a cluster of canopies and tents, including a red one for supplies and a pink one for a mess hall.

The camp also featured an improvised pig pen made of rough-cut branches, filled with seven pigs that Abrenica, Baylon and Velasco had 'purchased' from the natives with cowrie shells dropped by the supply plane. One pig was a runt, 'cute as a button,' Margaret wrote. The sergeants named it 'Peggy' in her honour.

'Peggy must have thought she was a dog,' Margaret wrote. 'She followed everyone around, and the moment any of us sat down, climbed on our laps. The paratroopers scrubbed Peggy every day until she shone.'

The most elaborate structure was a pyramidal tent outfitted as VIP and officers' quarters. One section, partitioned off for Margaret's privacy, had a deep bed made from dried, golden valley grass, over which hung a canopy made from a yellow cargo parachute. Artfully arranged mosquito netting completed the fit-for-a-queen decor. Lest her feet touch ground without shoes, empty parachute bags became a bedside rug.

'I was so touched I wanted to cry,' Margaret wrote in her diary. 'Everything about the camp was deluxe, including a bathroom! The three sergeants had even made a tub of empty, waterproof ration cartons. They had dug a well nearby, and filling the tub was very easy work.'

As officers, McCollom and Walter were assigned bunks on the men's side of the pyramidal tent. But Walter insisted that his bed go to Decker, to speed the sergeant's ongoing recovery. Walter and his men strung up jungle hammocks, amusing Margaret with the sight of the oversized captain squeezing his frame into the hanging sack.

On the first full day that all fifteen of them were together at the base camp, the paratroopers celebrated by roasting two suckling pigs in a Filipino lechon* feast, slowly turning them on spits until they were golden brown. Margaret made sure that 'Peggy' was spared this fate. The meal reminded Walter of his boyhood; almost a decade had passed since his last lechon. 'After making a pig of myself

* A lechon feast consists of a pig roasted on a spit and is traditional to the Philippines.

Young warriors from different worlds. The Filipino-American soldiers are (from left) Camilo Ramirez, Custodio Alerta, Don Ruiz and Juan 'Johnny' Javonillo.

(on pig), I staggered over to the supply tent and laid down in agony,' Walter wrote in his journal. 'The boys are really great cooks.'

The following day, the survivors and paratroopers indulged Alex Cann in his role as filmmaking auteur. Although he was supposed to be making a fact-based documentary, Cann was not above a bit of Hollywood staging. He had missed the survivors' entrance into base camp, yet he wanted the arrival as a plot point in his film. He persuaded everyone to recreate the last leg of the journey. No one wanted to lug a seventy-five-pound backpack up and down the mountain, so they filled their bags with empty ration boxes that gave the appearance of bulk without the weight.

This time they discarded the sanitary towels too.

Twenty-three

Gliders?

After their initial exhilaration at the survivors' discovery in the jungle wore off, Colonel Elsmore and his staff at Fee-Ask struggled to devise the best way to empty Shangri-La of US Army personnel and, now, a filmmaker for the Dutch government.

Throughout their deliberations, the planners' top priority was safety. Fifteen lives depended on their judgement. More, really, taking into account the risk to pilots, crew and anyone else who took part in the operation. Yet the planners also must have known that success or failure would affect their own lives, as well, personally and professionally. They cared about the survivors and the paratroopers not just as soldiers but as individuals, and they were responsible for Alex Cann. Also, they knew how the military worked: there would be hell to pay if the widely publicized story of Shangri-La ended tragically because of a poorly planned or executed rescue effort.

Elsmore and his team debated numerous possibilities, rejecting one after another as impractical, illogical, impossible, or just doomed to fail. After crossing off rescue by dirigible, helicopter, amphibious plane, PT boat, and overland hike back to Hollandia, they briefly debated dropping into the valley members of a Navy Construction Battalion – the Seabees – with small bulldozers to create a temporary landing strip. That plan foundered when Elsmore decided that landing a C-47 at high altitude on a short, improvised airstrip, then trying to take off again over the surrounding mountains, carried too great a risk of a second plane crash in this remote valley.

Next they discussed using a small, versatile plane called the L-5 Sentinel, affectionately known as 'The Flying Jeep'. Used throughout the war for reconnaissance missions and as front-line airborne ambulances, Sentinels had what the Army called 'short field landing and takeoff capability'. That meant they might be useful on the bumpy ground of the valley floor, without the need for an improvised runway. But Sentinels had drawbacks, too.

One concern was that a flight from Hollandia to the valley would take a Sentinel approximately three hours and consume all its fuel. Cans of fuel would have to be parachuted to the valley floor for each return trip. Also, each Sentinel could carry only a pilot and one passenger, which meant that fifteen round trips would be needed, with each flight carrying the same risk. Still, the planners kept the L-5 Sentinel under consideration.

As Elsmore weighed the Sentinel's pros and cons, he sought advice from an expert: Henry Palmer, a thirty-one-year-old lieutenant from Baton Rouge, Louisiana. Palmer, a lanky country boy nicknamed 'Red', had extensive experience with Sentinels and other light aircraft. He was stationed nearby, at an airstrip on the tropical island of Biak, off the northern coast of New Guinea.

Elsmore arranged for Palmer to fly low over Shangri-La in a B-25 bomber to assess the situation. One pass convinced Palmer that the Sentinel was wrong for the job.

He had another idea, involving another type of aircraft altogether. Like the Sentinel, it was designed to land in tight spaces, on rough terrain. But Palmer thought this other type of aircraft had a better chance of safely clearing the mountains with passengers aboard. In addition, it would not require a drop of fuel.

When Palmer returned to Hollandia, he walked into the planners' headquarters and headed for a blackboard. With chalk dust flying, Palmer drew what must have looked like a child's illustration of a mother plane and a baby plane, connected by an umbilical cord.

The sketch, he explained, depicted a motorless aircraft being pulled through the sky by a twin-engine tow plane. Lieutenant Palmer had just made a case for the highest-altitude and downright-strangest mission in the history of military gliders.

The first motorless flight is credited to Icarus, whose mythical journey ended with melted wings and a fatal plummet into the sea. Military glider pilots, an especially wry bunch, considered Icarus a fitting mascot. Their aircraft seemed to have been designed for crash landings, too. In the words of General William Westmoreland: 'They were the only aviators during the Second World War who had no motors, no parachutes, and no second chances.'

The Wright brothers and other aircraft pioneers experimented with gliders on the path to motorized flight. But after the Wrights' triumph at Kitty Hawk, gliders became almost-forgotten second cousins to aeroplanes. During the early decades of the twentieth century, gliders were used primarily for sport, by enthusiasts who competed for distance records and boasting rights. Still, glider *aficionados* built larger and more elaborate craft, capable of carrying multiple passengers and soaring long distances once in flight with the help of motorized aeroplanes.

In the 1930s, Germany became a leader in glider technology, largely because after its defeat in the First World War the country was banned from having a motorized air force. Hitler overturned this ban in 1935, but he did not forget about German glider pilots. His generals began plotting possible uses for them in war. German engineers designed gliders that resembled small aeroplanes without motors, able to carry a pilot and nine soldiers or a ton of equipment. They could land on rough fields in the heart of combat zones, as opposed to the manicured runways needed by planes. Equally appealing to the Nazis, manned gliders could be released from tow planes many kilometres from their destination; once freed from their tethers, they were silent in flight.

The Germans saw an opportunity to test their quiet war machines in May 1940, nineteen months before the United States entered the fight; with Poland and much of Germany's eastern border lands already under Nazi control, Hitler wanted to sweep through Belgium into France. Standing between him and Paris was Belgium's massive Fort Eban Emael, on the German-Belgian border. Dug deep into the ground, reinforced by a couple of metres of concrete, the newly built fort was considered impregnable. A traditional assault might have taken weeks, and success was hardly assured. Even if the Belgian fort fell, a long, costly battle would have spoiled the Germans' hope for *Blitzkrieg*, a surprise, lightning invasion. Helicopters might have speeded the effort, but the incessant noise from their rotors would have alerted the fort's defenders long before the German troops' arrival. The same disadvantages applied to planes delivering paratroopers, who would have been vulnerable as they floated under their parachutes to earth.

Gliders provided a stealth answer for the Germans' invasion plans. On 10 May 1940, tow planes from the Luftwaffe pulled a small fleet of gliders aloft into the skies approaching Belgium. The gliders, each carrying nine heavily armed German infantrymen, soared silently through the predawn darkness. Ten gliders landed on the 'roof' of the dug-in fort – a grassy plain the length of ten football fields. German soldiers poured out of the gliders ready to attack. Though badly outnumbered, they overwhelmed the stunned Belgians, deployed heavy explosives to destroy Fort Eban Emael's big guns, and captured the fort within the day. Columns of German tanks rolled past on their way to northern France.

The Belgian disaster at Fort Eban Emael was a wake-up call. It suggested that gliders might play a significant role in future combat. An American military glider programme began in earnest immediately after Pearl Harbor, with a sudden call to train one thousand qualified glider pilots, a number that within months rose to six thousand. Design work on military-grade gliders got under way at Wright Field in Ohio, where two young flight engineers, Lieutenants John and Robert McCollom, were soon stationed. The McCollom twins were not directly involved in the glider programme, but they watched with interest as it took shape.

The American aircraft industry was already at full capacity, trying to build enough planes to meet the military's growing demand. Consequently, the glider programme took a more entrepreneurial approach, and government contracts for motorless flying combat and cargo aircraft went to a mix of unlikely bidders, including a refrigerator manufacturer, a furniture company, and a coffin maker. Eventually, the military settled on the fourth version of a cargo glider made in Ohio called the Waco CG-4A, or the Waco for short.

Waco gliders were more fowl than falcon – clumsy, unarmoured flying boxcars made from plywood and metal tubing covered with canvas. Wacos had a wingspan of 25.5 metres, stood more than 3.5 metres high, and stretched more than 14.5 metres in length. Each glider weighed 1678 kilos empty but could carry a payload greater than its own weight in cargo and troops. Guided by a pilot and co-pilot, a Waco glider could transport up to thirteen fully equipped soldiers; or a quarter-ton truck; or a serious piece of artillery such as a 75 mm howitzer, complete with ammunition and two artillerymen. Most were towed into the air by thick, hundred-metre nylon ropes attached to C-47s, though some were pulled aloft by C-46s.

Before the war was over, the US military would take delivery of nearly fourteen thousand Wacos. Ironically, for a motorless aircraft, a major supplier was the Ford Motor Company, which built the gliders for about fifteen thousand dollars each. For the same price as one glider, the government could have bought seventeen deluxe, eight-cylinder Ford sedans.

A Waco CG-4A glider in flight.

Wacos got their first taste of combat in July 1943 during the invasion of Sicily. A year later, gliders delivered troops in the Normandy landings on D-Day, though scores fell prey to three-metre-high wooden spikes that German Field Marshal Erwin Rommel had ordered placed in French fields where he thought Wacos might land. Gliders also participated in Operation Dragoon in southern France and Operation Varsity in Germany. They delivered supplies during the Battle of the Bulge and were used in a variety of other combat missions in Europe. They also served in the Eastern theatre in China, Burma and India, as well as in Luzon, in the Philippines.

A major advantage of Waco gliders as troop-delivery aircraft was that, if the pilot braked hard enough on landing, he could stop quickly – within two hundred metres of touch down – on uneven ground. Not infrequently, however, the glider came to rest with its nose buried in the dirt and its tail in the air. More than a few flipped over completely. Many others missed their intended landing zones entirely, as a result of weather, broken tow cables, pilot error, and other mishaps. Even when everything worked perfectly, Waco gliders made slow, fat targets for enemy anti-aircraft guns.

In short order, Wacos earned the nicknames 'flak bait', 'bamboo bombers', and 'flying coffins'. Glider pilots were known as 'suicide jockeys' who made oxymoronic 'controlled crash landings'. When they gathered to drink, glider pilots saluted each other with a mordant toast: 'To the Glider Pilots – conceived in error, suffering a long and painful period of gestation, and finally delivered at the wrong place at the wrong time.'

In September 1944, a young London-based reporter for United Press named Walter Cronkite was assigned to fly in a Waco glider during Operation Market Garden in Holland. Years later, Cronkite admitted, 'I came close to disgracing myself' by refusing the mission. He ultimately agreed only to save face with his fellow reporters. 'I had seen what had happened to the gliders in Normandy. The wreckage of hundreds of them was scattered across the countryside.' Cronkite landed safely, but he never forgot the experience: 'I'll tell you straight out: If you've got to go into combat, don't go by glider. Walk, crawl, parachute, swim, float – anything. But don't go by glider!'

During the early phase of the war, Waco gliders were regarded as almost disposable – once they landed and discharged their troops or supplies, they were abandoned. But as costs mounted, efforts were made to retrieve Wacos that had not been reduced to kindling. However, because most touched down in areas far from conventional airstrips, their tow planes could not simply land, reconnect their tethers, and pull the gliders aloft. As a solution, engineers developed a retrieval system in which low-flying aircraft – low, as in six metres off the ground – could zoom past and 'snatch' a Waco glider back into the air.

Nearly five hundred glider retrievals were executed from battlefields in France, Burma, Holland and Germany, with nearly all the gliders empty except for the pilots. But in March 1945, two Wacos retrofitted as medevac aircraft landed in a clearing near Remagen, Germany. Twenty-five wounded American and German soldiers were loaded aboard the two gliders. C-47s snatched the Wacos off the ground, and soon after they landed safely at a military hospital in France.

Now, three months after those successful snatches, Lieutenant Henry Palmer wanted to borrow a page from that mission, albeit with a higher degree of difficulty.

Palmer's scheme was a plan only the military or Hollywood could love. Fortunately for Palmer, it just so happened that both had representatives in Shangri-La.

As Palmer envisioned it, the operation would begin in Hollandia. A C-46 would pull a Waco airborne and tow it 240 kilometres into the skies over the valley. Once safely through the mountain pass, the glider pilot would disengage from the tow plane and guide the Waco down to the valley floor, where passengers would board. At such a high altitude, at least 1600 metres above sea level, the glider would not be able to carry its usual load. Only five people would clamber aboard for each trip, with priority going to the survivors. Then the glider and its passengers would brace for the snatch.

The basic premise was that a C-47 would fly over the glider and, using a hook extending from the fuselage, pull the glider *back* into the air. Tethered together, the tow plane and the trailing glider would fly up and over the surrounding mountains and soar towards Hollandia. After separating, both pilots would make smooth landings and enjoy a celebratory welcome home, ticker tape optional.

This is how it worked on Palmer's blackboard. In practice, several dozen potential malfunctions or miscalculations could turn the gliders into freefalling kites, the tow planes into fireballs, and their passengers into fatalities. Beyond the usual dangers that came with gliders, an attempted snatch in Shangri-La carried a host of added perils.

No previous military snatch had occurred 1600 metres above sea level. The thinner air at higher altitude meant that, even if the snatch were successful, chances were increased that the C-47 would be slowed by the glider's weight to the point where the plane might stall. Depending on the C-47's altitude at that point, the glider might become the oversized equivalent of a paper airplane on a full-speed collision course with the valley floor. The same fate might befall the C-47.

Even if the plane didn't stall, no one knew whether a C-47, pulling a loaded glider in thin air, had the horsepower to climb to roughly 3000 metres quickly enough to make it through the pass that led out of the valley. In addition, the pilots of both aircraft would have to contend with the low clouds and the shifting winds that made getting in and out of the valley a challenge. Although the daily supply flights to Shangri-La made the trip seem routine, no pilot involved in the mission would forget that a momentary mistake had cost twenty-one lives aboard the *Gremlin Special*.

To top it off, if the first snatch succeeded, the rescuers would have to repeat the feat twice more, each time with the same dangers.

As Colonel Elsmore considered the idea, three factors played into its favour. First, Elsmore knew of no better or safer rescue option. Second, Palmer boosted confidence in the plan by volunteering to pilot the first glider himself. Third, Elsmore was a sky cowboy with a flair for the dramatic.

After consulting with his fellow planners, balancing the risks and rewards, Colonel Elsmore announced that Waco CG-4A gliders would be used to extract the fifteen temporary residents from Shangri-La.

Elsmore's decision set in motion a scramble to find pilots and qualified crew members for the tow plane. He also needed several other glider pilots to work with Palmer, assorted maintenance personnel, and hard-to-find glider pickup equipment. Gliders were used less extensively in the Pacific than in Europe, so the specialized gear was scattered all over the region, from Melbourne in Australia, to Clark Field in the Philippines.

The mission struck a piece of good luck when news of the planned glider pickup reached a young commander of the 33rd Troop Carrier Squadron based at Nichols Field, in Manila. At twenty-nine, an Eagle Scout from Decatur,

Illinois, Major William Samuels had been a pilot with United Airlines before the war. More important, he had been a glider snatch instructor at Bergstrom Field, in Austin, Texas. As far as Samuels knew, he was the most experienced glider pickup pilot in the entire Southwest Pacific. When he volunteered to oversee equipment collection and crew training, as well as to pilot the snatch plane, Elsmore was so pleased that he turned over his own quarters to the major.

If everything went as hoped, Samuels would execute the first glider snatch from the cockpit of a C-47 known as *Louise*. The plane, an 'old bird' in Samuels' phrase, was borrowed from a unit that seemed glad to be rid of it. The engine nearly quit on the flight from Manila to New Guinea, and Samuels had to make an emergency landing en route for repairs. He renamed it *Leaking Louise* for its tendency to spray engine oil all over its wings.

The headquarters Elsmore chose for glider snatch training was tiny Wakde Island, a three-by-five-kilometre speck of land 160 kilometres off the coast of Hollandia. Wakde's most notable feature was a runway that ran almost its entire length. Another advantage was its isolation. If a glider fell on a deserted airstrip and no one was there to witness it, chances were excellent that it wouldn't make a sound.

Days passed with little progress. The effort seemed beset by delays caused by torrential rains, missing equipment, and a three-day case of dysentery suffered by Samuels. The delays gave glider pilot Henry Palmer plenty of time to think about the mission ahead. Eventually, he dubbed his Waco glider the *Fanless Faggot*, not as a slur but for its missing motor and its resemblance to a rough bundle of sticks.

To get a better idea of what they had volunteered for, Samuels and his co-pilot, Captain William McKenzie of La

Crosse, Wisconsin, flew over the valley to pick a spot for a glider landing and pickup strip. Neither liked the look of Shangri-La.

'What do you think, Mac?' Samuels asked.

'Well, Bill, we'll never know 'til we try,' McKenzie replied.

Samuels looked back to their crew, staring dubiously out the windows, assessing their chances of success, not to mention survival.

While the glider work crawled along, the three sergeants who organized the valley base camp, Abrenica, Baylon and Velasco, laid out a landing area to Samuels' specifications. They cut and burned brush – leaving it no more than thirty to sixty centimetres high – in a relatively flat area some 350 metres long and one hundred metres wide. They outlined the field with red cargo parachutes and used white paratrooper parachutes to make a centre line for the landing strip. Appropriately for a make-do operation, they laid out toilet paper in the shape of giant arrows that pointed the pilots towards the airfield.

On Wakde Island, much of the preparation was devoted to the most treacherous part of the operation: the snatch. When all the gear reached the island, crews installed equipment in the *Leaking Louise* that looked and functioned like a giant fishing reel, complete with line and hook. The reel, bolted to the cabin floor, was a huge winch, an 800-pound mechanical device the size of a washing machine. A crew member would use the winch to let out or pull in the line attached to the glider. The line, wrapped around the winch's drum, was 300 metres of 1.27-centimetre steel cable. The hook, attached to the end of the cable, was just that: a fifteen-centimetre-long steel hook.

When the time came to attempt a snatch, crew members on the *Leaking Louise* would unspool the cable and feed it hook-first down a wooden pickup arm, sometimes called a boom, that extended below the C-47's fuselage. The hook would be set at the end of the pickup arm, to hold it steady.

Meanwhile, the glider would be towed to the valley by another plane. After releasing their Waco from the tow plane and landing in Shangri-La, the glider's crew would erect two 3.5-metre poles, set some 6 metres apart. From the top of one pole to the top of the other, they would string a section of a 24-metre loop made from 2.5-centimetre-thick nylon rope. The result would resemble a pole-vault setup, with a section of the nylon loop as the crossbar. The remainder of the loop would hang down from the poles and be laid out neatly on the ground. Another nylon rope, about 70 metres long, would be attached to the ground end of the loop. Its far end would be fastened to the nose of the glider, parked 15 to 30 metres back from the poles. When the setup was complete, the loop of nylon rope hanging from two poles would be attached to the nylon tow rope, which would be attached to the glider.

In a successful snatch, the C-47 would swoop low over the pickup site. The steel hook at the end of the pickup arm would catch the nylon loop at the top of the poles. The C-47 would fly onward, with the pilot leaning hard on the throttles to gain altitude with the added drag of the glider. The winch operator inside the C-47 would consider speed, glider weight, and other factors to judge how many metres of steel cable to pay out from the reel to prevent the nylon rope from snapping. If he misjudged, the cable would rip off the glider's nose, snap its wings, or worse. Glider pilots described the sensation at the moment of the snatch as comparable to being shot out of a giant slingshot.

As the C-47 climbed, the glider would be jerked into the air from its parking spot within three seconds. It would be airborne within 18 metres, and its speed would go from zero to more than 160 kilometres per hour within seven seconds of the snatch. When the glider was airborne, the winch operator on the C-47 would reel in cable to draw it closer to the tow plane, so it trailed the C-47 by about 100 metres. The two aircraft would fly in graceful tandem, connected by the nylon-and-steel tether. In sight of Hollandia, the glider pilot would release his craft from the tow plane, and the Waco and the C-47 would make safe, separate landings.

This is how the planners envisioned it. In practice, the first trial runs of the *Leaking Louise* and the *Fanless Faggot* on Wakde Island were plagued by injuries, ruined equipment, and growing doubts about the wisdom of using gliders in the rescue attempt.

Twenty-four

Two Queens

AS JUNE 1945 WOUND DOWN, SO DID THE WAR. After the bloodiest battle of the Pacific, the Allies took Okinawa. Its capture on 21 June – after the deaths of 12,000 Americans and more than 100,000 Japanese – provided a staging area for an air and land attack on the main islands of Japan. That is, unless Emperor Hirohito could be persuaded to surrender. Secretly, America's leaders thought a new weapon, a bomb of unimaginable power, might accomplish that goal without sending troops to Tokyo. The bomb would be tested within weeks; if it worked, President Truman would decide whether to use it. Already, though, much of the world seemed eager to look beyond war. While the outsiders in Shangri-La awaited rescue, envoys from forty-four countries landed in San Francisco to sign a charter creating The United Nations.

While the glider crews worked, Camp Shangri-La played. Before an audience of natives, Decker shaved off six weeks' growth of beard. McCollom got a haircut from Ben

Bulatao, but he and Walter kept their non-regulation whiskers. Walter told the crew of the *three-one-one*: 'We want to look like we've been someplace after we get out of here.' They ate communal meals; explored the valley; posed for Alex Cann's camera; talked about their families; and read books, magazines, and letters dropped by the supply plane. One supply drop included a book on jungle survival techniques; it arrived so late the survivors were certain it was someone's idea of a joke.

A native man whom the paratroopers called 'Joe' oversaw daily meetings between the natives and the outsiders. When the market was up and running, five cowrie shells could be exchanged for a stone adze, the most sought-after souvenir. Walter established a going rate for other native weaponry, exchanging eighteen shells for sixty-two arrows and three bows. At first, a pig could be had for as little as two to four shells, but inflation crept in, and the price rose to fifteen shells. This proved costly when the pigpen built by the paratroopers collapsed and eight

A Dani tribesman tries on a uniform.

plump, fifteen-shell swine headed for the hills. So many shells changed hands that McCollom worried that the survivors and paratroopers were ruining the local economy.

In fact, the outsiders' use of cowrie shells as a kind of coin represented the natives' first tentative step towards a money-based economy.

Although they had long traded shells with people from outside their villages, to obtain twine, feathers or other goods that were not readily available, the natives did not treat shells as a universal currency. In their communal villages, there was nothing to buy from each other. They used shells and shell necklaces primarily to cement social bonds. At a funeral, for instance, mourners would briefly drape the dead body with gifts of shell necklaces. As a highlight of the ceremony, a village leader would redistribute those necklaces, creating obligations to him and shared remembrances of their previous owner.

McCollom's worry about the local economy was only the half of it. By tossing around shells as though their only value was as a means of trade, the outsiders risked undermining the glue that kept the community together.

Although most natives were willing to provide pigs, adzes, bows, and arrows in exchange for shells, some felt trepidation about the deals. 'We'd never seen so many shells. Our parents were telling us to be careful, don't take the shells,' said Lisaniak Mabel. He and his friends heeded the warning. 'The white guys got frustrated that we were rejecting the shells they were offering.'

One day, the native trader the paratroopers called Joe brought three women to the camp. Confused at first, Alex Cann and the paratroopers concluded that they were being offered the women in exchange for shells.

'Walt, you've got to be careful,' Cann told Walter, 'because he wants to sell you the women.'

'Hell, I've got enough trouble,' Walter replied. 'I don't want a bunch of women running around!' Walter's men cracked up when they heard that.

Walter wrote in his journal: 'He [Joe] is quite a money monger, and by the looks on the women's faces, they were little impressed by us.' The feeling was mutual. Walter waved off the deal.

The man the outsiders called 'Joe' was Gerlagam Logo, a son of the chief named Yali Logo and a warrior with a fierce reputation. Many years later, tribe members remembered Gerlagam as having been friendly with the outsiders. But they doubted that he ever tried to sell them women. Gerlagam had a wife and two daughters. Perhaps, they said, he wanted his new acquaintances to meet his family.

Each day when the supply plane flew overhead, Walter and McCollom placed orders for food and provisions. Sergeant Ozzie St George, a reporter for the Army magazine *Yank* who covered the mission alongside civilian journalists, made a sport of tracking the cargo drops. Among the items he recorded were: twenty pairs of shoes, 136 kilos of medical supplies, fourteen .45 calibre pistols with 3000 rounds of ammunition; six Thompson submachine guns; knives; machetes; tents; cots; clothes for the survivors; seventy-five blankets; camp stoves; gasoline; canteens; water; seventy-five cases of ten-in-one rations; rice; salt; coffee; bacon; tomato and pineapple juice; and 'eggs that landed unscrambled'.

Walter continued his amateur anthropology. He searched for signs of religion, with no luck. 'They're believers in mankind and that's about all the religion they seem to have,' Walter told Major Gardner by walkie-talkie.

While walking with his men and some natives near the Baliem River, Walter arranged a running race on the riverbank to test their speed. Earlier he had recorded his disappointment with their potential as porters, complaining in his journal that they tired more quickly than the Filipino bearers he recalled from his boyhood. The race did nothing to improve his view. 'Natives not very fast,' he wrote, 'as we outran them with equipment on.' He did not record whether the Dani men might have been amused, confused or both by the notion of running full speed when they were not chasing a lost pig or escaping a deadly enemy.

During one stroll, Walter and the survivors found corpses from recent warfare. 'One warrior had been shot through the heart with an arrow,' Margaret wrote. 'Another had died from a spear driven through his head.' Separately, Walter and McCollom found the skeleton of a man they thought must have stood more than 1.8 metres tall and weighed more than ninety kilos. It was the closest they ever came to seeing one of the 'giants' they'd heard so much about.

Captain Earl Walter and Lieutenant John McCollom examine a native jawbone they found in the valley.

After a walk with Alex Cann, Walter estimated the valley's population at five thousand and concluded that the natives belonged to 'a dying race'. He based that assumption on his observations of few children and some overgrown sweet potato fields. In fact, Walter's population estimate was about one-tenth to one-twentieth the actual number, and he had not understood that, as good farmers the Dani people left old fields fallow to regain their nutrients. However, his point about children was accurate. It was the custom of Dani women to abstain from sex for up to five years after childbirth, which led to a birthrate which was not as high as in some other native populations.

The natives reached mistaken conclusions about their guests, as well, beyond their belief that the visitors were spirits. Decades later, several old men who were boys and teenagers in June 1945 swore that they had witnessed a strange miracle. As they described it, after the paratroopers ate pig meat, the animals emerged whole and alive when the men defecated. Narekesok Logo said: 'You could see where the cuts were on the pig' after its rebirth.

During his weeks at the base camp, Alfred Baylon – 'Weylon' to the natives – made regular medical calls in the nearby hamlets. The sergeant earned the natives' trust by treating minor wounds, pig bites, and a variety of skin ailments, including a form of athlete's foot. He treated their dandruff, too. 'In the Army, they say to make the most of what you have,' Baylon told a reporter. 'So I smeared their heads with mosquito repellant. It seemed to work surprisingly well.' When a woman with an infection on her breast began to heal within days of treatment, Baylon became the tribespeople's favourite outsider. The feeling was mutual. 'They are a wonderfully carefree people,' he said. 'Living in a land of perpetual summer, they never worry about their next meal.'

Walter encouraged the sergeant, to a degree. When a local woman went into labour, the natives came running for Baylon. 'But the captain forbade it,' Margaret wrote in her diary, 'fearing that if anything happened to the woman or the baby, the natives might turn on all of us.'

Before the others reached the valley, Baylon usually visited the village alone or with Sergeant Velasco, who became relatively adept at the native language. Now, Alex Cann, Walter, and the three survivors joined the sergeants on their rounds. But as they headed towards the nearest village, an old man blocked their way.

'He was a man of dignity and authority,' Margaret wrote. 'He knew and liked Sergeants Velasco and Baylon, and there was no ill will and nothing threatening in the chief's attitude. But he made it abundantly clear that he didn't want his village invaded all the time.'

When a pantomime negotiation went nowhere, Margaret tried a charm offensive: 'I pouted as prettily as I knew how and I batted what few stubby little eyelashes had begun to grow back after the originals were singed off in the plane crash.'

'Aw, Chief, don't be mean,' she told the native leader.

Margaret laughed about it in her diary: 'Walter, McCollom, Decker and the sergeants stared at me as if I had lost my mind. But it worked. Right before our eyes, the old chief melted.'

Still, the native leader had limits. He allowed the two sergeants, Margaret and Alex Cann into the village, but he turned away Walter, McCollom and Decker. Rather than risk an incident, Walter and the two male survivors returned to camp.

That day, Margaret met a woman in the village whom she described as 'regal in manner'. Based on her belief that the woman was a village leader's wife, or at least one of his wives, Margaret called her 'the queen'.

The meeting and its aftermath revealed a profound change in Margaret since the crash. She had flown aboard the *Gremlin Special* hoping to see strange creatures she believed were 'primitive'. During her time in the jungle clearing, she came to see them as people. Since reaching the base camp, her views had evolved further. No longer did she describe natives in her diary as savages or child-like, for instance. Upon getting to know 'the queen', Margaret's outlook took an evolutionary leap. Any remaining hint of superiority vanished. In its place came respect.

'The queen and I liked each other immediately,' she wrote. They spent long stretches together: 'All we lacked, from the American point of view, was a front porch and a couple of rocking chairs.' Margaret described their ability to communicate as 'a case of understanding the heart, for neither of us was ever able to understand a word of the other's language'.

The native woman invited Margaret into the long hut the village women used as a communal cookhouse. She fed Margaret hot sweet potatoes, declining the butter that

The native woman Margaret called 'The Queen' greets her outside a hut.

Margaret brought with her from the base camp. Margaret, too, hesitated to abandon her traditional ways. The native woman tried to persuade her to strip down to what Margaret called a 'G-string of woven twigs worn by herself and her ladies in waiting'. Margaret demurred: 'I just clutched my khaki tighter around me.' The queen did not seem to mind.

After a few days, the native woman was so eager for Margaret's visit that she met her halfway between the camp and the village. 'Occasionally the trail was rough or we would have to cross small streams with precarious log bridges,' Margaret wrote. When Margaret feared she might fall, she would appeal to the nimble-footed woman for help: 'She always knew what I meant. The queen would take my hand in hers and give me an assist along the way.'

When the sergeants teased Margaret for slowing their pace en route to the village, the queen sensed that the men were making fun of her friend. 'She turned on them, and there was no mistaking the fact that they were getting a royal dressing down, for such unseemly behavior toward a royal guest.' The same tongue-lashing befell a group of native girls and young women working in the sweet potato gardens who giggled when the two women walked past.

Walter noticed Margaret's growing connection. With a combination of envy and admiration, he told the men in the supply plane: 'The natives will take stuff from her, but they won't take anything from the rest of us.'

The more Margaret came to appreciate the locals, the more she admired them for refusing the paratroopers' goods. 'The natives of Shangri-La are a wise people,' she wrote. 'They are happy. They know when they're well off. They are too smart to permit a few chance visitors from Mars to change the rhythm of centuries.'

Walter, meanwhile, tried repeatedly to trade machetes, knives and other modern conveniences for an ornate necklace of small shells arranged in vertical rows on a strip of rawhide that hung from the wearer's throat to his breastbone. Each time he failed.

Soon Walter had bigger worries than souvenirs. Reports on the glider snatch tests, delivered via walkie-talkie, sounded grim.

After the pickup equipment was installed in the *Leaking Louise*, the four pilots agreed on what sounded like a straightforward plan. First, they would make a few practice runs on Wakde Island to test the gear, get in sync with each other, and hone the glider and pickup crews. Then, the *Leaking Louise* would tow the *Fanless Faggot* halfway across New Guinea to Mount Hagen, a large, accessible valley at the same 1600-metre altitude as Shangri-La. By testing it there, they thought, the first high-altitude Waco glider pickup snatch would not involve crash survivors as guinea pigs and reporters as witnesses.

The plan unravelled almost immediately. On the first trial run on Wakde Island, Samuels came in too low with the *Leaking Louise*. No one was hurt, but the snatch failed.

Keaugi Walela wearing the necklace that Earl Walter tried unsuccessfully to obtain.

Worse, the C-47's propellers severed the nylon tow rope, and the radio compass mast was knocked off the underside of the plane. After repairs, Samuels tried again. On the second effort, the steel tow cable broke, destroying the winch. No one was hurt, but replacing it caused more delays. Then calamity struck.

The *Tribune*'s Walter Simmons had flown to Wakde Island to witness the tests. Despite the danger, Simmons volunteered to be one of eight passengers aboard the *Fanless Faggot* for the third trial run. Just after the snatch, the steel cable inside the *Leaking Louise* again snapped as the crew tried to reel in the glider. 'The winch just blew up,' said McKenzie, the co-pilot.

The broken cable whipped around the C-47's cabin like an angry snake, tearing through the wall of the navigator's compartment. The slashing cable struck the winch operator, Master Sergeant Winston Howell, in the head. Only days earlier, Howell had told the AP's Ralph Morton he was certain they would have no trouble. The cable slashed the radio operator, Sergeant Harry Baron, across the back.

'A shower of aluminum, wood, glass and smoke inundated the cockpit,' Samuels wrote in a self-published memoir. 'I looked back to ask if the boom was retracted so we could land. All I could see was everyone lying down and much blood.' The injuries to Howell and Baron weren't life-threatening, but both were hospitalized.

Before the other half of the broken steel cable could slice through the *Fanless Faggot,* glider pilots Palmer and Allen detached the Waco and made an emergency landing. Walter Simmons and the other glider passengers and crew emerged shaken but unhurt. Later, Allen blamed the accident on the hastily scavenged snatch equipment, saying it 'was unused for several years and was badly rusted'.

Alarmed, Colonel Elsmore put out a call for another replacement winch and flew to Wakde Island to supervise.

He told Walter Simmons that if they encountered more problems, he might cancel the glider snatch altogether. In the meantime, Elsmore quietly revived the idea of inviting the Seabees to build a runway in Shangri-La; it would take longer than a glider snatch and pose its own problems, but he would not have to worry about exploding winches, snapping cables, and the other perils inherent with 'flying coffins'.

Even before the snapped cable, Walter and his men were unsettled by the idea of a glider ride. They were blasé about jumping out of airplanes. But gliders were something else entirely, and the Waco's reputation preceded it. In his daily radio conversations with the supply plane, he told the planners not to rush: 'We wouldn't want any haphazard attempt made to get us out of here ... We are perfectly willing to wait until everything is set ... We don't want to take any chances by pushing the thing to get out of here before the pickup and glider pilots are ready.' After learning of the accident and injuries, Walter repeated those messages with more urgency.

Adding to his anxiety was the need for multiple pickups to get all fifteen people out of the valley. 'Each trip increased the possibility of a bad accident, trouble, whatever,' Walter said. He spoke privately with his top sergeant, Sandy Abrenica, about trying to march out, or 'whether we had to come up with other ways to get out of there, if the glider pickup didn't work'. Without telling Elsmore, Walter and Abrenica made rough calculations of how many more men they would need to mount a trek during which they might face headhunters, hiding Japanese troops, or both.

Margaret turned to prayer. The night she learned about the broken glider cable, she huddled in her private corner of the big tent: 'I said my Rosary over and over, asking God that no one be hurt in trying to save us.' Major Samuels, the snatch pilot, had the same idea. He later told Margaret that he had gone to Sunday services and asked a chaplain to pray for their mission.

The first threat to Margaret's friendship with the native woman came one day in the village when she pulled out a comb and absentmindedly ran it through her hair. The queen was mesmerized: 'She had never seen a comb before or anyone doing such queer things to their hair. The other natives were equally delighted with this toy. Half the village gathered 'round and I combed my hair until my arm was tired.'

Margaret handed the comb to her friend. Rather than use it on herself, the woman 'carefully combed my hair down over my face'. Margaret smiled as the woman completed the styling. Then Margaret combed her hair back off her forehead to its usual swept-back arrangement. The queen took the comb and again plastered Margaret's hair over her face. Alex Cann captured the comic back-and-forth scene on film. But the woman's husband became involved, and it stopped being funny.

'Sergeant Velasco was about to put a stop to this beauty business when the chief decided to join the game,' Margaret wrote. 'He started to run his hands through my hair. This was a goodwill gesture from which I shrank inwardly. But I didn't want to offend him and his followers. So I sat still a moment and said, "Unh, unh, unh" at what I deemed were appropriate intervals in the conversation.'

Velasco kept an eye on Margaret's friend. The native woman began speaking in what sounded like an agitated tone, and he sensed that she was growing jealous.

'Scram,' Velasco told Margaret, and they ran together from the village.

On their way back to base camp, he said: 'I guess you might have been queen. But I also suspect you might have been dead.'

Margaret worried the friendship was ruined. But on her next visit to the village, the woman was her usual gracious self. From the woman's improvised sign language, it appeared that she wanted Margaret to move from the base camp into the women's hut. 'Velasco and Baylon told me they were certain she wanted to adopt me. But I didn't think my father back in Owego would like that very much,' Margaret wrote. She politely declined.

On another visit, with Decker and McCollom in tow, several women approached Margaret and motioned for her to hold out her right hand. 'As I did so, one of the women raised a stone ax,' Margaret wrote. 'I was so amazed by this first sign of violence in the natives that I could scarcely move.'

Realizing what was happening, McCollom shoved Margaret out of the way.

Afterward, McCollom tried to explain what he believed was afoot: 'When a girl is of marriageable age, they chop off the tips of all the fingers on her right hand. I guess this is a hint to you to nab off one of us handsome guys.'

Margaret brushes back her hair after a native salon treatment.

McCollom had added one and one but got three. Having noticed that nearly all the women in the village who had reached sexual maturity had lost several fingers, he assumed there was a relationship between the two.

In fact, the Dani people of Koloima were trying to help Margaret mourn.

Unlike the natives near the jungle campsite, the villagers in the valley did not know about the plane crash; news of an event so many kilometres away would have had to pass through the territory of enemies with whom communication usually occurred at spear-point. Instead, the natives in the valley assumed that Margaret and the other visitors had escaped from some terrible event in their world. The people of Koloima were so sure of this, their name for Margaret was Nuarauke, which meant 'fleeing'.

By their logic and experience, whatever tragedy caused Margaret to seek refuge in the valley must have involved death. To honour and appease the dead, they assumed that Margaret would want to sacrifice her fingers. When she declined, the natives were not insulted; any reprisal against Margaret would come not from them, but from the spirit world.

Margaret also apparently misunderstood when she thought that the native leader wanted to take her as his bride. To the contrary, the natives thought the male survivors and paratroopers wanted to give Margaret in marriage to a native leader named Sikman Piri. 'The white men said to him, "Sleep with this woman,"' said Hugiampot, who was a teenager at the time. 'She said, "Sleep with me." But Sikman Piri said, "No, I am afraid." So he didn't take her as a wife.'

Margaret/Nuarauke wasn't the only outsider given a native name. Sergeant Caoili was called Kelabi – a rough pronunciation of his surname that had no meaning in the

Dani language. Other names included Bpik, Pisek, Araum, Mamage, and Suarem, though the passage of time blurred which name belonged to whom. Some natives knew Alex Cann as Onggaliok, but others remembered him as Elabut Muluk, a Dani phrase that means 'big belly'.

When Walter first arrived in the base camp with the survivors, he was happy to see the people of Koloima. The captain wrote in his journal: 'All of the natives appreciate our help, as we do theirs.' But three days later, Walter sensed tension bordering on hostility. The change was subtle; fewer smiles, fewer visitors loitering close to the base camp.

That night, he heard angry shouts coming from the village. He put the camp on alert and for the first time in weeks posted guards throughout the night. 'It is good to be prepared,' he wrote in his journal. 'The natives have been less friendly the last few days. However, with our weapons we can stand here easily. And so we prepare for our first uneasy night since we got here.'

Morning arrived without incident, but Walter ordered his men to remain vigilant. He kept closer tabs on the survivors' movements, ordering them to stay close to base camp.

Walter tended to be cautious, but in this case he was not imagining things. As much as the natives appreciated the medical care and liked Margaret, the outsiders' presence had disturbed their routines, their wars in particular.

The base camp was in the middle of the no-man's land the natives regularly used as a battlefield. As long as the outsiders were there, the Dani people of Koloima could not satisfy their desire to confront their enemies in open combat. In addition, some local leaders didn't like how Walter and his men handed out fistfuls of shells, fired their frightening guns, and wandered wherever they pleased. For many years, the native leader named Yali Logo had been

Regional 'big man' Yali Logo (centre).

the regional big man. Now the outsiders behaved as big men, and Yali didn't like it.

Unaware that the outsiders were preparing to leave the valley, Yali began plotting their departure on his terms. He visited the base camp by day, where Walter photographed him standing calmly, though unsmiling, with his tribesmen. But, according to his tribesmen, at night Yali sent a messenger to his sworn enemy and frequent battlefield opponent, a legendary big man in the neighbouring territory named Kurelu.

'At night the enemies talked,' said Ai Baga, a teenager at the time. 'Yali wanted to drive them out, and he wanted Kurelu to help. But Kurelu said no.'

It is possible, said several Dani men who witnessed the events, that Kurelu was pleased to see Yali's authority undermined by the outsiders; as a result, Kurelu had no incentive to join a conspiracy.

As days passed with no sign of gliders, Yali kept plotting and Walter kept posting guards.

Twenty-five

Snatch

UPON ARRIVING AT WAKDE ISLAND, COLONEL Elsmore cancelled the original plan to practise a 1600-metre glider snatch at Mount Hagen. Instead, they would focus on fixing the problems and conduct exercises to perfect the manoeuvre at sea level on Wakde. To compensate for the higher altitude in Shangri-La, they would overload the glider during the trial runs, filling it with nine passengers and 136 kilos of sandbags.

Elsmore believed the maxim that a leader should not ask his troops to do anything he would not do himself. He sat in the glider's co-pilot seat for the last three snatch tests. It is not clear whether Elsmore's hands-on approach reflected confidence that nothing would go wrong or lingering doubts that something might. Either way, those runs went off without a hitch. Satisfied, Elsmore declared that the snatch was on.

The plan called for three glider drops into Shangri-La, and three subsequent snatches, to get all fifteen people out of the valley. Bad weather added several more days of delays, so the glider and tow crews cooled their heels in

Hollandia. In the valley, the temporary inhabitants waited in nervous anticipation, only to be told to stand down until the cloud cover cleared.

They awoke early on the morning of 28 June 1945 to clear skies with wisps of clouds that the *Tribune*'s Walter Simmons compared to 'puffs of cigar smoke'.

The first plane into the valley was the supply plane.

'Does the queen think she wants to pull out of there today?' Major Gardner asked via walkie-talkie.

'She's been wanting to get out of here for a week,' Walter replied.

'I suppose that goes for everybody,' Gardner said.

The major told Walter that Colonel Elsmore would supervise the mission from the cockpit of his own plane, a B-25 bomber. Instead of bombs, however, Elsmore had loaded the plane with enough reporters for a media circus, with him as ringmaster. After telling Walter about the colonel and the correspondents, Gardner relayed a message to Walter that almost certainly came directly from the press-conscious Elsmore: 'We should like it very much if on the first trip out, you, Mac, Maggie, and Decker could be on that glider.'

Walter knew that he would get enormous attention as a hero if he stepped out of the first glider as the rescue leader alongside the three survivors. Only weeks earlier, he had repeatedly noted in his journal how much he valued such exposure: 'If this deal is getting all the publicity it appears to be, I am sure that my prayers on the future will be answered.' Worldwide front page coverage of him with Margaret, McCollom and Decker – perhaps with Colonel Elsmore patting him on the back or pinning a medal on his chest – might have made it impossible for the brass to ignore Walter's combat requests. Just as important, after the war he could show the stories and photos to his hero father. Walter also knew that he might have only one chance to bask in the acclaim; days might pass before the second and third glider pickups, and by then the media train might have rolled on.

None of that mattered as much as it once did. Walter was not the same man who parachuted into the valley six weeks earlier, hungry for a mission and focused on his own career. He was no less gung-ho, but he was more mature; for the first time since he was drafted, he felt he had proved his mettle. Not only to the Army brass; not only to his men; not only to the imagined eyes of his father; but to himself. Walter understood what it meant to be a leader, and rushing to the front of the line would not do.

'I will not be on the first glider,' Walter answered, according to a transcript of the ground-to-air exchange. 'I will send the three survivors and one or two of my men on the first glider. I will be the last man to leave here with my master sergeant and a couple of tech sergeants.'

Major Gardner could have ordered him aboard the first glider run, but he let it drop. Gardner turned the conversation to wind speed on the valley floor. Walter assured him that it was minimal. That was the last discussion about when Walter would leave the valley.

A few minutes later, the radio in the supply plane crackled with word that the *Fanless Faggot* was en route to Shangri-La, gliding at the end of a tow cable pulled by a C-46. Elsmore joined the conversation, reporting from his B-25 cockpit that the glider was making good time. He corrected the tow plane's course, and within minutes the C-46 cleared the last ridge and entered the valley with the glider trailing a hundred metres behind on its nylon leash.

When he saw Shangri-La spread out below him, Lieutenant Henry Palmer grabbed an overhead lever in the glider cockpit. He pulled down, releasing the *Fanless Faggot* from the tow cable.

Within seconds, the glider slowed from more than 160 kilometres per hour to less than 130. As the C-46 flew off, engine noise faded away. Glider pilots Palmer and G. Reynolds Allen could hear the wind rushing past as they gently banked the engineless aircraft to further reduce speed. They lined up the glider's nose between the red parachutes that outlined the makeshift landing strip and touched down. As they slowed to a stop, the glider's tail rose like a whale's fluke, then eased back down for a perfect landing. Alex Cann captured the moment for posterity.

'We were all out on the field, jumping up and down with happiness,' Margaret wrote in her diary. Dozens of natives gathered around, whooping and hollering at the sight. 'This was their first chance to see, close up, one of those monsters of the air that had been so terrifying to them at first. Now they gazed at it with no more fear than we did.'

Henry Palmer knew that Major Samuels had only enough fuel in the *Leaking Louise* to circle a few times before attempting the snatch. Samuels also worried about a new cloud bank settling over the mountains surrounding the valley. Over the radio, he warned: 'We haven't too

Glider pilot Lieutenant Henry Palmer inspects a native axe after landing the *Fanless Faggot* in the valley.

much gas or time.' Samuels was serious about his concern. Before leaving Hollandia, he and his men had tossed out their heavy boots, their .45 calibre side arms, the plane's Thompson submachine guns, and every other nonessential item to lighten the load.

As the clouds thickened, Samuels expressed doubts that a snatch attempt would be possible that day. The glider crew might have to sleep in the base camp overnight, and they would try again the following morning, weather permitting.

Colonel Elsmore would not hear of it: 'It looks like a damn good day to me,' he said.

Samuels relented, and the *Leaking Louise* began to prepare for a pickup. He announced over the radio that he wanted to try a couple of 'dry runs' – swooping low over the field without grabbing the glider. Again Elsmore objected.

'You better not try a dry run,' the colonel commanded. 'If you're short on gas, don't take the time. You can make it OK without a dry run.'

While Samuels and Elsmore sparred overhead, Lieutenant Palmer jumped down from the glider and called to the survivors: 'You ready to go? This express takes off here on schedule in thirty minutes.'

'Thirty minutes?' Margaret said. 'Why, I'm not even packed.' Neither were McCollom, Decker and the two paratroopers Walter had chosen for the flight: Sergeants Fernando Dongallo and Ben Bulatao. By putting 'Doc' on the first glider, Walter wanted to focus attention on the medics who had risked their lives by jumping into the jungle.

As the survivors and the sergeants hurriedly gathered their belongings and souvenirs, the glider pilots went to work setting up the snatch poles. With the camp bustling, Alex Cann aimed his camera at a remarkable scene: twenty or more tribesmen pitched in to help Walter and the paratroopers roll the *Fanless Faggot* into position for the snatch. Leaning forward, their hands pressed against the glider's canvas skin, the modern warriors and the Stone Age warriors worked together, shoulder to shoulder, to muscle the Waco into place on the no-man's-land-cum-battlefield-cum-improvised-glider-landing strip.

With the clock ticking and the snatch plane's fuel tanks emptying, Palmer hustled the five passengers on to the glider. Margaret realized she had not said goodbye to the natives. 'But they understood that we were going,' she wrote. Margaret was especially sorry to leave without a final visit with 'the queen'.

The native leader Yali Logo was not sorry to see them leave, but Margaret felt certain that some of the tribesmen were distraught: 'Tears streamed down their black faces. They felt they were losing friends, and I knew I was losing some of the best and kindest friends I would ever have. I blew my nose rather noisily, and discovered that McCollom and Decker were doing the same thing.'

It is possible that the weeping natives were sad to see Margaret climb aboard the glider. It is also possible that

Native tribesmen help push the *Fanless Faggot* into position for a snatch attempt.

their tears reflected complex emotions among the people of Koloima.

The glider fascinated them, but according to several witnesses, they did not understand until later that their new acquaintances intended to fly away forever. They thought the glider's arrival was the last sign of the Uluayek legend. Frightened, they appealed to their ancestors.

'We had a crying ceremony,' said Binalok, a son of Yali Logo. 'It was to say, "Oh, we feel this deeply." As we cried, we named our dead ancestors. We thought we would be going back to the ways of our ancestors.'

Almost nothing had changed for generations in the valley, where the people lived and farmed and fought as their forefathers had. One exception involved styles of penis gourds and women's wrapped skirts. After the crying ceremony, the men of Koloima stopped storing tobacco in the tips of their penis gourds, reverting to the practice of their elders. Native women changed how they wrapped their grass skirts, adopting a more traditional style. The changes might have seemed slight to an outsider, but not to a Dani. Unable to imagine what a new age would look like or how dramatically it would affect their lives, the people of Koloima hoped that the upheaval would be relatively minimal. Nothing more than a return to older styles of gourds and skirts.

In the end, the natives were right about Uluayek but wrong about its effects. In a relatively short time, the world would come to Shangri-La, and the valley would change in ways they could never imagine.

Inside the glider, Palmer snapped Margaret out of her thoughts about the natives with a sharp warning: 'Don't be surprised if the tow rope breaks on the first try.'

'What happens if it does?' McCollom asked.

Palmer laid on a Louisiana accent: 'Well, suh, the Army's got me insured for ten thousand dollars.'

Margaret was not laughing. She gripped her Rosary and looked around the glider cabin, so flimsy when compared to the plane that brought her to the valley nearly seven weeks earlier. She told her diary: 'I wondered if we had survived a hideous plane crash and so much hardship, illness and pain, only to be killed when rescue was so near.'

Palmer helped to fasten their seat belts and showed them where to hold on, to avoid any whiplash when the snatch came. They held tight as the *Leaking Louise* grew closer.

Major Samuels circled the C-47 at 450 metres above the valley floor. His crew made sure the pickup arm was in place, hanging below the plane's belly, to grab the nylon loop. Peering through the windshield, he looked to the horizon and saw clouds closing in on the valley.

'I don't think I can pick up today,' he radioed to Elsmore in the *Ray Jr* and also to the crew in the supply plane.

Relying on his rank and his expertise, gained from a year of flying into and out of Shangri-La, Elsmore commanded otherwise: 'This is the best weather I've seen in the valley in many a day. You can do it. Go right down there and pick up the glider. You'll never get much better weather here.' Samuels knew better than to argue.

At one point during the conversation, Samuels turned away from the radio and asked his co-pilot, Captain William McKenzie: 'Are you nervous, Mac?'

'Hell, yes,' McKenzie said. 'Are you?'

'I guess you could say that.'

Samuels wrenched his neck to look into the cabin. 'You guys all ready back there?' he asked the crew. They responded with thumbs up.

'OK, here we go. Lower the boom.'

Samuels pulled back on the throttles, slowing the C-47 to 220 kilometres per hour. He pushed forward on the control wheel, guiding the plane down to six metres above the valley floor and headed towards the spindly posts with the nylon loop draped across them.

At 9.47 a.m., the steel hook caught hold of the loop. Samuels slammed the throttles forward to gain power as he pulled back on the control wheel to gain altitude.

Inside the glider, the passengers and crew felt a neck-snapping jolt.

Watching from his B-25 at 1800 metres, Colonel Elsmore spat a machine-gun litany into his radio: 'Oh boy. Oh boy. Oh boy, Oh boy, OH BOY!'

The drag from the glider slowed the *Leaking Louise* to a dangerous 169 kilometres per hour. The snatch plane was flying barely above the speed at which a C-47 was doomed to stall, a failure almost certain to be fatal.

Making matters worse, just before becoming airborne, the left wheel of the *Fanless Faggot* snagged one of the parachutes laid down the centre of the field. The white cloth billowed and thrashed against the glider's underbelly as it struggled to gain altitude at the end of the tow rope. Lieutenant Palmer's black humour about Army life insurance now seemed more relevant and even less funny. If it were even possible, an emergency landing in the *Fanless Faggot* would likely be a twisting, uncontrolled affair.

Margaret prayed harder as the glider swept treacherously low towards the jungle-covered mountains. Over 200 metres of steel cable had spun out from the winch inside the *Leaking Louise*. Added to the 100 metres of nylon rope from the loop and the towline, the *Fanless Faggot* trailed the C-47 by about 300 metres, or 100 metres farther than ideal. With Samuels struggling to gain altitude, the longer distance between the two aircraft meant that the glider was being tugged too low towards the jungle-covered mountains. Samuels pulled back harder on the control wheel and applied full power. Still the tow rope dragged through the trees – pulling the glider and the seven people on board through the upper branches.

As the *Fanless Faggot* moved forward at the end of the nylon cable after the snatch, a parachute used as a field marker caught on the glider's wheel.

When the glider grazed a tree top, Margaret clenched in fear. Her mind raced back to the sound of branches scraping against the metal skin of the *Gremlin Special* just before it crashed.

The *Leaking Louise* clawed for altitude, climbed, and hauled the damaged *Fanless Faggot* into the clear. 'When the glider swayed into our line of vision,' Samuels reported, 'we could see pieces of fabric fluttering off in the wind.'

The trees were only the first obstacles. His hands sweating, Samuels fought to bring the C-47 up to 3000 metres, the altitude he knew would be needed to clear the surrounding ridges. As Samuels overheated, the twin engines of the *Leaking Louise* did so, too. The plane began losing altitude.

'I've pushed her as far as she can go,' he radioed. Samuels announced that he wanted to cut the glider loose to avoid killing the C-47's engines – along with everyone aboard both aircraft.

Elsmore demanded that the major do no such thing. Watching from a higher altitude in his B-25, he believed the *Leaking Louise* had climbed high enough to clear the pass. He radioed back: 'Let 'em heat up. Keep goin'!'

Clouds shrouded the highest ridges, blocking Samuels' vision.

Inside the *Fanless Faggot*, the five passengers were exhaling with relief over the tow rope's refusal to break in the trees. But while congratulating each other on their apparent survival, they heard a persistent slap-slap noise from underneath the glider. The sound came from the parachute that had snagged on the wheel during take-off. As it whipped against the glider's belly, the chute tore through the canvas-covered floor, adding to the damage caused by the sweep through the trees. Strapped in their seats, the passengers looked through ragged gashes to the jungle over a thousand metres below. The chute kept thwacking, the canvas kept shedding, and the holes kept growing.

Nearing panic, Margaret tried not to look, but she could not stop herself. It reminded her of a ride on a glass-bottomed boat, only with no bottom.

John McCollom, who had twice re-entered the burning *Gremlin Special*, who had swallowed the grief over his dead twin to lead Margaret and Decker down the mountain, who had walked across a log to confront the axe-wielding natives, had one more task thrust upon him.

McCollom unbuckled his seat belt and dropped to his knees. He crawled towards the tail of the glider, the wind pounding against his face. Hanging on to keep from plummeting to his death, McCollom reached through the hole and grabbed a handful of parachute cloth. He pulled it inside, then grabbed another handful, then another, until the parachute was safely stowed away.

In the cockpit of the snatch plane, Samuels' struggles continued. He obeyed Elsmore's order not to cut loose the glider, even as he watched a temperature gauge on the dashboard show that the cylinder heads of both engines were overheating.

The view from the *Fanless Faggot* as the *Leaking Louise* pulled the glider out of Shangri-La, en route to Hollandia.

With help from co-pilot William McKenzie, Samuels flew the equivalent of a high-altitude tightrope, with a dozen lives in two aircraft hanging in the balance. He throttled back just enough to keep the engines from seizing while maintaining enough altitude for both his C-47 and the trailing Waco glider narrowly to clear the valley walls.

'We dropped her down to eight thousand feet,' Samuels said, 'and ... we were practically brushing the mountain tops.'

But the plane remained aloft, and so did the glider. As they flew through the final mountain pass out of the valley, the overheating *Leaking Louise* and the damaged *Fanless Faggot* passed over the charred wreckage of the *Gremlin Special*.

Even with a half-metre-wide hole in the glider floor, Margaret, McCollom and Decker could not spot the crash site. But they knew, under the jungle canopy, pressed into the moist soil, there stood twenty white wooden crosses and one Star of David, silently marking the loss of friends, comrades and family, left behind in Shangri-La.

Epilogue

After Shangri-La

AS COLONEL ELSMORE PREDICTED, THE REMAINDER of the ninety-minute trip was uneventful, with one small glitch. A pack of generals, VIPs, and reporters gathered at Hollandia's Cyclops Airstrip for the survivors' arrival, but the *Fanless Faggot* landed 400 metres away on Sentani Airstrip, completing a round-trip begun seven weeks earlier with the *Gremlin Special*. The greeting party raced to Sentani, where the survivors posed for photos with the crews of the glider and tow planes. Later they gave a press conference that made the front pages of newspapers around the world. Asked what they wanted to do next, the trio played it cute:

'Get a haircut and shave, and then go up to Manila,' McCollom said.

'A haircut and a shower will do me,' Decker said.

'I'd like a shower and a permanent,' Margaret said.

The *Fanless Faggot* was too damaged to fly again, so a new glider was used the following day in a snatch that brought out Alex Cann and five paratroopers: Corporal Custodio Alerta and Sergeants Alfred Baylon, Juan

The three survivors of the *Gremlin Special* crash upon their return to Hollandia.

Javonillo, Camilo Ramirez, and Don Ruiz. Two days later, on 1 July 1945, out came the third and final group – Walter called them 'The Four Musketeers' – Sergeants Santiago Abrenica, Hermenegildo Caoili and Roque Velasco, and Walter himself. Along with souvenirs of bows, arrows, and axes, they decorated their caps with pig tusks and feathers to make a grand entrance. They left behind the tents and most of their supplies, but took their weapons.

The paratroopers tried to convince several native boys to board the glider, without success. 'We were excited to go,' said Lisaniak Mabel. 'We said, "Let's go!" but our parents said, "We don't want to lose you."'

The paratroopers had better luck with the little pig named 'Peggy'. Squealing and wriggling, it left Shangri-La on the last glider flight to Hollandia. Peggy's subsequent fate is unknown.

Four months after the rescue, Shangri-La and the 'Grand Valley' discovered in 1938 by Richard Archbold were formally acknowledged to be one and the same. As the journal *Science* reported: 'The identity of the valley came about through a comparison of photographs taken by the Army just before the survivors were rescued with airplane photographs taken by the Archbold expedition. The identity is acknowledged by the Army, and particularly by Colonel Ray T. Elsmore, who directed the recent rescue operations.'

Archbold never returned to New Guinea, never married, and never engaged in further exotic expeditions. He devoted the remainder of his life, and his considerable fortune, to the Archbold Biological Station, a 5000-acre preserve near Lake Placid, Florida, dedicated to ecological research and conservation. He died in 1976 at sixty-nine.

Just as the Uluayek legend foretold, a new age dawned after the return of the sky spirits. Changes in the valley during the ensuing decades have been dramatic, but whether for better or worse is a matter of debate.

Spurred in part by news stories about the natives during coverage of the *Gremlin Special* rescue, Christian missionaries established camps in the valley in the decade after the war. They flew in aboard new amphibious planes that could land and take off from a straight stretch of the Baliem River. After initially reacting with hostility, in time a majority of native families accepted Christianity. Today, more than a dozen large churches dot the valley's one town of any size, Wamena, a dusty former Dutch government post with rubbish-strewn streets and a population of ten thousand and rising. Wamena is also now the site of a small airport; aircraft remain the only way in and out, but the valley's former isolation has surrendered to a timetable of regular scheduled flights.

After the missionaries came Indonesian troops, who arrived in force in the 1960s and 70s, after the Netherlands ended colonial control over the western half of New Guinea. Dutch New Guinea is now an Indonesian province called Papua.* Hollandia has been renamed Jayapura. Shangri-La is now the Baliem Valley.

Tribal affiliations remain intact among valley people, but natives throughout the province are collectively called Papuans. A low-intensity independence movement has sputtered along seeking a 'Free Papua'. But hundreds of kilometres from the Baliem Valley, mining companies are extracting significant gold and copper deposits. The Indonesian government has no intention of ceding control over Papua or its resources.

Years of persuasion by missionaries and force by Indonesian authorities put an end to the perpetual wars that formerly defined native life in the Baliem Valley. But an absence of war has also meant an absence of strong leaders, and peace has not led to prosperity. The province has the highest rates of poverty and AIDS in Indonesia. Health care is woeful, and aid workers report only sporadic attendance at school by valley children. The Indonesian government provides financial support, but much of the money ends up in the hands of non-native migrants who run virtually all the businesses of Wamena.

Elderly native men in penis gourds walk through Wamena begging for change and cigarettes. Some charge a small fee to pose for photos, inserting boar tusks through passages in their nasal septums to look fierce. More often, they look lost.

One village near Wamena earns money by displaying a mummified ancestor to the few tourists who obtain special government permits to visit the valley. Younger men and women have largely abandoned penis gourds and twine

* The eastern half of the island of New Guinea is a separate country, called, confusingly, Papua New Guinea.

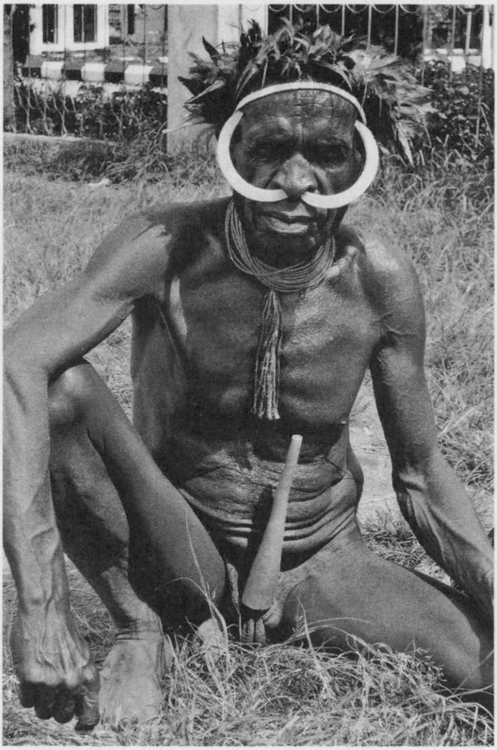

A Dani tribesman photographed in the Baliem Valley city of Wamena in 2010.

skirts. Instead they wear Western castoff shorts and t-shirts with unfamiliar logos and images. In February 2010, a young man walked towards his remote village wearing a t-shirt that displayed a portrait of Barack Obama. Asked if he knew the identity of the man on his shirt, he smiled shyly and said no.

Robert Gardner, a documentary filmmaker who first visited the valley in 1961 to film the Dani people in their original state, despairs at the changes during the past half-century. 'They were warriors and independent people,' he said. 'Now they're serfs in their own country.' Others, however, say the transition to modern ways, though difficult, will eventually lead to improved opportunities and standards of living.

Outside Wamena, large parts of the landscape remain unchanged from scenes depicted in photographs taken by Earl Walter and the movie made by Alex Cann. Families still live in thatch-roofed huts and grow sweet potatoes and other root crops, and they still count their wealth in pigs.

Logging companies have stripped some nearby mountainsides of trees, but the Ogi ridge where the *Gremlin Special* crashed remains pristine. Large pieces of wreckage can still be found there by anyone willing to make an arduous trek up the mountain, using moss-covered logs as bridges over small ravines, cutting through thick vines, and avoiding missteps that could send them over cliffs. Buttons, belt buckles, and pieces of human bones can be found in the muddy tomb where the wreck sits. Not long ago, a boy digging with friends turned up a silver dog tag. It was stamped with the name, address and serial number of WAC Sergeant Marion McMonagle, a widow from Philadelphia who had no children and whose parents died before her.

The tale of the plane crash and the sky spirits is still told by those who remember it, though their numbers are dwindling. When the author of this book visited in early 2010, Yunggukwe Wandik, whose pig was killed by falling cargo, refused to talk about the episode for nearly an hour. She only relented when an apology was offered on behalf of his countrymen. She never asked for money, but after she shared her memories, she accepted a few dollars as long-belated compensation for her first pig.

Throughout this visit, natives crowded around to view copies of Earl Walter's photos. When Helenma Wandik saw a photo of Wimayuk Wandik, known to the survivors as Pete, his eyes welled with tears. He held the photo close to his face, then stroked it with his long, bony fingers. 'This is my father,' he said in Dani, drawing it to his chest. He accepted a copy of the photo and offered a polished stone in exchange.

After the war, the Army tried to send troops to Shangri-La to recover the crash victims' remains. Plans for this were scuttled in 1947 when two amphibious planes that were supposed to be used in the mission were destroyed in a typhoon. No one was hurt. In letters to the victims' families, the Army declared that 'the many extreme hazards involved in this plan posed serious threats to the lives of the members of this proposed expedition'. The bodies from the *Gremlin Special* were declared 'non-recoverable' and their common gravesite received an official name: 'USAF Cemetery, Hidden Valley, No. 1', at longitude 139 degrees 1' east, and latitude 3 degrees 51' south.

However, a decade later, a Dutch team searching the jungle for the wreck of a missionary plane stumbled upon the *Gremlin Special*. The finding was reported by the Associated Press, prompting a search and recovery mission by the US Army. Using detailed directions from John McCollom and Earl Walter, the Army team located the crash site in December 1958. The bodies of Sergeant Laura Besley, Captain Herbert Good, and Private Eleanor Hanna were identified and recovered. As for the eighteen others, in the words of an Army officer who notified the next-of-kin, 'segregation was not possible'. The team collected as many bones and personal effects as possible and marched out.

Herbert Good was buried at Arlington National Cemetery. Eleanor Hanna was buried in a private cemetery in Pennsylvania. Her Chinese coin bracelet, and the two others she had left behind in her tent, were returned to her family.

Laura Besley was buried at the National Memorial Cemetery of the Pacific, in Hawaii. Her second funeral was on 13 May 1959, the fourteenth anniversary of the crash. Every WAC then stationed in Hawaii served as an honorary pallbearer. A few weeks later, one WAC who attended the funeral returned to be sure a proper grave marker had been installed. To her surprise, a lei of vanda orchids rested on Laura Besley's grave. She never learned who left them.

The eighteen others were buried together on 29 June 1959, at the Jefferson Barracks National Cemetery in St Louis. Their remains rest under a large granite headstone inscribed with their names, ranks, birthdates, and home states. Among the mourners were Colonel Peter Prossen's two sons, Peter Jr and David. John McCollom attended the ceremony with his brother's widow, Adele, and her fourteen-year-old daughter, Dennie.

Robert McCollom's wedding ring, found among the remains, was returned to his widow. She never remarried. After her death the ring passed to their daughter, who wore it to feel connected to her parents. It was stolen from her home in 1991, but she still hopes it will turn up.

James Lutgring, whose place on the *Gremlin Special* crew was taken by Melvin 'Molly' Mollberg, never forgot his best friend. Lutgring knew that, months before his death, Mollberg had tried unsuccessfully to join a unit that flew P-47 Thunderbolts. As a tribute, Lutgring and some friends arranged to nickname a P-47 'Molly'. They took pictures of themselves gathered around the fighter's nose, its name painted in flowing script. Lutgring also named his son after his lost pal, though Melvyn Lutgring never learned why his parents substituted a 'y' for the 'i'. Melvyn Lutgring served in Vietnam as an Army helicopter mechanic.

Lieutenant Henry E. Palmer received an Air Medal for Meritorious Achievement for piloting the *Fanless Faggot*. He returned to Louisiana after the war, married, had four daughters, and became Registrar of Voters in East Feliciana, Louisiana. In that role, he played a small part in a much larger historical event: the investigation into the assassination of President John F. Kennedy. In 1967, New Orleans District Attorney Jim Garrison charged a businessman named Clay Shaw with conspiring with Lee Harvey Oswald to kill the president. Henry Palmer was called to testify during Shaw's trial, as part of the prosecution's effort to establish a connection between Shaw and Oswald. Witnesses said Oswald tried to register to vote in Palmer's office on a day when Shaw was nearby. Shaw was found innocent, but Henry Palmer continued to field questions about the case from conspiracy theorists until he died in 1991 at seventy-seven.

For piloting the *Leaking Louise*, Major William J. Samuels received a Distinguished Flying Cross, given for 'heroism or extraordinary achievement while participating in aerial flight'. Shortly afterward, he was offered a choice: go to Okinawa and be promoted to lieutenant colonel or go home. He chose the latter and spent the next thirty-three years as a pilot for United Airlines. He died in 2006 at ninety-one.

After the war, Colonel Ray T. Elsmore co-founded Transocean Air Lines, an upstart company created by aviation mavericks to fly unscheduled routes that other carriers couldn't or wouldn't. He served as a Transocean director and executive vice president from 1946–52. Elsmore later became president of Western Sky Industries in Hayward, California. His military honours included the Legion of Merit, the Distinguished Service Medal, the Commendation Award, and six Presidential Unit Citations.

An obituary published in the *New York Times* recalled how Elsmore arranged General MacArthur's flight from the Philippines and 'directed the dramatic rescue of a

Women's Army Corps member and two service men from the wilds of the "Valley of Shangri-La" in Netherlands New Guinea'. He died in 1957 at sixty-six. There's no evidence he ever set foot in the valley.

A year later, the *Times* published the obituary of George Lait, one of the reporters who flew with Elsmore in 1944 and named the valley Shangri-La. Fittingly, Lait went to Hollywood after the war and became a top publicist in the movie business. He died at fifty-one.

Ralph Morton remained Australia bureau chief for the Associated Press until 1948, after which he worked on the AP's foreign desk in New York and taught at the Columbia University School of Journalism. In 1954, he and his wife founded the weekly *Dartmouth Free Press* in Nova Scotia. He died in 1988 at eighty.

Walter Simmons of the *Chicago Tribune* stayed in the Far East for a decade after the rescue. He wrote one of the first accounts of North Korean soldiers crossing the 38th parallel at the start of the Korean War. He returned to Chicago in 1955 and became the newspaper's features editor, Sunday editor and Sunday magazine editor before his retirement in 1973. He died in 2006 at ninety-eight.

Alexander Cann edited his film into an eleven-minute quasi-documentary called *Rescue from Shangri-La*. It opens with images of forbidding mountains shrouded by clouds, then Cann begins the narration: 'High in the mountains of Dutch New Guinea, beneath these clouds, an American Army plane crashed some time ago.' The film climaxes with the glider snatch.

After the war, Cann married for a fourth and final time, had two sons and a daughter, and continued making documentaries in Australia. His wife, theatrical agent June (Dunlop) Cann, told a reporter that he 'stopped off to be an alcoholic for twelve years', so she left the film industry to raise their children. Late in life, he sobered up and returned to acting, winning roles on the television series *Skippy*, about a heroic kangaroo, and in the 1970 movie *Ned Kelly*, starring Mick Jagger. Cann died in 1977 at seventy-four.

At the urging of Earl Walter, medals were awarded to all ten enlisted paratroopers from the 1st Recon – Santiago Abrenica, Custodio Alerta, Alfred Baylon, Ben 'Doc' Bulatao, Hermenegildo 'Superman' Caoili, Fernando Dongallo, Juan 'Johnny' Javonillo, Camilo 'Rammy' Ramirez, Don Ruiz and Roque Velasco. All but Bulatao and Ramirez received the Bronze Star. The two medics received the Soldier's Medal, the Army's highest non-combat award, for risking their lives to save the three survivors. Bulatao and Ramirez left few public traces after the war. In September 1945, Ramirez travelled to Kelso, Washington, to see Ken Decker. During the visit, Decker's parents hosted a wedding reception for Ramirez and a Texas woman named Lucille Moseley with whom he had been exchanging letters for several years. A brief news story about the wedding described her as 'a twenty-eight-year-old night club entertainer'. The marriage didn't last. Ramirez died in 2005 at eighty-seven. Ben Bulatao got married in Reno, Nevada, in 1968, and divorced in California in 1984. He died in 1985 at seventy-one.

After the rescue, Earl Walter and the men of the 1st Recon finally shipped out to the Philippines. By then the islands were secure. On 15 August 1945, six days after an atomic bomb was dropped on Nagasaki, the Japanese announced their surrender. The same day, General MacArthur dissolved the 1st Recon in a letter expressing gratitude for battalion members' service.

Walter completed his bachelor's degree at the University of Oregon. He rose through the sales department at the

Mail-Well Envelope Company, where he worked for thirty-seven years. He became a major in the US Army reserves and raised three daughters and two sons with his wife Sally, whom he lost to a heart attack in 1989. Walter regained his passion for swimming and became a US Masters champion, winning medals into his eighties.

Like the two medics, Walter received a Soldier's Medal. In 2009, a few weeks after his eighty-eighth birthday, Walter showed it to a visitor in his apartment in an assisted-living complex near the Oregon coast. The octagonal medal, about the size of a Kennedy half-dollar, hung beneath a faded red, white and blue ribbon. A framed citation that hung on the wall credited Walter with 'exceptional courage and leadership'. It described the mission, then concluded: 'Captain Walter's heroism in personally leading the rescue party was directly responsible for the safe return of these survivors.'

After the war, he showed the medal to his father. 'He asked, "Did you earn that?"' Without hesitating, C. Earl Walter Jr told C. Earl Walter Sr: 'Yes, Dad, I did.'

In the last entry in his journal, dated 3 July 1945, Walter wrote: 'And so temporarily we close the tale of The United States Army Outpost at Shangri-La, Dutch New Guinea, and hope that in the years to come we can still look back and say it was a job well done and let it go at that.'

In early 2010, he learned from this book's author that some older natives in New Guinea still remembered him and his men. Walter choked up at the rush of memories. After a long pause, he cleared his throat and said: 'It was the highlight of my life.'

In the spring of 1995, Walter met John McCollom and Ken Decker in a Seattle restaurant to mark the fiftieth anniversary of the crash. They posed with photos taken of their younger selves in Shangri-La. They laughed and reminisced,

From left, John McCollom, Ken Decker and Earl Walter in 1995.

filling gaps in each other's stories. Decker, at eighty-four, flirted with a waitress. They raised a glass to each other, to the paratroopers of the 1st Recon, and to the 'Queen of Shangri-La', who couldn't be with them.

After the snatch, Ken Decker spent several months in the hospital recovering from his injuries. Once healed, he enrolled in the University of Washington, where he received a degree in engineering. He worked for the Army Corps of Engineers then joined the Boeing Company, where he remained until his retirement in 1974.

He married late in life and had no children. Decker seldom spoke publicly about the crash, in part because he never regained any memory of what happened between the time the *Gremlin Special* took off and when he stumbled out of the wrecked plane.

Before he died in 2000 at age eighty-eight, Decker received a telephone call every year on 13 May, his birthday and the anniversary of the crash. On the other end of the line was his old friend John McCollom.

For as long as McCollom lived, the memory of Captain Baker wagging the wings of his B-17 brought tears to his eyes.

He left the Army in 1946, but was called back to active duty during the Korean War. He spent thirty-eight years as a civilian executive at the Wright-Patterson Air Force Base in Ohio. After retiring, McCollom became an aerospace consultant and vice president of the Piper Aircraft Company.

He married, had a son and a daughter, divorced, then remarried, acquiring four stepchildren. At the wedding of his twin brother's daughter, Dennie, he stood in for Robert and gave her away. He became a surrogate grandfather to her two sons.

Visitors to his home couldn't miss a wall of photos of John and Robert, young, nearly indistinguishable and completely inseparable, at least in memory. McCollom rarely spoke publicly of his twin, lest the enormity of the loss overwhelm him. When he acknowledged feeling survivor's guilt, he would spread it among all the people who died aboard the *Gremlin Special*: 'Why wasn't I killed instead of them?' he would say. Most often, when asked about what happened, he would answer, 'I was lucky.'

Yet pain has a way of finding an outlet, and the deepest pain for McCollom was reserved for thoughts about his twin. On rare occasions, he'd admit that a sorrowful thought wormed its way into his mind: 'Maybe it should have been me instead of my brother, who was married and had a baby daughter he had never seen.'

For a long time after the crash, he regularly dreamed that he, Decker and Margaret hiked back through the

John McCollom and his niece, Dennie McCollom Scott, in 1998.

jungle to the wreckage. And there was Robert, alive, waiting for them to return.

In August 2001, near the end of his life, McCollom's legs were too weak to carry him upstairs to an office over his garage. One day, his wife Betty came home from the grocery store to an empty house. Worried, she called to him. He replied: 'I'm upstairs.'

She went to the office and asked: 'How'd you get up here?'

'One step at a time, on my back end. I was looking for something,' he said.

John McCollom died several days later. He was eighty-two. When Betty McCollom went to the office, she discovered that he had assembled all his insurance, deeds, titles, and other important documents. Among his papers was the certificate from Colonel Elsmore inducting him into the 'Shangri-La Society'. McCollom also authored his own obituary, at one point writing simply: 'In May of 1945, his airplane crashed in New Guinea. He was rescued in June

1945 but his twin brother was killed in the accident.'

After her husband's death, Betty McCollom created a scholarship for aerospace engineering students at the University of Minnesota. She knew he would not have wanted the tribute alone. She called it the John and Robert McCollom Memorial Scholarship.

'Mac was determined,' she said. 'A number of tough things happened in his life. He just gritted his teeth and took it, and then he'd go forward. He was amazing.'

Three weeks after the snatch, Margaret returned to the United States a star. Describing her reception, a *Los Angeles Times* correspondent pronounced her 'the most celebrated young woman of the war'. Not to be outdone, the *Boston Sunday Advertiser* declared: 'She's blonde. She's cute. She's the No. 1 adventure girl in World War II.'

Photographers tracked her stops en route from Hollandia to Manila to California to New York City; radio shows jockeyed to interview her; a newspaper syndicate purchased her diary; her hometown paper announced that she was fielding offers from 'promoters, exhibitionists, theatrical agents, circus booking agents, publicity experts, columnists, commentators and just plain reporters'. A national magazine, *Calling All Girls*, won the Army's permission to publish a 'true comic' about her experiences in Shangri-La. As a publicity stunt, a newspaper arranged for Margaret to make her long-overdue date with Sergeant Walter 'Wally' Fleming. Instead of swimming in the surf off Hollandia, they dined at Toots Shor's, the landmark New York restaurant. They saw each other once or twice afterward, then called it quits.

A crowd estimated at three thousand people – the entire village, really – stood in sweltering heat to greet Margaret's train when it pulled into the Owego station. The Owego Free Academy band struck up a rousing march as she stepped from the train into her father's arms. The president of the Chamber of Commerce proclaimed her 'Owego's Number One Citizen'. No detail was too small for reporters to capture: 'Tanned and with a fresh wave in her feather-cut bob, Margaret wore a smart WAC summer silk uniform and alligator pumps.' A representative from a New York talent agency let slip that Margaret was choosing among several movie offers. A gossip columnist wrote that Hollywood beauty Loretta Young wanted the role, but others expected Margaret to star as herself. Neighbours pushed through a police line seeking autographs and cheered as she rode to her home on McMaster Street with her father and sisters in a convertible. Margaret's most lasting memory of her parade was two old women sitting on a porch, waving their handkerchiefs and crying.

At the end of a thirty-day furlough, the Army decided not to ship Margaret back to New Guinea. Instead, the brass sent her on a nationwide tour hawking Victory Bonds. During one six-week stretch, she spoke in fourteen

Margaret Hastings flanked by her sisters, Catherine and Rita, during the parade upon her arrival home in Owego, New York.

different states. Over time, she gave more than two hundred speeches. At each stop, she repeated a brief version of her ordeal and posed with celebrities and generals, including Dwight Eisenhower. Her mailbox swelled with thousands of fan letters, poems, autograph requests, and proposals from unknown suitors, including a young man who boasted that he was his town's champion spitter. One letter came from Sergeant Don Ruiz, the paratrooper whom Walter believed Margaret tried to seduce. The letter is chaste, catching her up on news of the paratroopers and describing the photos Walter took in the valley. 'You look swell standing by your golden grass mattress bed and also in the little pup tent back in the potato field,' he wrote. The closest Ruiz came to flirting was to write about the beautiful women he danced with at a party. He signed off: 'Long live the Queen of Shangri-La.'

Not everyone appreciated the attention lavished on Margaret. The mother of the *Gremlin Special* co-pilot, Major George Nicholson, lodged a complaint with the Army. 'She developed a lot of resentment toward Margaret Hastings,' said John McCarthy, George Nicholson's first cousin, once removed. Margaret Nicholson apparently feared that her son would be blamed for the crash. In response to one of her letters, a colonel in the War Department's Public Relations Office wrote: 'I have the deepest sympathy for your bereavement, and I can well understand your concern that nothing be published that would tend to minimize the sacrifice made by your gallant son. You can be sure that anything which would be of this nature would be disapproved for publication.' Nicholson's wife, Alice Nicholson, asked to speak directly with Margaret, but Margaret declined. John McCarthy explained: 'My great aunt Alice said, "Do you refuse to see your commander's wife?" Margaret Hastings replied, "I refuse to see my commander's widow."'

The criticism added to Margaret's growing disenchantment with fame. She did not consider herself a hero, just a fortunate survivor, and she longed for her old routines. Her wish came true when movie plans fizzled. 'The war ended and they were overwhelmed with war stories,' said Margaret's sister, Rita Callahan. 'Once they wanted to make a B movie and she wouldn't sign up for it.'

A year after the snatch, a reporter for the *Los Angeles Times* found Margaret living contentedly on McMaster Street. 'Almost any morning, she can be seen in faded GI pants and shirt, sweeping and dusting inside the green frame house that she shares with her father,' he wrote. 'Margaret is not writing a book about her experiences. She has no movie ambitions. She signs no testimonials for canned goods, cigarettes or camping equipment. The biggest thing in her life right now is a plan – to go to Syracuse University for a degree.'

Margaret spent more than two years at Syracuse, but left without graduating. She married Robert Atkinson, whom her sister Rita described as a former Olympic bobsledder turned insurance salesman. They had a son, but separated when Margaret was pregnant a second time, with a daughter. They divorced and Margaret raised her children on her own, in Rome, New York, where she worked in an administrative job on the Griffiss Air Force Base. Now and then, reporters sought her out, most often on anniversaries of the crash. They also called when Michael Rockefeller, the son of New York's governor and scion of the storied family, disappeared in New Guinea. 'He'd have an excellent chance of surviving, if he didn't drown,' she told them.

Margaret's last public appearance as the 'Queen of Shangri-La' came in 1974, when she, McCollom and Decker became honorary members of the National World War II Glider Pilots Association. Three decades after their ordeal, the three survivors embraced, laughed and reminisced during a reunion at the glider pilots' convention that year. During brief remarks, Margaret described a lesson she carried with her from the valley. 'Fear is something I don't think you experience unless you have a choice. If you have a choice, then you're liable to be afraid. But without a choice, what is there to be afraid of? You just go along doing what has to be done.'

Someone asked Margaret if she would like to return to New Guinea. Without hesitating, she answered, 'You bet!'

She never made it. Four years later, Margaret was diagnosed with uterine cancer. 'She put up a good fight,' her sister said. 'She never felt sorry for herself. When she knew she was going to lose, she took herself off treatments and came home.'

Margaret Hastings died in November 1978 at sixty-four. She is buried next to her parents, in a pretty little cemetery dotted with American flags, a short walk from McMaster Street.

The survivors, pilots, paratroopers and, in Margaret's lap, 'Peggy' the pig, after the rescue from Shangri-La. (Ken Decker is missing because he was being treated for his injuries when this photograph was taken.)

CAST OF CHARACTERS

(In alphabetical order)

SANTIAGO 'SANDY' ABRENICA – Master sergeant in US Army 1st Reconnaissance Battalion (Special). Right-hand man to Captain C. Earl Walter Jr.

CUSTODIO ALERTA – Corporal in the 1st Reconnaissance Battalion (Special). Volunteered for rescue mission following *Gremlin Special* crash.

G. REYNOLDS ALLEN – Captain in the US Army Air Forces and pilot of the Waco glider dubbed the *Fanless Faggot*.

RICHARD ARCHBOLD – Biological researcher and sponsor/organizer of the 1938 expedition that 'discovered' the New Guinea valley later nicknamed 'Shangri-La'.

WILLIAM D. BAKER – Captain in Army Air Forces and pilot of B-17 search plane that spotted the survivors in the jungle clearing.

ALFRED BAYLON – Sergeant in the 1st Reconnaissance Battalion (Special). Volunteered for rescue mission following *Gremlin Special* crash.

LAURA BESLEY – Sergeant in the Women's Army Corps from Shippenville, Pennsylvania. Passenger aboard the *Gremlin Special*. Close friend of Margaret Hastings.

BENJAMIN 'DOC' BULATAO – Sergeant in US Army 1st Reconnaissance Battalion (Special). Lead medic in volunteer rescue mission following *Gremlin Special* crash.

ALEXANDER CANN – Canadian-born filmmaker for the Netherlands Indies Government Information Service. Former Hollywood actor and failed jewel thief.

HERMENEGILDO CAOILI – Sergeant in the 1st Reconnaissance Battalion (Special). Volunteered for rescue mission following *Gremlin Special* crash.

KENNETH DECKER – Tech Sergeant from Kelso, Washington, who worked as a draftsman in the engineering department of the Far East Air Service Command. Passenger aboard the *Gremlin Special*.

FERNANDO DONGALLO – Sergeant in the 1st Reconnaissance Battalion (Special). Volunteered for rescue mission following *Gremlin Special* crash.

RAY T. ELSMORE – Colonel and commander of the 322nd Troop Carrier Wing of the US Army Air Forces. Confirmed Major Myron Grimes's report of a large valley in central New Guinea and subsequently became the US military's leading authority on the region. Directed rescue operations following *Gremlin Special* crash.

WALTER 'WALLY' FLEMING – Army sergeant based in Hollandia, New Guinea, and sometime boyfriend of Margaret Hastings.

GEORGE GARDNER – Major in the US Army Air Forces who supervised supply runs to the *Gremlin Special* survivors.

HERBERT F. GOOD – Army captain from Dayton, Ohio. Passenger aboard the *Gremlin Special*.

MYRON GRIMES – Major in the Army Air Forces who was the first US military pilot to 'discover' the New Guinea valley later nicknamed 'Shangri-La'.

JACK GUTZEIT – Sergeant and radioman on C-47 search and supply plane, the *three-one-one*, following the *Gremlin Special* crash.

ELEANOR HANNA – Private in the Women's Army Corps from Montoursville, Pennsylvania. Passenger aboard the *Gremlin Special*.

MARGARET HASTINGS – Corporal in the Women's Army Corps from Owego, New York. Secretary to Colonel Peter Prossen, close friend of Laura Besley. Passenger aboard the *Gremlin Special*.

PATRICK HASTINGS – Widowed father of Margaret Hastings. Foreman in shoe factory in Owego, New York.

EDWARD T. IMPARATO – Colonel in the US Army Air Forces and pilot of plane that dropped C. Earl Walter Jr's paratrooper team into Shangri-La.

JUAN 'JOHNNY' JAVONILLO – Sergeant in the 1st Reconnaissance Battalion (Special). Volunteered for rescue mission following *Gremlin Special* crash.

HELEN KENT – Sergeant in Women's Army Corps from Taft, California. Passenger aboard the *Gremlin Special*.

GEORGE LAIT AND HARRY E. PATTERSON – War correspondents who flew over the New Guinea valley with Colonel Ray T. Elsmore and coined the nickname 'Shangri-La'.

YALI LOGO – Leader of the Logo-Mabel clan who plotted to murder the *Gremlin Special* survivors.

JOHN AND ROBERT MCCOLLOM – Twin brothers from Trenton, Missouri, both lieutenants in the maintenance section of the Far East Air Service Command. Passengers aboard the *Gremlin Special.*

WILLIAM G. MCKENZIE – Captain in the US Army Air Forces from La Crosse, Wisconsin. Co-pilot to Major William Samuels in glider snatch plane.

HERBERT O. MENGEL – Captain in the US Army Air Forces from St Petersburg, Florida, and pilot of the *three-one-one* supply plane.

MELVIN MOLLBERG – Private in the Army Air Forces from Baudette, Minnesota. Assistant engineer on the *Gremlin Special.* Joined the crew as a favour to his best friend, Corporal James 'Jimmy' Lutgring, who didn't want to fly with Colonel Peter Prossen.

RALPH MORTON – War correspondent for the Associated Press who led coverage of the *Gremlin Special* crash along with Walter Simmons of the *Chicago Tribune*.

GEORGE H. NICHOLSON JR – Major in the Army Air Forces from Medford, Massachusetts. Co-pilot on the *Gremlin Special.*

HENRY E. PALMER – Lieutenant in the US Army Air Forces from Baton Rouge, Louisiana. Glider pilot aboard the *Fanless Faggot*.

PETER J. PROSSEN – Colonel in the Army Air Forces from San Antonio, Texas. Chief of the maintenance section of the Far East Air Service Command in Hollandia, Dutch New Guinea. Pilot of the *Gremlin Special.*

CAMILO 'RAMMY' RAMIREZ – Corporal in the US Army's 1st Reconnaissance Battalion (Special). Volunteer medic in rescue mission following *Gremlin Special* crash.

DON RUIZ – Sergeant in the 1st Reconnaissance Battalion (Special). Volunteered for rescue mission following *Gremlin Special* crash.

WILLIAM J. SAMUELS – Major in the US Army Air Forces and commander of the 33rd Troop Carrier Squadron, from Decatur, Illinois. The most experienced US pilot in the Southwest Pacific in 'snatching' gliders from the ground into the air.

WALTER SIMMONS – War correspondent for the *Chicago Tribune* who led coverage of the *Gremlin Special* crash along with Associated Press reporter Ralph Morton.

ROQUE VELASCO – Sergeant in the 1st Reconnaissance Battalion (Special). Volunteered for rescue mission following *Gremlin Special* crash.

C. EARL WALTER JR – Captain in the US Army's 1st Reconnaissance Battalion (Special), from Portland, Oregon. Was awaiting a combat posting with his Filipino-American paratroopers when he volunteered to lead the rescue mission into Shangri-La.

WIMAYUK WANDIK – Known to the *Gremlin Special* survivors as 'Pete', a leader of the native village of Uwambo.

ADDITIONAL PASSENGERS AND CREW KILLED IN THE CRASH OF THE *GREMLIN SPECIAL*, 13 MAY 1945:

Major Herman F. Antonini of Danville, Illinois; Major Phillip J. Dattilo of Louisville, Kentucky; Private Alethia M. Fair of Hollywood, California; Captain Louis E. Freyman of Hammond, Indiana; Private Marian Gillis of Los Angeles; First Lieutenant Lawrence F. Holding of Raleigh, North Carolina; Private Mary M. Landau of Brooklyn, New York; Sergeant Marion W. McMonagle of Philadelphia; Corporal Charles R. Miller of Saint Joseph, Michigan; Sergeant Belle Naimer of the Bronx, New York; Private George R. Newcomer of Middletown, New York; Sergeant Hilliard Norris of Waynesville, North Carolina; and Corporal Melvyn Weber of Compton, California.

THE FILIPINO REGIMENTS

THE MEN OF THE 1ST RECON HAD A RIGHT TO BE upset at finding themselves sidelined in New Guinea. Every soldier of Filipino descent had followed a difficult road to service in the American military.

The roots of the tangled relationship between Filipinos and Americans dated back nearly fifty years, to 1898 and the Treaty of Paris, which marked the end of the Spanish-American War. The treaty gave the United States control over the Philippines, much to the chagrin of the Filipino people, who ached for independence after three centuries under Spanish rule. But America was feeling its imperialist oats as a world power. President William McKinley declared in his famous if sometimes disputed quote that it was the United States' duty to 'educate the Filipinos, and uplift and Christianize them'.

Within weeks of the treaty, American and Filipino patrols traded fire on the outskirts of Manila, triggering a forty-one-month clash that became known as the Philippine-American War, the most overlooked conflict in United States history. Before it was over, the United States suffered more than four thousand combat deaths. The Philippines lost perhaps five times as many soldiers, as well as more than one hundred thousand civilians who died from famine and disease. President Theodore Roosevelt declared victory on 4 July 1902, and the Philippines became a US territory, though skirmishes continued for years. Atrocities by American soldiers were whitewashed, and Roosevelt's secretary of war congratulated the Army for conducting 'a humane war' in the face of 'savage provocation' by 'a treacherous foe'.

The next three decades saw an influx of Filipino immigrants to the United States, with a majority of the newcomers heading to California and Hawaii. At the same time, a mutually beneficial trading relationship developed across the Pacific. One resource the Americans especially valued was hardwood, which is how C. Earl Walter Sr came to manage a lumber company in Mindanao. But for many Filipinos, the United States was hardly welcoming. Anti-Filipino sentiment ran high, and Filipinos experienced racially motivated attacks and legal restrictions against owning land. Anti-miscegenation laws in Western states prevented them from marrying white women. For most, economic opportunities were limited to field work, service occupations, manual labour, and jobs in canneries and factories.

Meanwhile, the drive for Philippines independence continued. In 1934, President Franklin D. Roosevelt signed a law establishing a ten-year transition period, at the end of which the Philippines would have its own US-style democracy. Until then, new immigration by Filipinos would be severely limited and repatriation laws would pressure Filipinos living in the United States to return to the islands.

Then came 8 December 1941. One day after Pearl Harbor, Japan launched a surprise air-and-land attack on the Philippines, centred on the island of Luzon. The outnumbered Philippine and American forces, under General MacArthur's command, quickly withdrew to the Bataan Peninsula and the island of Corregidor, at the entrance to Manila Bay. The US–Philippine forces surrendered in April 1942, and with help from none other than Colonel Ray Elsmore, MacArthur escaped to Australia to begin plotting his return. Surviving American and Filipino forces and the Filipino people weren't so fortunate; they suffered through the Bataan Death March and a brutal occupation.

News of the attacks on Pearl Harbor and the Philippines made Filipinos in the United States eager to fight the Japanese. By then, more than one hundred thousand transplanted Filipinos lived in Hawaii and on the US mainland. But they were in a strange limbo. They were legal US residents, but they weren't eligible for citizenship, so they could neither be drafted nor volunteer for military service.

Individually and through their representatives in Washington, Filipinos petitioned Roosevelt, his secretary of war, and members of Congress for the right to fight. Some wanted to serve for practical reasons, such as the opportunities and benefits they expected would come to veterans after the war. But more spoke of vengeance. Although the United States had been attacked by air at Pearl Harbor, the Philippines had been invaded. Sounding like a Colonial recruit in the Revolutionary War, one Filipino volunteer declared: 'Life is so small a property to risk as compared to the fight incurred for the emancipation of a country from ... foul, ignominious, barbaric, inhuman treatments.'

Within weeks of the Japanese invasion, Roosevelt signed a law that allowed Filipinos to join the US military. The Army responded by creating the 1st Filipino Battalion, which from the outset was expected to help in the battle to retake the islands through overt and covert action. By May

1942, more than two thousand men of Filipino descent had volunteered. So many new recruits volunteered that the battalion was upgraded to the 1st Filipino Regiment. Soon after, the Army created a 2nd Filipino Regiment. Eventually, more than seven thousand men of Filipino descent served in the two regiments. Roosevelt rewarded their fervour by making Filipino soldiers in the US military eligible for citizenship, and several thousand took the oath.

An American reporter who caught up with the Filipino-American troops a few months after their induction described them with unreserved admiration: 'The men of this Filipino regiment are taking the business of sudden death seriously. Their American officers have commended their amazing conscientiousness and ardour, and have encouraged them to add a purely Filipino fillip to the orthodox warfare methods. In simulated jungle fighting, these sons and grandsons of guerrilla warriors ... like to creep close to the enemy with bayonets tightly gripped in their mouths, and then jump at him, wielding their bayonets as if they were their native bolos.'

In spring 1944, the 2nd Filipino Regiment was merged into the 1st Filipino Regiment and sent overseas as the 1st Filipino Infantry Regiment. Its members made it to the Philippines in February 1945. In one battle on Samar Island, the regiment reported killing 1572 Japanese soldiers while losing only five of its men. In May 1945, while Walter and his men were still in Hollandia awaiting an assignment, the 1st Filipino Infantry Regiment moved into heavy combat against the Japanese on Leyte Island.

ACKNOWLEDGEMENTS

THIS STORY WAITED A LONG TIME TO BE TOLD, BUT IT didn't wait untended. A remarkable collection of people lovingly preserved documents, letters, scrapbooks, maps, photographs, movies and, most of all, memories.

I am indebted above all to C. Earl Walter Jr, without whom I would never have attempted to write this book. Earl welcomed me into his home; shared his scrapbooks, photos and journals; and poured out stories of Shangri-La. Thanks also to his daughter Lisa Walter-Sedlacek.

Buzz Maxey provided indispensable help during my trip to the Baliem Valley, aka Shangri-La. He guided me to the surviving witnesses, translated their accounts, and interpreted the cultural meaning of their responses. I admire his dedication to the welfare of the people of Papua, and I encourage others to follow his path. Thanks also to Myrna, Ben and Dani Maxey. Tomas Wandik skilfully guided me up the mountain and through the jungle to the crash site. His daughter Nande Mina Wandik made an ideal hiking companion. I'm deeply grateful to Helenma Wandik, Yunggukwe Wandik, Ai Baga, Lisaniak Mabel, Hugiampot, Narekesok Logo and Dagadigik Walela for their eyewitness accounts.

Emma Sedore, historian of Tioga County, NY, provided priceless assistance and suggestions. Without her, much of Margaret Hastings' story might have been lost. Thanks also to Roger Sharpe and Kevin Sives at the Tioga County Historical Society.

The lovely Betty 'B.B.' McCollom gave me rich insight into her late husband John and graciously shared his scrapbooks and photographs. Dennie McCollom Scott provided invaluable information and suggestions. Rita Callahan told me stories about her sister Margaret Hastings and their father, Patrick Hastings. She directed me to Margaret's childhood friend Mary Scanlon, whose memories enriched me and this book.

Peter J. Prossen Jr helped me to understand his father, and I admire his candour. Maryrose Condon, John McCarthy and Michael McCarthy helped me to know their cousin, Major George H. Nicholson Jr. Roberta Koons kindly shared memories of her sister, Eleanor Hanna. Gerta Anderson helped me to know Laura Besley. My new friend Melvyn Lutgring generously told the story of his father's guilt over giving his job on the flight crew to his best friend, Melvin 'Molly' Mollberg. Alexandra Cann delighted me with yarns about her larger-than-life father, for whom she was named.

Documentary filmmaker Robert Gardner spent time in the 1990s researching this story as a possible follow-up to *Dead Birds*, his brilliant film about the Dani people. He gave me rare files that would have been impossible to replicate. His unaired interviews with John McCollom enabled me to see and hear Mac from beyond the grave. Thanks also to Michael Hutcherson for reproducing the interview tapes.

My understanding of the Dani was greatly enriched by Dr Myron Bromley, whose close reading of this manuscript and thought-provoking suggestions are sincerely appreciated. I also thank James Sunda, who along with Myron was among the first missionaries to enter the valley. Professor Karl Heider's impressive research on the Dani, amplified by his email correspondence, was enlightening.

Dona Cruse learned of the crash through her mother, Ruth Coster, who was supposed to be aboard the flight. Dona shared her voluminous knowledge and research of these events. Colonel

Pat Jernigan (retired) was a remarkable, indefatigable resource who answered my questions and provided valuable insight.

Major Myron Grimes (retired) never got much credit for being the first US Army Air Forces pilot to spot the valley from the air. He made me feel as though I was in the cockpit with him, and I'm thankful for the ride. George Theis of the National Association of World War II Glider Pilots saved me from gliding into a fusillade of errors.

At the end of World War II, Gene Hoops was an Army corporal sent to the base in Hollandia as part of a clean-up patrol. His job was to destroy all military files, but when he opened a metal drawer and found photos from the crash site he knew they were worth saving. For the next six decades he did just that, and I'm thankful that he did.

In his excellent film, *An Untold Triumph*, documentary filmmaker Noel 'Sonny' Izon brought to light the contributions of Filipino-American soldiers during World War II. He generously shared information about the Filipino paratroopers who bravely jumped into the valley.

The late Colonel Edward T. Imparato, who played an important role in the supply and rescue effort, published verbatim documents, transcripts, Walter's journal, news stories, and his own reflections in his book, *Rescue from Shangri-La* (Paducah Kentucky: Turner Publishing, 1997). Colonel Imparato died before I had a chance to meet him, but I salute him for his work in the valley and on his book.

Justin Taylan, director of PacificWrecks.org, was an enormous help throughout. Thanks to Professors Alex Fabros and Dan Gonzales for teaching me about Filipino-American soldiers; Jette Flipse for her helpful suggestions; Robert Knox for sharing his great-uncle's stirring account of a C-47 crash; James W. Zobel at the MacArthur Memorial Archives; Ed Christine and Tom Wilbur at the *Binghamton Press & Sun*; Norm Landis at the *Rome Daily Sentinel*; Sissy Burge at *The Watchman* of Clinton, Louisiana; Lynn Gamma at the Air Force Historical Research Agency; David Freece at the Cowlitz County Historical Museum; Heidi Reutter of the University of Central Arkansas; Mary Jane Vinella of the Bellevue, Wash., Regional Library; Lisa Rickey of the Dayton, Ohio, Metro Library; telegraphy historian Thomas C. Jepsen; transcriptionist Steve Wylie; intrepid traveller Jan Versluis; and my graduate assistant, Roxanne Palmer.

My colleagues and students at Boston University indulged and encouraged me throughout this project. Special thanks to Dean Tom Fiedler and Professor Lou Ureneck for their support and the sabbatical that enabled me to complete this book, and to Bob Zelnick and Isabel Wilkerson for setting such inspiring examples.

At a crucial moment, Helene Atwan of Beacon Press convinced me to trust my instincts. She made me an author a decade ago, and I'm forever grateful. Richard Abate is the best friend and agent any author could ask for. He stuck with me as I searched for the right idea, and then he found the ideal home for this book.

My editor Claire Wachtel embraced me and this story from start to finish. She improved this book with her ideas, her insights and her confidence. Thanks also to Jonathan Burnham, for everything. I'm grateful to Melissa Kahn of 3Arts, who believed, and to the entire team at HarperCollins and Harper UK, including Elizabeth Perrella, Diane Aronson, Miranda Ottewell, Arabella Pike and Sophie Goulden.

Deep thanks to my own tribe: Brian McGrory; Ruth, Emily, and Bill (Air William) Weinstein, whose generosity sent me to New Guinea in comfort; Colleen Granahan, Dan Field, and Isabelle and Eliza Granahan-Field; Jeff Feigelson, who should have been an editor; Kathryn Altman; Dick Lehr; Chris Callahan; Nancy and Jim Bildner; Naftali Bendavid; the late Wilbur Doctor; Allan Zuckoff, and the extended Kreiter and Zuckoff clans.

Special thanks to my parents, first teachers, and first readers: Sid and Gerry Zuckoff.

I was struggling with a much different writing project when my beloved daughters informed me that I was lost in the wrong jungle. 'That's not the kind of story you like,' Isabel said. Eve agreed. 'Write about Margaret and Shangri-La,' she said. Smart girls.

My wife, Suzanne (aka Rose, aka Trixie) Kreiter, makes life the closest thing I'll find to Shangri-La.

NOTES ON SOURCES AND METHODS

THIS IS A WORK OF NONFICTION. NO LIBERTIES have been taken with facts, dialogue, characters or chronology. All quoted material comes from interviews, reports, diaries, letters, flight logs, declassified military documents, news stories, books or some other source cited in the notes below. Descriptions of people and places are based on site visits, interviews, written materials, photographs and newsreel images. Unless noted, the author conducted all interviews, either in person or by phone. Interviews with natives of the Baliem Valley, or Shangri-La, were translated by Buzz Maxey, an American missionary relief and development manager who has lived there most of his life.

Abbreviations of key source materials:

IDPF – Individual Deceased Personnel File, an official US Army document generally running more than one hundred pages, detailing the circumstances of death, recovery and identification of remains, dispersal of belongings, and burial. IDPFs for nineteen of the *Gremlin Special* victims were obtained using the Freedom of

Information Act. Army officials said they could not locate files for Laura Besley and Louis Freyman.

CEW – C. Earl Walter Jr's daily journal, which he wrote during his weeks in Shangri-La. Walter granted permission for its use here. Much of the journal was reproduced by Colonel Edward T. Imparato in *Rescue from Shangri-La* (Paducah, KY: Turner Publishing Co., 1997).

MACR – Missing Air Crash Report No. 14697, the declassified US Army Air Forces account of the incident, including survivors' sworn statements taken upon their return to Hollandia; the names, ranks and home addresses of the victims; a map showing the crash location; and an official account of the flight, the crash, and the search and rescue.

SLD – 'Shangri-La Diary' is an account of the crash and rescue written by Margaret Hastings in secretarial shorthand while in the valley. Inez Robb of the International News Service helped to expand it into a serial distributed to newspapers in the summer of 1945. *Reader's Digest* published a condensed version in December 1945. Tioga County Historian Emma Sedore transcribed the version of the diary used here. In an unaired interview with documentary filmmaker Robert Gardner, John McCollom vouched for its accuracy. C. Earl Walter Jr agreed, with one exception: he denied singing 'Shoo, Shoo Baby' as he entered the survivors' camp. However, in a joint interview in 1998, McCollom insisted that it was true and Walter relented. Walter acknowledged as much to the author. Walter's initial denial might be traced to the ribbing he took from friends and family about singing in the jungle.

TCHS – Tioga County Historical Society, in Owego, NY, which preserved Margaret Hastings' personal scrapbook, letters, telegrams, photographs, and other materials.

NOTES

Chapter 1: Missing

2 grew up a farm boy: Description comes from interviews with Margaret Hastings' sister Rita Hastings Callahan, on 1 August 2009.
2 visible signs of her absence: Ibid.
2 walked into a recruiting station: Margaret Hastings' enlistment records at NARA.
3 combat death toll: United States Department of Veteran Affairs Fact Sheet, dated November 2008. Retrieved 27 January, 2010, at www1.va.gov/opa/fact/amwars.asp.

Chapter 2: Hollandia

5 usual five-thirty a.m. reveille: Details of Margaret Hastings' daily routine in New Guinea are contained in SLD, Part Two. Also, Margaret Hastings, 'Owego WAC Writes of Her Life in New Guinea', letter to Verna Smith, published in the *Owego Gazette*, 8 March 1945.
6 just 1.56 metres: Margaret Hastings, Shangri-La Diary, Part Eleven. Hereafter: SLD. Margaret notes her height in comparison with the native women, pleasantly surprised that they are shorter than her 'five-feet, one-and-one-half inches'.
6 teenage nickname: 1932 Owego Free Academy Tom-Tom Yearbook, p. 18, at TCHS.
6 hitchhiked when she wanted: Interview with Mary Scanlon, 2 August 2009.
7 'drank liquor ... liked the boys': Undated college paper written by Margaret Hastings, titled 'A Tribute To Mother', found in correspondence file at Tioga County Historical Society, hereafter TCHS.

7 'To tell the truth': James R. Miller, 'Reconversion of a Heroine', the *Los Angeles Times Magazine*, 7 July 1946, p. 5.

7 more exciting than Atlantic City: Margaret Hastings, SLD, Part One.

7 'blood, toil, tears and sweat': John Lukacs, *Blood, Toil, Tears and Sweat; The Dire Warning: Churchill's First Speech as Prime Minister* (New York: Basic Books, 2008), p. 11.

8 'The western world has been freed': Harry S. Truman, transcript of speech announcing the surrender of Germany, found at Miller Center of Public Affairs, University of Virginia, retrieved 3 January 2010, at http://millercenter.org/scripps/archive/speeches/detail/3340.

8 House Speaker Sam Rayburn: C.P. Trussell, 'Blackout Lifted on Capitol Dome', *New York Times*, 9 May 1945, p. 1.

8 'It will be a busy summer ...': Hanson W. Baldwin, 'A New Phase Now Opens In The Pacific War', *New York Times*, 13 May 1945, p. E5.

8 Between sunrise and sunset: Day-by-day chronology of World War II Pacific History, compiled by US Air Forces and provided by Justin Taylan of PacificWrecks.org, http://www.pacificwrecks.com/60th/1945/5-45.html, retrieved 11 October 2009. Also, a chronology from http://www.onwar.com/chrono/index.htm, retrieved 11 October 2009.

10 named the island after an African country: Karl Heider, *Grand Valley Dani: Peaceful Warriors*, Third Edition (Belmont, California: Wadsworth Group, 1997), p. 1.

10 Sri Lankan potentates: Tim Flannery, *Throwim Way Leg* (New York: Grove Press, 1998), p. 3.

10 Captain Cook visited in 1770: Hobart M. Van Deusen, 'The Seventh Archbold Expedition', *BioScience*, July 1966, p. 450.

11 'Operation Reckless': Samuel Eliot Morison, *History of U.S. Naval Operations in World War II, Vol. 8: New Guinea and the Marianas, March 1944–August 1944* (Champaign, IL: University of Illinois Press, 2002), pp. 68–90. Also, Stanley Sandler, *World War II in the Pacific: An Encyclopedia* (New York: Garland Publishing, 2001), pp. 400–403.

11 'Release a Man for Combat': Ibid, p. 184.

11 'my best soldiers': Stanley Sandler, *World War II in the Pacific: An Encyclopedia*, p. 1050.

12 a sidearm to keep under her pillow: Dona Cruse interview, 11 August 2009. Dona is the daughter of WAC Ruth Coster Cruse, who passed up a chance to fly over Shangri-La on 13 May 1945. Also, Steven Mayer, 'Taft veteran killed in crash only woman listed on wall', *Bakersfield Californian*, 12 Nov. 2007, at www.bakersfield.com/102/story/283703.html, included in the Ruth Coster Collection at the University of Central Arkansas.

12 'Hey Joe – hubba, hubba ...': Colonel Ray T. Elsmore, 'New Guinea's Mountain and Swampland Dwellers', *National Geographic Magazine*, December 1945, Vol. 88, No. 6, p. 676.

12 precautions' real aim: Judith A. Bellafaire, *The Women's Army Corps: A Commemoration of World War II Service*', US Army Center of Military History Publication 72–15. See also the definitive history of the WACs, Mattie E. Treadwell's *The Women's Army Corps* (Washington: Office of the Chief of Military History, Dept. of the Army, 1954 [c1953]), p. 422. Also, Selene H.C. Weise, *The Good*

Soldier: The Story of a Southwest Pacific Signal Corps WAC (Shippensburg, PA: Burd Street Press, 1999).

12 'blanket parties': Margaret Hastings' letter to Kitty Dugan, 2 February 1945, in archives at TCHS.

13 The letter didn't give away: A notation on the envelope indicates the letter to Kitty Dugan was 'Censored by Lt. Margaret V. Bogle', the same officer who informed Margaret Hastings about the trip to Shangri-La.

13 enlisting in August 1942: Background information on Laura Besley from US World War II Army Enlistment Records, retrieved at www.ancestry.com on 11 September 2009, and Harrisburg, Pa., City Directory (R.L.Polk & Co.: 1936–37), p. 62. Also, 1930 US Federal Census Records.

13 a 'sassy' young woman: Interview with Gerta Anderson, 26 April 2010. Laura Besley's mother and Gerta Anderson's maternal grandmother were sisters. Laura was named 'Earline', after her father, Earl, but took the name Laura from her grandmother.

13 tables made from boxes and burlap: Margaret Hastings, 'Owego WAC Writes of Her Life in New Guinea', letter to Verna Smith, published in the *Owego Gazette*, 8 March 1945.

14 silky blue parachute: Margaret Hastings' letter to Kitty Dugan, 2 February 1945. Details of WAC tents in Hollandia also from Mary L. Eck, 'Saga of a Sad Sack', self-published pamphlet recounting military life in New Guinea and elsewhere, 1979.

14 double electric light socket: Margaret Hastings, SLD, Part Two.

15 'Get skinny in Guinea': Ibid, p. 16.

15 Margaret showered at least twice a day: Margaret Hastings, 'Owego WAC Writes of Her Life in New Guinea', letter to Verna Smith, published in the *Owego Gazette*, 8 March 1945.

15 'in order to keep respectable': Ibid.

15 'There was "jungle rot" ...': Lieutenant Colonel Anne O'Sullivan (retired), 'Recollections of New Guinea', *Women's Army Corps Journal*, October–December 1974, Vol. 5, No. 5, p. 14.

16 almost enough to make her feel cool: Margaret Hastings, SLD, Part Two.

16 the health of military women: Mattie E. Treadwell, *The Women's Army Corps* (Washington: Office of the Chief of Military History, Dept. of the Army, 1954 [c1953]), p. 446.

16 several hundred WACs: Mattie E. Treadwell, *The Women's Army Corps* (Washington: Office of the Chief of Military History, Dept. of the Army, 1954 [c1953]), p. 427.

16 a letter to his family: All quotes from Colonel Peter J. Prossen come from his letters to his wife on 12 and 13 May 1945, copies of which were provided by his son, Peter J. Prossen Jr.

17 his elder son knew him: Interview with Peter J. Prossen Jr, 28 July 2009.

18 hundred or so men and twenty-plus WACs: John McCollom, unaired interviews with filmmaker Robert Gardner, Dayton, Ohio, October 1997.

19 Coca-Cola syrup and fresh fruit: Eck, p. 29.

19 sightseeing flights up the coastline: John McCollom, unaired interviews with filmmaker Robert Gardner, Dayton, Ohio, October 1997.

Chapter 3: The Hidden Valley of Shangri-La

20 a more direct, low-altitude pass: Elsmore, *National Geographic*, p. 671. Also, unaired interviews with John McCollom, conducted by documentary filmmaker Robert Gardner, Dayton, Ohio, October 1997.

20 'Colonel, if we slip ...': Elsmore, *National Geographic*, p. 671.

21 a mostly flat, verdant valley: Major Myron J. Grimes (retired), interview on 31 August 2009.

21 stamped the area 'unknown' or 'unexplored': Ozzie St George, 'Rescue From Shangri-La', *Yank: The Army Weekly*, 17 August 1945, p. 6. Also, Gordon L. Rottman, *World War II Pacific Island Guide: A Geo-Military Study* (Westport, CT: Greenwood Press, 2001), p. 148.

21 'estimated 14,000-foot peak': Ozzie St George, 'Rescue From Shangri-La', *Yank: The Army Weekly*, 17 August 1945, p. 6.

21 a mountain might be hiding inside: Elsmore, *National Geographic*, p. 671. (At one point Elsmore writes of a cloud bank, 'We could see the occasional rift, but we knew that peaks lurked in its innocent white walls.')

21 a flying instructor during the First World War: 'Ray Elsmore, 66, Helped M'Arthur', *New York Times*, 19 February 1957, p. 31.

21 MacArthur's evacuation flight: 'Ray Elsmore, 66, Helped M'Arthur', *New York Times*, 19 February 1957, p. 31.

22 the Southwest Pacific: Rottman, pp. 146–152.

22 prepared to veer up and away: Major Myron J. Grimes (retired), interview on 31 August 2009.

23 'Push on through': Elsmore, *National Geographic*, p. 673.

23 'a riot of dazzling color': Ibid, p. 674.

23 'Crops were in full growth ...': Elsmore, *National Geographic*, p. 674.

24 'diving into the drainage ditches': Ibid.

25 'one of the most impressive sights': Ibid, p. 676.

26 'a pilot unfamiliar with this canyon': Colonel Ray T. Elsmore, secret letter (since unclassified) to General George C. Kenney, dated 29 May 1944, titled 'Route Survey'. Located at MacArthur Memorial Archives, Norfolk, Va.

26 'anxious to avoid incidents and bloodshed': Elsmore, *National Geographic*, p. 677.

26 models of sinewy manhood: 'The Hidden Valley', *Pulse: A 27th General Hospital Publication*, Vol. 3, No. 46, 8 July 1945, Supplement, p. 1. The publication was a hospital bulletin saved by Capt. Earl Walter. Also, Mary L. Eck, 'Saga of a Sad Sack', self-published pamphlet recounting military life in New Guinea and elsewhere, 1979.

26 the size of ponies: Lieutenant William Jeff Gatling Jr, 'Shangri-La' letter home to his family, published in the *Arkansas Gazette*, 20 May 1945, no page given. Found in the Ruth Coster Collection at the University of Central Arkansas.

27 had ever set foot in the valley: Elsmore, *National Geographic*, p. 677.

27 'I suppose I would have regretted it ...': Gatling, 'Shangri-La' letter, 20 May 1945.

28 His father: Jack Lait was the best man at George Lait's wedding: Unbylined story, 'George Lait Weds; War Correspondent Takes Jane

Peck Harrington as Bride', *New York Times*, 8 September 1945, p. 18. Also, see unbylined obituary, 'Jack Lait, 71, Dies; Editor of Mirror', *New York Times*, 2 April 1954, p. 27. Also, 'The Press: Blue Bloomers and Burning Bodies', *Time magazine*, 26 July 1948.

28 a correspondent for the International News Service: Ibid.

28 knocked out cold: Unbylined International News Service story, 'Newsman Kayoed In London Raid', published in *St Petersburg Times*, 20 April 1941, p. 9.

28 blown out of a car seat: Ernie Pyle, column called 'Rambling Reporter', published in the *Pittsburgh Press*, 27 March 1941, p. 21.

29 'As a war correspondent': Inez Robb, column called 'Robb's Corner', published in the *Reading Eagle*, 29 January 1958, p. 14. It's fitting that Robb wrote this tribute to George Lait, who helped to name the valley Shangri-La. When Margaret Hastings turned her diary into an eighteen-part newspaper series in 1945, Robb was brought on as a professional writer to help.

29 a dispatch rich in description: Donald Collier, 'U.S. Fliers in New Guinea Discover a Shangri-La', *Chicago Natural History Museum Bulletin*, Nos 3–4, March–April 1945, quoting a story by George Lait 'published in a New Guinea news sheet of the *Army*'. Retrieved 30 August 2009, at www.archive.org/stream/bulletin16chic/bulletin16chic_djvu.txt.

29 Patterson's story: Harry E. Patterson, 'Real Shangri-La in New Guinea', *Milwaukee Journal*, 11 March 1945, p. 2.

30 disappointed by the name 'Hidden Valley': Elsmore, *National Geographic*, p. 680.

31 'matched a whole army': James Hilton, *Lost Horizon* (New York: Pocket Books, 1933, 1936, renewed 1960), p. 157.

31 'He foresaw a time ...': Hilton, *Lost Horizon*, p. 158.

31 a 1937 speech: President Franklin D. Roosevelt's 'Quarantine the Aggressors Speech', delivered in Chicago on 5 October 1937. Roosevelt paraphrased slightly, changing the tense from 'would' to 'will'. The result was to make the prediction even more ominous. Text located at http://fletcher.tufts.edu/multi/texts/historical/quarantine.txt, retrieved 1 September 2009.

Chapter 4: Gremlin Special

32 comically ornate certificate: Membership in the 'Shangri-La Society' was extended to survivors of the 13 May 1945 crash and their rescuers. Margaret Hastings' was found at TCHS, and John McCollom and C. Earl Walter kept theirs in their personal scrapbooks. Ken Decker's was not located.

32 'leading authority on the valley': Walter Simmons, 'Glider Takes Six More Out of Shangri-La', *Chicago Tribune*, 1 July 1945, p. 3.

33 'a case of "head you lose"': Ray Zeman, 'Pilot Finds Shangri-La', *Los Angeles Times*, 16 October 1944, p. A1.

33 'fully equipped with bargaining trinkets': Harold Streeter, 'Pacific Reporter: Shangri-La', Associated Press story published in *Hartford Courant*, 13 May 1945, p. 12.

33 'navigational training': MACR, p. 1.

33 Prossen's first trip to Shangri-La: John McCollom, unaired interviews conducted by documentary filmmaker Robert Gardner, Dayton, Ohio, October 1997.

33 a date after work: Margaret Hastings, SLD, Part One. In her published diary, Margaret says she had been informed of the flight a day earlier by Colonel Prossen, but in her sworn statement after the crash, dated 29 June 1945, in the MACR, she said she was invited that morning.
33 desperate to visit Shangri-La: Margaret Hastings, SLD, Part Two.
33 she leapt at Prossen's offer: Prossen issued the invitation through the chain of command, so it was delivered by Lieutenant Margaret V. Bogle, according to Margaret Hastings' sworn statement, dated 29 June 1945, in the MACR.
34 prizes at local dog shows: Margaret Hastings, SLD, Part Two.
34 savouring each cold spoonful: Margaret Hastings, SLD, Part Two.
35 leather and hydraulic fluid: Details of the C-47 from www.boeing.com/history/mdc/skytrain.htm, retrieved 5 September 2009. Also, www.warbirdalley.com/c47.htm.
35 built at a cost of $269,276: Copy of Aircraft Record Card #41-23952, from US Air Force Historical Division, Research Studies Institute, Maxwell Air Force Base, Alabama.
35 *Merle* or *Gremlin Special*: The MACR lists *Merle* as the nickname, but *Gremlin Special* is cited in an account of the crash in Michael John Clarinbould's *The Forgotten Fifth: A Photographic Chronology of the U.S. Fifth Air Force in World War II* (Hyde Park, NY: Balus Design, 2007), pp. 103–104.
35 *The Gremlins*: Roald Dahl, *The Gremlins* (Milwaukie, Oregon: Dark Horse, 2006 reprint edition).
36 'Let the girls in first': Margaret Hastings, SLD, Part Two.
36 caught Laura's eye and winked: Margaret Hastings, SLD, Part Two.
37 spent time in a German prisoner-of-war camp: Background information on Eleanor Hanna from her sister, Roberta (Hanna) Koons, interview on 11 September 2009.
37 singing wherever she went: Margaret Hastings, SLD, Parts Two and Four.
37 'Isn't this fun!': Ibid, Part Two.
37 bracelet made from Chinese coins: Eleanor Hanna's US Army Individual Deceased Personnel File contains a Xerox image of part of the bracelet, which was found in the grave she shared with Laura Besley. At first it wasn't clear to whom it belonged, but a 14 May 1959 letter in the file from her father to the Army Quartermaster General makes a claim on the bracelet and refers to the two others she owned just like it.
37 daughter of a newspaper publisher: Unbylined story, 'Pfc. Gillis from East Orange', *New York Times*, 9 June 1945, p. 2. Although the *Times* said she was from New Jersey, the MACR lists a hometown of Los Angeles.
37 fleeing from Spain with her mother: Ibid.
37 grieving the death of her fiancé: Unbylined story from the Associated Press, 'Airfield is Built to Rescue a Wac And 2 Men in New Guinea', *New York Times*, 9 June 1945, p. 1.
37 relieve her loneliness: Information about WACs Helen Kent and Ruth Coster from interviews with Dona Cruse, 11 August 2009, and 4 September 2009. Dona is the daughter of Ruth, who died in 2003.
37 tell her what it was like: Ibid.
37 Four more WACs: World War II enlistment records, from www.ancestry.com, retrieved 1–3 November 2009.

38 trailed by his co-pilot: Background on George H. Nicholson from MACR. Also, 1920 and 1930 US Federal Census, retrieved at www.ancestry.com, 11 September 2009. Also, interviews with Maryrose Condon, a first cousin of Major Nicholson, and John and Michael McCarthy, first cousins once removed, on 13 September 2009.

38 graduated from Boston College then received master's degrees: Interviews with Maryrose Condon and John McCarthy, 13 September 2009. Also, 'Major Geo H. Nicholson Killed in Plane Crash', *Malden (Mass.) Evening News*, 31 May 1945, p. 1, and 'Maj. George H. Nicholson, Killed in Pacific Plane Crash', undated newspaper clipping saved by Nicholson's family.

39 served under Lord Mountbatten: 'Major Geo H. Nicholson Killed in Plane Crash', *Malden (Mass.) Evening News*, 31 May 1945, p. 1.

39 skipped a 'Victory in Europe' party: Letter from Alice K. Nicholson Cadley to friends and family, dated 'Mother's Day 1995', in which she marked the fiftieth anniversary of the crash by distributing copies of Nicholson's letter.

39 a vivid, fifteen-page narrative: Letter from George H. Nicholson to his wife, Alice K. Nicholson (later Cadley), dated 9 May 1945, provided by his cousin Maryrose Condon.

41 three other crew members: MACR, p. 3, crew list.

41 a month earlier: Unbylined, undated newspaper clipping, 'Melvin Mollberg Killed In Plane Crash in the Pacific', provided by Melvyn Lutgring.

41 Corporal James Lutgring: Interview with Melvyn Lutgring, 5 January 2010. Lutgring was named for Melvin Mollberg, despite the different spelling of their first names.

43 asked her on a date: Margaret Hastings, SLD, Part Two.

44 'The Inseparables': Interview with Betty McCollom, widow of John McCollom, 1 August 2009. Also, information about John and Robert McCollom from Marjorie Lundberg, 'Baby Girl's Father Killed, But Uncle is Dad's Replica', *St Paul Dispatch*, 8 June 1945, no page listed, from John McCollom's personal scrapbook.

44 Eagle Scouts together: John S. McCollom's obituary, published in the *Dayton Daily News,* 21 August 2001, p. 10, provided by Betty McCollom.

44 a wedding photo: Undated story and photographs published in the *St Paul Dispatch*, headlined 'Tragic Shangri-La Figures and Kin', found in John McCollom's personal scrapbook.

45 'Mind if I share this window ...': Margaret Hastings, SLD, Part Two. McCollom's location is confirmed in his sworn statement, dated 29 June 1945, in MACR.

Chapter 5: Eureka!

46 twisted in their seats for a look: Margaret Hastings, SLD, Part Three.

46 'Oh, what is so rare ...': Ibid.

46 'The Vision of Sir Launfal': The famous line from Lowell's 1848 poem is, 'And what is so rare as a day in June?'

47 a heading of 224 degrees: John McCollom, MACR, sworn statement, p. 1.

49 standing in the narrow radio compartment: Ibid.

49 Major Nicholson was alone at the controls: Ibid.

49 an altitude of about 300 metres: Ibid.
49 120 metres: Margaret Hastings, SLD, Part Three.
49 'Eureka!': Ibid.
49 'I want to come again': Ibid.
50 'Give her the gun and let's get out of here': Ibid.
50 thought he was joking: Ibid. Margaret wrote, 'I thought he was joking. So did everyone else.'
50 applying full power to climb: John McCollom, MACR, sworn statement, p. 1.
50 learned to fly only three years earlier: 'Maj. George H. Nicholson Killed In Pacific Plane Crash', undated newspaper clipping saved by Nicholson's family.
51 Turbulent air was common: the MACR does not make an official determination whether the cause of the crash was pilot error, a sudden downdraught or a combination of factors.
51 high-altitude valleys ... especially treacherous: Colonel Edward T. Imparato, *Rescue from Shangri-La* (Paducah, KY: Tuner Publishing, 1997), p. 170. Imparato knew the terrain from flying over it.
51 'a sudden down-draft of air current': Declassified document titled 'Historical Data Regarding the Loss of a FEASC C-47 and the Rescue of Survivors of the Crash', prepared by the US Air Force Historical Division, Research Studies Institute, Maxwell Air Force Base, Alabama, dated 17 November 1952.
52 'flat on the deck': Margaret Hastings, SLD, Part Three.
52 'This is going to be darn close, but I think we can get over it': John McCollom, MACR, sworn statement, p.1.
52 The cabin crumpled forward: This account of the crash is taken from the sworn MACR statements of John McCollom and Margaret Hastings, as well as photographs of the wreckage provided to the author by Eugene M. Hoops. At the end of World War II, Hoops was part of an American military unit sent from the Philippines to New Guinea to clean up the base at Hollandia and to destroy remaining files. Upon opening a metal file drawer, he discovered a set of photographs from the 13 May 1945 crash and its aftermath. Despite orders to destroy the material, Hoops believed the photos might be significant and he decided to preserve them for history.
53 turning somersaults as he fell: John McCollom, MACR, sworn statement, p. 1.
53 momentarily blacked out: John McCollom, unaired interviews conducted by documentary filmmaker Robert Gardner, Dayton, Ohio, October 1997.
53 flattened down like a tin can: Ibid.
53 'all by myself on a Sunday afternoon': Ibid.
53 spoiled by a plane crash: Margaret Hastings, SLD, Part Three. She writes that she was 'indignant because this thing had happened to me!'
54 thick arms around her: Ibid.
54 'My God! Hastings!': Ibid.
54 McCollom doubted it would explode: John McCollom, unaired interviews conducted by documentary filmmaker Robert Gardner, Dayton, Ohio, October 1997.
54 'Give me your hand!': Margaret Hastings, SLD, Part Three.
55 Her hair still crackled with burning embers: John McCollom, MACR, sworn statement, p 2.

55 a bloody gash: Decker details his injuries in his MACR sworn statement, p. 2. Also, Margaret Hastings, SLD, Part Four and John McCollom, MACR, sworn statement, p. 2.
55 'My God, Decker, where did you come from?': Margaret Hastings, SLD, Part Four.
55 crawled out from under the plane: Kenneth Decker, MACR, sworn statement, p. 1.
55 catapulted through the cockpit and out through the windshield: John McCollom, unaired interviews conducted by documentary filmmaker Robert Gardner, Dayton, Ohio, October 1997.
55 'Helluva way to spend your birthday': Ibid.
56 'Hastings, can't you do something for these girls?': Margaret Hastings, SLD, Part Four.
56 seared off all Eleanor's clothes: John McCollom, unaired interview with filmmaker Robert Gardner, Dayton, Ohio, October 1997.
56 'Let's sing': Margaret Hastings, SLD, Part Four.
56 only superficial burns: Ibid.
57 McCollom invited him to join in the fun: John McCollom, unaired interview with filmmaker Robert Gardner, Dayton, Ohio, October 1997.
57 tangled in the roots of a tree: John McCollom, MACR, sworn statement, p 2.
57 They left Good's body where it fell: Photograph of the wreckage, courtesy of Eugene M. Hoops.
59 wedding ring: Letter to Mrs Cecelia A. McCollom from Lt Col Donald Wardle, chief of the Army Disposition Branch, Memorial Division, dated 13 May 1959. Also, letter to Louis Landau, father of Private Mary Landau, from Lt Col Donald L. Wardle, dated 1 May 1959, about the recovery of remains and personal items from the crash site. Contained in Mary Landau's Individual Deceased Personnel File, provided by the US Army under a Freedom of Information Act request.

Chapter 6: Charms

60 'surrounded by fire if we don't': Margaret Hastings, SLD, Part Four.
60 'You're all right': Ibid.
61 'Everything in the jungle had tentacles': Ibid, Part Six.
62 pulled off her khaki shirt: Ibid, Part Four.
62 arms draped over his shoulders: John McCollom, unaired interview with filmmaker Robert Gardner, Dayton, Ohio, October 1997.
62 still dangled from her burned wrist: Eleanor Hanna's IDPF notes that the bracelet was found in the grave she shared with Laura Besley, which means it remained in her possession after the crash. She had no clothes, and therefore no pockets, so it stands to reason the bracelet remained on her wrist.
62 a broken rib: John McCollom, unaired interview with filmmaker Robert Gardner, Dayton, Ohio, October 1997.
63 help McCollom with Eleanor Hanna: Ibid, also MACR, sworn statements of Kenneth Decker, p. 1, and John McCollom, p. 2.
63 compounding their misery: Margaret Hastings, SLD, Part Four. She writes: 'Now the daily and eternal rain of New Guinea began to fall. Soaked clothing was added to our miseries.'
63 .45 calibre pistol: John McCollom, MACR, sworn statement, p. 2.

63 Cracker Jack-sized boxes of 'K' rations: Jerold E. Brown, *Historical Dictionary of the U.S. Army* (Westport, CT: Greenwood Press, 2001), p. 270.
64 burn until the middle of the next day: John McCollom, MACR, sworn statement, p. 3.
64 no one would have survived: John McCollom, unaired interview with Robert Gardner, Dayton, Ohio, October 1997.
64 could not find any flares: The survivors gave separate accounts of the contents of the life rafts. Margaret Hastings, in SLD, Part Four, said the kit contained flares, but in his sworn statement in the MACR, John McCollom states: 'I looked all over the life raft equipment, but I never could find any flares.' He later writes about trying to use Margaret's mirror to signal planes, adding veracity to his account.
65 'Let's sing': Margaret Hastings, SLD, Part Four.
65 the plane was still aflame: John McCollom, unaired interview with Robert Gardner, Dayton, Ohio, October 1997.
65 might be lightning: Colonel Edward T. Imparato, *Rescue from Shangri-La*, p. 184.
65 walking the 240 kilometres: Sergeant Ozzie St George, 'Hidden Valley', *Yank: The Army Weekly*, 10 Aug. 1945, Far East Edition, Vol. 3, No. 2, pp. 6–8.
65 yaps and barks of wild dogs: John McCollom, unaired interview with Robert Gardner, Dayton, Ohio, October 1997.
65 'Eleanor's dead': Margaret Hastings describes finding Eleanor Hanna dead in SLD, Part Four, while in his sworn statement in the MACR, John McCollom says only: 'I guess that Private Hanna died about 8 o'clock that night,' referring to the previous night.
66 'I can't stop shaking': Margaret Hastings, SLD, Part Five.
66 seventeen cans of water: Ibid. McCollom's MACR statement mentions the cots, but the more complete inventory is in Margaret's diary.
66 black electrical tape and a pair of pliers: Decker, MACR sworn statement, p. 1.
67 five-pointed white star: Photos of the downed C-47, taken shortly after the crash, provided by Dona Cruse.
67 impossible to see except from a short distance: Photograph of the wreckage, courtesy of Eugene M. Hoops.
67 no radio communication was exchanged: MACR, p. 1.
68 worked it furiously to flash snatches of sunlight: John McCollom, MACR sworn statement, p. 3. Also, Margaret Hastings, SLD, Part Five, and John McCollom, unaired interview with Robert Gardner, Dayton, Ohio, October 1997.
68 'Don't worry': John McCollom, unaired interview with Robert Gardner, Seattle, 13 May 1998.
68 at peace with her mother's death: Margaret Hastings, SLD, Part Five.
68 Margaret's middle name: Interview with Rita Callahan, 3 January 2010.
68 In a school essay: Undated college paper written by Margaret Hastings, titled 'A Tribute To Mother', found in correspondence file at TCHS.
69 hugging tightly to keep from falling off: Margaret Hastings, SLD, Ibid.
69 'Everyone else is dead and we're very lonely, aren't we?': Ibid.
70 'Laura has died!': Margaret Hastings, SLD, Part Five.

70 'Don't be a dope, Hastings': Ibid.
70 'Now the shoes belong to me': Ibid.
72 hated the nickname: Margaret Hastings, SLD, Part Fifteen.
72 lit a cigarette and handed it to her: Ibid, Part Five.
72 'No night will ever again be as long': Ibid.

Chapter 7: Tarzan

73 a course they could follow: John McCollom, MACR sworn statement, p. 3. Also, John McCollom, unaired interview with Robert Gardner, Dayton, Ohio, October 1997.
74 an officer wrote back: Susan Sheehan, *A Missing Plane: The Dramatic Tragedy and Triumph of a Lost and Forgotten World War II Bomber* (New York: Berkeley Books, 1986), p. 210.
74 more missing planes than any country on earth: Sheehan, p. 9. Sheehan focused her work on the eastern half of the island, but in the estimation of Justin Taylan of Pacific Wrecks, this was true for all of New Guinea.
74 *Flying Dutchman*: This account of the 10 November 1942 crash and cargo door diary is based on: Claringbould, p. 39. Also, 'Agony of the Flying Dutchman', at www.aerothentic.com/historical/Unusual_Stories/C47FlyingDutchman.htm, retrieved 23 August and 14 September 2009, and 'C-47A Flying Dutchman', at www.pacificwrecks.com, retrieved 23 August 2009.
75 'so light he "felt like a baby"': 'Agony of the Flying Dutchman,' at www.aerothentic.com/historical/Unusual_Stories/C47FlyingDutchman.htm, retrieved 23 August 2009.
77 two tins of water and a few cellophane-wrapped sweets: Margaret Hastings, SLD, Part Five. Margaret Hastings' account is the primary source of the trio of survivors' journey through the jungle to the clearing. McCollom corroborated significant parts and added important details in his October 1997 interview with Robert Gardner, and also in newspaper interviews he gave over the years.
77 Later, writing in her diary: Ibid.
77 'Let's go': Ibid.
78 crawling on their hands and knees: Jack Jones, 'Survivor Recalls Crash, 47 Days in Wild Jungle', *Dayton Daily Camera*, 10 June 1959, p. 20.
78 'a three-inch "feather" bob': Margaret Hastings, SLD, Part Five.
79 never complained: John McCollom, unaired interview with Robert Gardner in Dayton, Ohio, October 1997.
79 'It is foolish to think that we could have cut our way out': Margaret Hastings, SLD, Part Six.
79 they intended to fill their stomachs: Ibid.
80 returned with a new idea: Ibid.
81 'Damned if I ever thought I'd understudy Johnny Weissmuller': Ibid.
81 'the old mother hen instinct': Remarks of Colonel Jerry Felmley at John McCollom's retirement dinner, 23 September 1980, Wright Patterson Air Force Base Officers' Club. Felmley interviewed Decker for the occasion.
82 a fresh human footprint: John McCollom, unaired interview with Robert Gardner in Dayton, Ohio, October 1997.
82 strange barking sounds: Sergeant Ozzie St George, 'Rescue From Shangri-La', *Yank: The Army Weekly*, 17 August 1945, p. 6.

Chapter 8: Gentleman Explorer

83 brusque manner: Roger A. Morse, 'Richard Archbold and the Archbold Biological Station' (Gainesville, FL: University Press of Florida, 2000), p. 61.

84 'Why don't you collect mammals?': Ibid, p. 4.

84 learned from his many mistakes: Ibid, p. 4. Archbold's autobiographical notes indicate that, in Morse's words, he 'botched the job'.

84 his grandfather had been a major benefactor: Ibid, p. 9.

84 put his inheritance to work: Ibid, pp. 11–14.

85 'a comprehensive biological survey of the island': Richard Archbold, A.L. Rand, and L.J. Brass, 'Results of the Archbold Expeditions, No. 41', *Bulletin of the American Museum of Natural History*, Vol. LXXIX, Art. III, 26 June 1942, p. 201.

85 frustrated by logistical challenges: Morse, p. 15.

85 largest privately owned plane in the world: Ibid, p. 23. The plane is sometimes called the *Guba II,* because it was the successor to a similar flying boat that Archbold sold to the Soviet Union, with US permission, to help the Russians search for a plane that crashed while trying to fly over the North Pole. Archbold called the second plane simply the *Guba* in his accounts in the *New York Times* and elsewhere.

86 a range exceeding 6500 kilometres: Richard Archbold, 'Unknown New Guinea', *National Geographic Magazine*, Vol. LXXIX, No. 3, p. 315.

87 nearly two hundred people: Ibid.

87 'convict carriers': Morse, p. 25. Also, Susan Meiselas, *Encounters with the Dani: Stories from the Baliem Valley* (New York: Steidl/International Center for Photography, 2003), p. 8.

87 collecting mammals, birds, plants and insects: A.L. Rand, 'The Snow Mountains – New Guinea Group in the American Museum of Natural History', *Scientific Monthly*, Vol. 52, No. 4, April 1941, pp. 380–382. Also, Richard Archbold, 'Expedition Finds Rats 3 Feet Long and Kangaroos That Climb Trees', *New York Times*, 1 January 1939, p. 18.

88 'a pleasant surprise': Richard Archbold, A.L. Rand, and L.J. Brass, 'Results of the Archbold Expeditions, No. 41', *Bulletin of the American Museum of Natural History*, Vol. LXXIX, Art. III, 26 June 1942, p. 211.

88 called it a *Groote Vallei*: L.J. Brass, 'Stone Age Agriculture in New Guinea', *Geographical Review*, Vol. 31, No. 4, October 1941, p. 556.

88 expeditions in 1907, the early 1920s, and 1926: H. Myron Bromley, *The Phonology of Lower Grand Valley Dani*, a publication commissioned and financed by the Government of Netherlands New Guinea, 1961, pp. 1–2.

88 the light-skinned men, who must really be ghosts: Denise O'Brien, 'The Economics of Dani Marriage: An Analysis of Marriage Payments in a Highland New Guinea Society', Dissertation Presented to the Faculty of the Graduate School of Yale University in Candidacy for the Degree of Doctor of Philosophy, pp. 7–8.

89 'the last time in the history of our planet': Tim Flannery, *Throwim Way Leg*, p. 4.

89 'Forestation is so heavy ...': Editor's note attached to Richard Archbold, 'Unknown New Guinea', *National Geographic Magazine*, Vol. LXXIX, No. 3, p. 318.
90 rough weather prevented him from changing course: L.J. Brass, 'Stone Age Agriculture in New Guinea', *Geographical Review*, Vol. 31, No. 4, October 1941, p. 556.
90 L.J. Brass described what they saw: Ibid, p. 557.
91 farm country ... central Europe: Richard Archbold, 'Unknown New Guinea', p. 316.
91 'One was evidently a man of some importance': Ibid, p. 321.
91 started their treks at opposite ends of the valley: Ibid, p. 321.
92 the natives practised cannibalism: Archbold, Rand, and Brass, 'Results of the Archbold Expeditions, No. 41', p. 253.
92 would discourage the explorers from travelling to the next village: Archbold, 'Unknown New Guinea', p. 324.
92 tribesmen 'in large numbers': Susan Meiselas, *Encounters with the Dani*, p. 12. The remainder of the Van Arcken reports from 9 and 10 August 1938, also come from Meiselas, pp. 12–15. In her translation, she uses 'Papuan' rather than 'native'.
93 'Here the natives seemed to take our party for granted': Richard Archbold, 'Unknown New Guinea', p. 336.
93 the most awful moment: The details of this incident were explored vividly by Susan Meiselas in her insightful book. Meiselas reprints original copies of Van Arcken's patrol reports and the map he drew of the valley, including his obfuscating label showing the location where 'one Papuan died due to a lance attack'. Meiselas declares, 'The colonial government forbade Archbold from discussing the August 10 shooting in exchange for Archbold's continued access to the region.' Credibility for that claim is enhanced knowledge that colonial rule was already under challenge, as well as by a brief item in the *New York Times* on 8 March 1940, reporting that Archbold had been appointed 'Officer of the Order of Orange Nassau' by Dutch Queen Wilhelmina.
93 significance would be overlooked: Richard Archbold, A.L. Rand, and L.J. Brass, 'Results of the Archbold Expeditions, No. 41', *Bulletin of the American Museum of Natural History*, Vol. LXXIX, Art. III, 26 June 1942. Roughly six of the report's ninety-one pages are devoted to Teerink's and Van Arcken's journeys, based on their diaries.
94 'where more than a show of force was necessary': Ibid, p. 219.
94 'one native died due to a lance attack': Meiselas, p. 15.
94 'reception the natives will extend is unpredictable': Archbold, Rand, and Brass, 'Results of the Archbold Expeditions, No. 41', p. 205.

Chapter 9: Guilt and Gangrene

96 'this aching, miserable night': Margaret Hastings, SLD, Part Seven.
96 'a sickening sight': Ibid.
96 'evil-smelling running sores: Ibid, Part Ten.
97 She walked in agony: Ibid, Part Seven, in which she wrote: 'I forced myself to walk back and forth ... it was agony.'
97 burns on the left side of her face: Ibid, Part Nine.
98 the only one left alive: Pat Pond, 'Reunion: Thirty Years After', *Women's Army Corps Journal*, October–December 1974, Vol. 5, No. 5, p. 19.

98 'as much for myself as for them': Undated John McCollom letter to Colonel Edward T. Imparato, reprinted in *Rescue from Shangri-La*, p. 160.

98 walk all the way to the ocean: Joint interview of John McCollom and C. Earl Walter, conducted and taped by Robert Gardner but never aired, Seattle, 13 May 1998. McCollom says, 'I never even doubted that even if they didn't find me, that I was going to make it – if I had to walk to the ocean.'

98 separated the Charms by color: Sergeant Ozzie St George, 'Rescue From Shangri-La', *Yank: The Army Weekly*, 17 August 1945, p. 6.

99 'delicious battery acid': Margaret Hastings, SLD, Part Seven.

99 'we're going to starve to death': Ibid.

100 'I doubted him for a moment': Ibid.

100 Several hundred US women had already died: Information on the deaths of women in World War II was provided by Retired Colonel Pat Jernigan, who has done notable work on the history of women in the military, and also by http://www.nooniefortin.com/earlierwars.htm, retrieved 2 October 2009.

101 six nurses killed by German bombing and strafing: Ibid.

101 'a handful of icicles': The story of the homemade WAC flag comes from Retired Colonel Pat Jernigan and also from Mary L. Eck, 'Saga of a Sad Sack', a self-published pamphlet by a former WAC who served in New Guinea, pp. 29–30. Also, letter titled 'I Am Proud', by WAC Margaret Durocher, in Margaret Hastings' correspondence file at TCHS.

102 calls were made to Allied landing strips: US Army document, titled Report of Circumstances Surrounding Flight and Search for C-47 Aircraft Number 41-23952, from MACR, contained in Individual Deceased Personnel Files of the crew and passengers who died.

102 'a forced landing': Ibid.

102 twenty-four planes took part: Ibid.

102 A volunteer crew member: Interview with Melvyn Lutgring on 5 January 2010.

102 'this is it': Margaret Hastings, SLD, Part Seven.

103 flew away without spotting them: John McCollom, MACR sworn statement, p. 4. In her diary, Margaret Hastings does not record the first plane they saw at the clearing. Decker's MACR statement is vague, but he seems to agree with McCollom by writing that they reached the clearing around 11 a.m. and 'we were spotted by a plane that same noon'.

103 'Get out the tarps!': Margaret Hastings, SLD, Part Seven.

103 brought along an unusual passenger: Ibid, Part Thirteen.

104 'They see us by now': Ibid, Part Seven. Margaret Hastings' SLD is the source of the entire dialogue following their discovery by Captain Baker in the B-17.

104 'a limitless sea of green': Sheehan, p. 214.

104 saved them in the middle of a jungle: 'End of Adventure is Only Beginning, McCollom Finds', undated story in Trenton, Missouri, newspaper, from John McCollom's personal scrapbook.

104 they were not alone: Interview with Helenma Wandik, 1 February 2010.

105 drop two life rafts: Russell Brines, 'Shangri-La On New Guinea', Associated Press story datelined Manila, 8 June 1945, from Earl Walter's personal scrapbook. Also, Sergeant Ozzie St George,

'Rescue From Shangri-La', *Yank: The Army Weekly*, 17 August 1945, p. 6.
105 a message to the Sentani Airstrip: Ibid. Also, MACR, p. 4.
105 'back in Hollandia by Sunday': Margaret Hastings, SLD, Part Seven.
105 'the damn hard candy': Ibid.
106 a faraway pack of dogs: John McCollom, unaired interview with filmmaker Robert Gardner, Dayton, Ohio, October 1997.
106 'Do you hear something funny?': Margaret Hastings, SLD, Part Seven.
107 the noise that native children made: Ibid.
107 'a tasty dinner was waiting in the camote patch': Ibid.
107 dozens of nearly naked black men: John McCollom, unaired interview with filmmaker Robert Gardner, Dayton, Ohio, October 1997. In his account, McCollom places the number of natives at 'about forty'. In SLD Part Eight, Margaret Hastings writes there were 'about a hundred men'.

Chapter 10: Earl Walter, Junior and Senior

109 'enough equipment to stock a small country store': Sergeant Ozzie St George, 'Rescue From Shangri-La', *Yank: The Army Weekly*, 17 August 1945, p. 6.
109 outfitting an overland trek: Sergeant Ozzie St George, 'Rescue From Shangri-La', *Yank: The Army Weekly*, 17 August 1945, p. 6. Also, Gerard M. Devlin, *Silent Wings: The Saga of the U.S. Army and Marine Combat Glider Pilots During World War II* (New York: St. Martin's Press, 1985), p. 354.
110 the 503rd recaptured the island of Corregidor: Gordon L. Rottman, *World War II Pacific Island Guide* (Westport, CT: Greenwood Press, 2002), p. 305.
111 the 511th had carried out a lightning raid: Larry Alexander, *Shadows in the Jungle: The Alamo Scouts Behind Enemy Lines in World War II* (New York: NAL Caliber, 2009), p. 261.
111 taught biology and chaired the science department: Unbylined story, 'Col. Babcock Will Head Black-Foxe', *Los Angeles Times*, 20 May 1962, p. H3.
113 'We had been hiking all day': C. Earl Walter Jr interview, 7 July 2009.
113 'old enough to wonder about women': Ibid.
113 'that might straighten me out': C. Earl Walter Jr interview, 7 July 2009.
114 Buster Keaton, Bing Crosby, Bette Davis, and Charlie Chaplin: Steven Mikulan, 'Men of the Old School', *LA Weekly*, 17 May 2001.
114 'sleep-away school for the sons of Hollywood rich people': Valerie J. Nelson, 'Sydney Chaplin dies at 82; stage actor and son of Charlie Chaplin', *Los Angeles Times*, 6 March 2009, p. A30.
114 'more money than I knew what to do with': C. Earl Walter Jr interview, 7 July 2009.
115 'no interest in anybody else': Ibid.
116 a fellow guerrilla leader: John Keats, *They Fought Alone* (New York: Pocket Books, 1965), pp. 170–171. The book focuses on Colonel Wendell Fertig and is based on his recollections, diaries and reports. Forty years after its publication, in January 2003, the accuracy of the

book, including the account involving C. Earl Walter Sr, was challenged in the *Bulletin of the American Historical Collection*, Vol. 31, No. 1 (123), by Clyde Childress, a retired Army officer. Retrieved on 25 October, 2009, at http://ahcf.virtual-asia.com/html/pdf/123_Wendell_Fertig_s.pdf.

116 Elizalde … sent word to the younger Walter: Document dated 15 July 1944, titled 'Summary of Interview with Lt. Col. L.E. Parks, For Commander Vining, Per Cecil E. Walter Jr, 1st. Lt., Inf., C-1314597'. Located at MacArthur Memorial Archives, Norfolk, Va.

116 'make me proud of his work': Ibid.

117 the 5217th Reconnaissance Battalion: Rottman, p. 39.

118 'do my bit in their extermination': Document dated 15 July 1944, titled 'Summary of Interview with Lt. Col. L.E. Parks, For Commander Vining, Per Cecil E. Walter Jr, 1st. Lt., Inf., C-1314597'. Located in Walter's personnel file at MacArthur Memorial Archives, Norfolk, Va.

118 'my liking for combat': Ibid.

Chapter 11: Uwambo

121 a single word that could describe both time and place: Douglas Hayward, 'Time and Society in Dani Culture', *Irian: Bulletin of Irian Jaya Development*, June and October 1983, Vol. XI, No. 2–3, pp. 31–32.

121 terms for only two [colours]: Eleanor R. Heider, 'Probabilities, Sampling, and Ethnographic Method: The Case of Dani Colour Names', *Man*, New Series, Vol. 7, No. 3 (Sep., 1972), pp. 448–466.

121 ignored the canopy of stars: Hayward, p. 35.

121 'Let me eat your faeces': Karl G. Heider, *Grand Valley Dani: Peaceful Warriors*, p. 9.

121 natives … organized themselves: Ibid, pp. 67–69.

122 Their enemies were *dili*: Ibid, pp. 94–95.

123 'We people of the Baliem': H.L. Peters, 'Some Observations of the Social and Religious Life of a Dani Group', *Irian: Bulletin of Irian Jaya Development*, June 1974, Vol. IV, No. 2, p. 76.

123 a moral obligation: Douglas Hayward, *Dani of Irian Jaya Before and After Conversation* (Sentani, Indonesia: Regions Press, 1980), p. 102. See also Peters, p. 77.

123 'If there is no war, we will die': Peters, p. 76.

123 different parts of speech: Ibid, p. 77.

124 ghosts, called *mogat*: K. Heider, p. xi.

124 flesh of their enemies: Interview with Yali elder Helenma Wandik, 1 February 2010. Also, see Russell T. Hitt, *Cannibal Valley: The heroic struggle for Christ in savage New Guinea – the most perilous mission frontier in the world* (New York: Harper & Row, 1962), pp. 120–129.

125 hoot of a cuckoo dove: K. Heider, p. 101.

125 hurled insults across the front lines: K. Heider, p. 99.

125 gained social standing: Peters, p. 78.

125 abstained from sex for up to five years: K. Heider, p. 22. See also Karl G. Heider, 'Dani Sexuality: A Low Energy System', *Man*, New Series, Vol. 11, No. 2 (June 1976), pp. 188–201.

125 a source of pleasure and recreation: K. Heider, p. 104.

125 one party would simply move away: Ibid, p. 93.

126 leaving them half-blind: Karl Heider noted this in the 1960s. Even after the end of native wars, boys still played with bows and grass arrows, and several boys with missing eyes were seen in early 2010.
127 all thumbs: K. Heider, p. 134.
127 An anthropologist: Ibid.
127 greasy orchid fibres: Ibid, p. 59.
128 'These are clearly human beings': Margaret Mead, from a review of *Dead Birds*, included in a 'promotional flyer' for the film dated 18 November 1963. Reprinted in Meiselas, p. 67.
128 driven inland by subsequent arrivals: K. Heider, p. 1.
128 'In the beginning': Susan Meiselas, *Encounters with the Dani*, p. 2, quoting Peter Sutcliffe in 'The Day the Dani People Become Civilized, the Sun Will No Longer Rise', *Papua New Guinea Post-Courier*, 1972.
129 called themselves *iniatek,* the originals: Peters, p. 10.
129 humans became separate: K. Heider, p. 127.
129 men, like birds, must die: Ibid, p. 126. See also Peters, p. 114.
129 'dead birds': This idea explored most vividly by filmmaker Robert Gardner in his landmark 1964 documentary about the Dani, *Dead Birds*. Gardner understood the gap between the Dani and Westerners was not as large as it might seem. He once wrote: 'In *Dead Birds* my fondest hope was that my camera be a mirror for its viewers to see themselves.'
129 'Let us take revenge on our enemy together': Peters, p. 76.
130 spirits that lived in the sky: Interviews in January and February 2010 with Tomas Wandik, Yunggukwe Wandik and Helenma Wandik, in Papua, Indonesia, New Guinea. See also Peter Matthiessen, *Under the Mountain Wall: A Chronicle of Two Seasons in Stone Age New Guinea* (New York: Penguin Books, 1962, copyright renewed 1990), p. 105.
130 village the natives called Uwambo: Interviews in January and February 2010 with Tomas, Yunggukwe and Helmena Wandik, in Papua, Indonesia, New Guinea. This account of the natives' reaction to the plane also draws from interviews conducted by Buzz Maxey in 1999 with the same Yali tribespeople and several others in a group.
131 A village leader named Yaralok Wandik: This story was recounted by his son, Tomas Wandik, and also by his nephew, Helenma Wandik, in interviews on 1 February 2010. A separate version of these events that agreed with this account was given to Buzz Maxey in 1999 by Helenma and Tomas Wandik, and a group of other Yali men that included Miralek Walela, Yilu Wandik, Waragin Dekma, and two others whose first names were Yare and Wasue.

Chapter 12: 'Chief Pete'

134 The native men: Interviews with Helenma and Tomas Wandik, 1 February 2010.
134 tasted human flesh: Helenma Wandik, in an interview on 1 February 2010, confirmed that his people ate the hands of enemies killed in battle. Cannibalism among the valley people is discussed in numerous anthropological research papers, but perhaps the most vivid description is found in Russell T. Hitt's book, *Cannibal Valley*, pp. 120–129.

135 themselves, their allies, and their enemies: Bob Connolly and Robin Anderson, *First Contact: New Guinea's Highlanders Encounter the Outside World* (New York: Viking Penguin, 1987), p. 36.
135 come into contact with the Archbold expedition: Interviews with Helenma and Tomas Wandik, 1 February 2010.
136 Albert Einstein: This famous quote has many forms. The one used here is commonly accepted, though another frequently cited version is: 'I do not know how the Third World War will be fought, but I can tell you what they will use in the Fourth – rocks!' See Alice Calaprice, *The New Quotable Einstein* (Princeton, NJ: Princeton University Press, 2005), p. 173.
136 a native stew: Margaret Hastings, SLD, Part Eight. 'If I was going to end up in a jungle stew-pot, the natives would have to come and get me.'
136 'We haven't any weapon': Margaret Hastings, SLD, Part Seven.
137 McCollom watched: John McCollom, unaired interviews with Robert Gardner, Dayton, Ohio, October 1997.
137 more like one hundred: : Margaret Hastings, SLD, Part Eight. Except where otherwise noted, the account of the first meeting between the natives and the survivors, including dialogue, comes from this portion of the SLD.
137 'feed us before they kill us': Robert Pearman, 'Three Who Lived to Tell About It', *Milwaukee Journal*, 22 December 1961, p. 16.
137 He was wiry and alert: Photograph of the native the survivors called 'Pete', courtesy of Betty McCollom.
138 meet him halfway: In his interview with Robert Gardner, McCollom described the scene of the two of them on the log. In SLD, Margaret Hastings tells the story slightly differently, with the natives coming across the log to meet the survivors in the clearing. In other respects, their accounts agree.
138 McCollom reached out: John McCollom, unaired interviews with Robert Gardner, Dayton, Ohio, October 1997. In her SLD, Margaret Hastings credited the native leader with extending his hand, after which McCollom 'weak with relief, grabbed it and wrung it'.
139 a college classmate: John McCollom, unaired interviews with Robert Gardner, in Dayton, Ohio, October 1997, and in Seattle, 13 May 1998.
139 Wimayuk Wandik: The native the survivors called 'Pete' was identified as Wimayuk Wandik by his son, Helenma Wandik, on 1 February 2010, from a photograph taken by C. Earl Walter Jr. This was subsequently confirmed by Wimayuk Wandik's niece and nephew, Yunggukwe and Tomas Wandik.
141 He and his fellow villagers were traders: Interview with Helenma Wandik, 1 February 2010.
142 'Pete and his boys': Margaret Hastings, SLD, Part Nine.
142 a terrible smell: Interviews with Helenma and Tomas Wandik, 1 February 2010.
142 bit into the stalk: Ibid.
142 'The native who had the garden': John McCollom, unaired interviews with Robert Gardner, in Dayton, Ohio, October 1997.
145 bright blue eyes: Interviews with Helenma and Tomas Wandik, 1 February 2010.
145 'loved Pete and his followers': Margaret Hastings, SLD, Part Nine.

146 might dislodge his *etai-eken*: This discussion of the 'seeds of singing' and the treatment of wounds relies largely on Robert Gardner and Karl G. Heider, *Gardens of War: Life and Death in the New Guinea Stone Age* (New York: Penguin Books, 1974), pp. 88, 140–141. This treatment of wounds is also described in several places by Peter Matthiessen, in *Under the Mountain Wall*, p. 227.
147 'They took the chow': Sergeant Ozzie St George, 'Hidden Valley', *Yank: The Army Weekly*, 10 August 1945, Far East Edition, Vol. 3, No. 2, pp. 6–8.

Chapter 13: Come What May

149 Newspapers had detailed the atrocities: Authoritative reports about the Bataan Death March became common fare in early 1944. One example among many was an editorial published on p. E1 of the *New York Times* on 30 January 1944. Its headline: 'Revenge! The Nation Demands It.'
149 a daring escape: Undated interview with Camilo Ramirez by filmmaker Sonny Izon.
149 leading gruelling runs: C. Earl Walter Jr interview, 7 July 2009.
149 'As soon as I can get us there': Ibid.
150 the son of General Courtney Whitney: Letter dated 13 March 1945 from Captain C. Earl Walter Jr, to Brigadier General Courtney Whitney. Located in Walter's personnel file at MacArthur Memorial Archives, Richmond, Va. It's worth noting that Whitney was not universally admired. MacArthur's biographer, William Manchester, wrote, 'From the standpoint of the guerrillas, [Whitney] was a disastrous choice. Undiplomatic and belligerent, he was condescending toward all Filipinos except those who, like himself, had substantial investments in the islands.' See: William Manchester, *American Caesar: Douglas MacArthur, 1880–1964* (New York: Little, Brown & Co., 1978), p. 378.
150 a blunt letter: Ibid.
150 'a trait I inherited from my father': Ibid.
150 responded two weeks later: Letter dated 27 March 1945 from Brigadier General Courtney Whitney to Captain Cecil E. Walter Jr. Located in Walter's personnel file at MacArthur Memorial Archives, Richmond, Va.
151 He wrote to the general in response: Letter dated 2 April 1945 from Captain C. Earl Walter Jr to Brigadier General Courtney Whitney. Located in Walter's personnel file at MacArthur Memorial Archives, Richmond, Va.
151 frustrated to the point of distraction: Captain C. Earl Walter Jr (retired), interview on 7 July 2009.
151 'I was an only son': C. Earl Walter Jr interview, 7 July 2009.
151 Whether his father had such power: A personnel file for C. Earl Walter Sr at the MacArthur Memorial Archives in Norfolk, Va., contains only a single sheet of paper, confirming his commissioning as an officer, according to archivist James Zobel.
152 'I've got just the people to go in there': C. Earl Walter Jr interview, 6 July 2009.
153 a four-part warning: Ibid. Also, Colonel Edward T. Imparato, *Rescue from Shangri-La*, pp. 16–17.
155 each one took a step forward: C. Earl Walter Jr interview, 6 July 2009.

Chapter 14: Five-by-Five

156 'We can clear enough space': Margaret Hastings, SLD, Part Nine.
156 a C-47: John McCollom, unaired interviews with Robert Gardner, in Dayton, Ohio, October 1997, and in Seattle, 13 May 1998.
157 the 'walkie-talkie': The survivors didn't specify the model, but Margaret Hastings' description makes it likely that it was the Motorola SCR-300, a celebrated two-way radio used extensively in the Pacific during the war. See www.scr300.org and Harry Mark Petrakis, *The Founder's Touch: The Life of Paul Galvin of Motorola* (New York: McGraw-Hill, 1965), pp. 144–147.
157 'McCollom swiftly set it up': Margaret Hastings, SLD, Part Nine.
157 too choked up to speak: Sergeant Ozzie St George, 'Hidden Valley', *Yank: The Army Weekly*, 10 August 1945, Far East Edition, Vol. 3, No. 2, pp. 6–8.
157 'This is Lieutenant McCollom': Margaret Hastings, SLD, Part Nine.
157 Sergeant Jack Gutzeit: The crew members of the 311 supply plane were identified in the *Jungle Journal*, the newsletter of the Far East Air Service Command, Vol. 1, No. 4, 20 June 1945, p. 3.
158 'almost too weak to move': Margaret Hastings, SLD, Part Nine.
159 the natives had returned: The source of the scene and dialogue from the morning of Thursday, 18 May 1945 is SLD, Parts Nine and Ten.
160 'New Guinea housing project': Margaret Hastings, SLD, Part Ten.
161 permanently embittered one resident: Interview with Yunggukwe Wandik, 3 February 2010. After she reluctantly agreed to tell her story, the author paid her for the pig, on behalf of the people of the United States.
162 tomatoes and tomato juice: In SLD, Margaret Hastings only mentions tomatoes, but John McCollom, in his interview with Robert Gardner, said he and Decker found 'about a half-dozen big cans of tomato juice and tomatoes'.
162 'Come on, Maggie': Margaret Hastings, SLD, Part Ten.
162 tend more thoroughly to their wounds: Information and quotes about their first medical treatment, including quotes, come from Margaret Hastings, SLD, Part Ten.

Chapter 15: No Supper Tonight

166 the best soldier he'd ever met: C. Earl Walter Jr interview, 6 July 2009.
166 raced model airplanes: Unbylined story, 'Model Planes Continue Championship Flights', *Los Angeles Times*, 6 September 1938, p. 8. Background on Abrenica also comes from his immigration and enlisted records, accessed at www.ancestry.com, 29 November 2009.
167 more circuitous and perilous: Camilo Ramirez, undated interview with documentary filmmaker Sonny Izon. His enlistment records support Ramirez's account of his involvement with the Philippine Scouts; his tale of capture and escape is supported by contemporaneous newspaper accounts of his involvement in the rescue at Shangri-La, including an undated news story in Earl Walter's scrapbook headlined, 'Shangri-La Hero Here; Filipino Visits Pal, Claims U.S. Bride'.
167 'I will get through there': Ibid.

169 'his gung-ho attitude': C. Earl Walter Jr, undated interview with filmmaker Sonny Izon.
170 'That was a mess': C. Earl Walter Jr interview, 7 July 2009.
171 'Do you really want to do this?': C. Earl Walter Jr, undated interview with filmmaker Sonny Izon.
171 Walter noted in a journal: C. Earl Walter Jr's daily journal, hereafter CEW.
171 'Don't let anyone jump': Margaret Hastings, SLD, Part Eleven.
171 'I could no longer move': Ibid.
172 fleas in the blankets: Remarks of Colonel Jerry Felmley at John McCollom's retirement dinner, 23 September 1980, Wright Patterson Air Force Base Officers' Club. Felmley interviewed Decker for the occasion.
172 'Eureka! We eat!': Margaret Hastings, SLD, Part Eleven.
173 'Honest, Maggie': Ibid.
173 'He was in great pain': Ibid.
174 'They would chatter like magpies': Ibid, Part Nine.
174 sized up the native woman: Ibid, Part Eleven.
174 name was Gilelek: Interview with Helenma Wandik, 1 February 2010.
174 'They held out a pig': Margaret Hastings, SLD, Part Eleven.
175 'It is the remembrance of pigs': K. Heider, p. 39.

Chapter 16: Rammy and Doc

177 Flying in a C-47 over the survivors' clearing: C. Earl Walter Jr interview, 7 July 2009. This account also relies on Walter's undated, unaired interview with documentary filmmaker Sonny Izon.
177 'The reason I dropped five': C. Earl Walter Jr undated, unaired interview with documentary filmmaker Sonny Izon.
178 'it looked like hell': Ibid.
180 'It was patent to all of us': Margaret Hastings, SLD, Part Twelve.
180 'God bless you': Kenneth Decker, undated interview with Sonny Izon.
181 'I said more "Our Fathers"': Margaret Hastings, SLD, Part Twelve.
181 'a hundred feet above the jump zone': Camilo Ramirez, undated, unaired interview with documentary filmmaker Sonny Izon.
181 'The natives have spears': Ibid.
183 more harm than good: Margaret Hastings, SLD, Part Thirteen.
183 'work the bandages off': Ibid, Part Twelve.
184 'how shocked he was': Ibid.
184 'sorry-looking gams': Margaret Hastings, SLD, Part Twelve.

Chapter 17: Custer and Company

186 Colonel Edward T. Imparato: Imparato, p. 55.
186 take the plane in low: Interview with C. Earl Walter Jr, 7 July 2009.
187 'When we first landed': Ibid. Except where otherwise noted, the dialogue throughout this scene of the paratroopers' landing in the valley comes from the author's 7 July 2009 interview with Walter.
187 three hundred: Unbylined story, 'The Hidden Valley', *The Pulse* (Supplement), typewritten military newsletter, found in C. Earl Walter's scrapbook, p. 4.
187 'Custer's last stand': Interview with C. Earl Walter Jr, 8 July 2009.

188 'frightening, weird sound': Unbylined story, 'The Hidden Valley', *The Pulse* (Supplement), typewritten military newsletter, found in C. Earl Walter's scrapbook, p. 4.
188 'fully equipped for a combat mission': Ibid.
188 an area known to the natives as Wosi: Interview with Lisaniak Mabel, 2 February 2010.
189 'a vine from the sky': Ibid.
189 his name was Yali: The leader of the Logo-Mabel clans was identified in photographs taken by C. Earl Walter Jr by four separate witnesses interviewed 1–3 February 2010, including Yali's grandson, Reverend Simon Logo.
190 'I waved those damned leaves': Unbylined story, 'The Hidden Valley', *The Pulse* (Supplement), typewritten military newsletter, found in C. Earl Walter's scrapbook, p. 4.
190 Writing that night in the journal: C. Earl Walter Jr, CEW, dated 20 May 1945.
191 'never bathed': Interview with C. Earl Walter Jr, 6 July 2009.
191 'a lot of hugging': Ibid.
192 'let's take our pants down': Interview with C. Earl Walter Jr, 7 July 2009. Also, CEW entry, 21 May 1945.
192 'That's not mud': Interview with Ai Baga, 2 February 2010. The Dani reaction to the soldiers' nudity also relies on interviews the same day with Lisaniak Mabel and the following day with Narekesok Logo.
193 not welcome inside the fence: C. Earl Walter Jr, CEW, 20 May 1945.
194 'For six hours': Margaret Hastings, SLD, Part Thirteen.
194 scoured the jungle: John McCollom, unaired interview with Robert Gardner, in Dayton, Ohio, October 1997.
195 'A native came running into our camp': Margaret Hastings, SLD, Part Thirteen.
195 'with you by nightfall': Ibid.
195 'My beau, Wally': Ibid.
198 remembered her reaction: Camilo Ramirez, undated, unaired interview with documentary filmmaker Sonny Izon.

Chapter 18: Bathtime for Yugwe

199 sweat, blood, gangrenous shavings, and jungle grime: Margaret Hastings, SLD, Part Thirteen. This account of Margaret's bath also came from John McCollom's unaired interviews with Robert Gardner in Dayton, Ohio, October 1997.
200 'I looked around': Margaret Hastings, SLD, Part Thirteen.
201 'We saw she had breasts': Interview with Helenma Wandik, 1 February 2010.
201 'a man, a woman, and the woman's husband': Ibid.
201 'always heartily detested': Margaret Hastings, SLD, Part Thirteen.
202 'a short recon': C. Earl Walter Jr, CEW, dated 21 May 1945.
202 'one of the most interesting parts of our lives': Ibid.
202 'Fired a few shots': Ibid.
203 'just for the hell of it': Interview with C. Earl Walter Jr, 7 July 2009.
203 'our weapons can kill': C. Earl Walter Jr, CEW, dated 21 May 1945.
203 'One man, named Mageam': Interview with Lisaniak Mabel, 2 February 2010.

204 'Pika was shooting the gun': Interview with Ai Baga, 2 February 2010.
204 'our enemies didn't come': Interview with Narekesok Logo, 3 February 2010.
205 a house for *inalugu:* Interview with Ai Baga, 2 February 2010.
205 ate a hearty breakfast: C. Earl Walter Jr, CEW, dated 22 May 1945.
205 'God only knows': Ibid.
206 'A declaration, called a *maga*': Interview with Yunggukwe Wandik, 3 February 2010.
206 'came out on a path and stopped us': Interview with C. Earl Walter Jr, 6 July 2009.
207 'more bother than good': C. Earl Walter Jr, CEW, dated 23 May 1945.
207 'Did not understand': Ibid.
208 'Things look bad': Ibid, dated 24 May 1945.
208 'God only knows': Ibid.

Chapter 19: 'Shoo, Shoo Baby'

209 'Finally they are over us': C. Earl Walter Jr, CEW, dated 25 May 1945.
210 'Earl will get down there': John McCollom, unaired joint interview with C. Earl Walter Jr, conducted by documentary filmmaker Robert Gardner in Seattle, 13 May 1998.
210 'that yapping noise': Margaret Hastings, SLD, Part Fourteen.
211 'He looked like a giant': Ibid.
211 'I knew they were all right': C. Earl Walter Jr, unaired interview with documentary filmmaker Sonny Izon.
211 'His men worshipped Walter': Margaret Hastings, SLD, Part Fourteen.
211 'a pretty good-looking gal': Interview with C. Earl Walter Jr, 6 July 2009.
211 an American flag waved: Ibid, 7 July 2009.
211 'the lost outpost of Shangri-La': C. Earl Walter Jr, CEW, dated 29 May 1945.
211 'The Stars and Stripes now fly': Ibid, dated 31 May 1945.
212 'won and lost thousands of dollars': Margaret Hastings, SLD, Part Fourteen.
212 'Superman' and 'Iron Man': In her diary, Margaret Hastings refers to Caioli as 'Superman', but in captions on photos in his scrapbook, C. Earl Walter Jr uses the nickname 'Iron Man'.
213 'There ought to be a law': Margaret Hastings, SLD, Part Fourteen.
213 'Deuces wild, roll your own': Unbylined story, 'Here's a Soldier Who Refuses to Embrace a WAC', *Chicago Daily Tribune*, 12 July 1945, p. 4.
213 'don't know how to play cards': Interview with C. Earl Walter Jr, 6 July 2009.
213 'The captain played': Margaret Hastings, SLD, Part Fourteen.
214 'Walter was a personality kid': Ibid.
214 'leave the men alone': Interview with C. Earl Walter Jr, 6 July 2009.
215 'just walk away': Ibid.
215 'all the credit in the world': C. Earl Walter Jr, CEW, dated 25 May 1945.
215 burial duty: C. Earl Walter Jr, CEW, entries dated 27–29 May 1945.

216 a second Star of David: Document in the IDPF of Private Mary M. Landau, signed by her brother, Jack Landau, dated 29 June 1959.
216 helping to toss the funerary supplies: Oral History Interview with Ruth Johnson Coster, University of North Carolina, Greensboro, Object ID: WV0145.5.001.
217 trail of Margaret's hair: Margaret Hastings, SLD, Part Fourteen.
217 'There it is': John McCollom, unaired joint interview with C. Earl Walter Jr, conducted by documentary filmmaker Robert Gardner in Seattle, 13 May 1998.
217 'Lieutenant Mac's report': C. Earl Walter Jr, CEW, dated 29 May 1945.
217 'we buried Captain Good': C. Earl Walter Jr, CEW, dated 6 June 1945. News reports at the time said the burial service took place 26 May, but Walter's journal puts the date at 6 June. The credibility of his account is enhanced by previous entries in which he writes that he is waiting for orders about the disposition of remains.
218 'Out of the depth': Russell Brines, Associated Press Staff Writer, '"Shangri-La" On New Guinea', 9 June 1945, found in C. Earl Walter Jr's scrapbook.
218 'seemed to whisper a peace': Ibid.
218 'the saddest and most impressive funeral': Margaret Hastings, SLD, Part Fourteen.
220 'a long discussion on the world at war': C. Earl Walter Jr, CEW, dated 6 June 1945.
220 'When they climbed the mountain': Interview with Yunggukwe Wandik, 3 February 2010.
220 condolence letters: Copies of letters from General Douglas MacArthur, General Clements McMullen, and General H.H. Arnold provided by Major Nicholson's family.
221 'a corrected report': Letter to Patrick J. Hastings from General Robert W. Dunlop, dated 27 May 1945, in Margaret Hastings' archive file at TCHS.
222 'a very miraculous escape': Letter to Patrick J. Hastings from Chaplain Cornelius Waldo, dated 8 June 1945, in Margaret Hastings' archive file at TCHS.

Chapter 20: Hold the Front Page!

224 seeped into his journal: C. Earl Walter Jr, CEW, excerpted entries from 29 May to 8 June 1945.
226 Walter Simmons of the *Chicago Tribune*: Trevor Jensen, 'Walter Simmons: 1908–2006; Editor and War Reporter', *Chicago Tribune*, 1 December 2006, obituary, p. 18.
226 Reporting in May 1945: Headlines are from stories published in the *Chicago Tribune* under Walter Simmons' byline on 13, 17, 21 and 31 May 1945.
227 A native of Nova Scotia: Unbylined obituary, 'Ralph Morton, Former War Reporter', *Newsday*, 20 October 1988, p. 41.
227 more than fourteen hundred newspapers: *Encyclopædia Britannica*. Retrieved 22 February 2010, from www.britannica.com/EBchecked/topic/136280/Kent-Cooper. Also, www.encyclopedia.com/doc/1G2-3445000019.html.
228 'In a hidden valley': Walter Simmons, 'WAC, 2 Yanks Marooned in Hidden Valley', *Chicago Tribune*, 8 June 1945, p. 1.

228 'The crash of an Army transport plane': Associated Press story, 'Chutists Land in Shangri-La To Rescue Fliers', *Desert News*, 9 June 1945, p. 1.
228 *New York Times*: Byline Associated Press, 'Airfield Is Built to Rescue a Wac And 2 Men in New Guinea Crash', *New York Times*, 9 June 1945, p. 1.
229 'stop worrying and start praying': Transcript headlined 'Plane-to-Ground Conversations Reveal Details of Survivors' Life in Shangri-La Valley', *Trenton Republican-Times*, 13 July 1945, p. 1.
229 'the queen of the valley': Ibid.
230 'Shangri-La Gets Latest News': Ralph Morton, 'Shangri-La Gets Latest News From Associated Press', Associated Press story published in *[St Petersburg, Fla.] Evening Independent*, 13 June 1945, p. 6.
230 offered … one thousand dollars each: C. Earl Walter Jr, CEW, dated 16–18 June 1945.
230 a pang of jealousy: Ibid.
230 WAC Private Thelma Decker: Transcript headlined 'Plane-to-Ground Conversations Reveal Details of Survivors' Life in Shangri-La Valley', *Trenton Republican-Times*, 13 July 1945, p. 1.
230 bought a box of chocolates: 'Shangri-La Trio Hikes Out Today', Associated Press story published in *Salt Lake Tribune*, 14 June 1945, p. 2.
230 'she can go native': US Army air-to-ground transcript from 24 June 1945, reprinted in Imparato, p. 120.
231 'clawed at the aluminum door frame': Walter Simmons, 'Crew Supplying Hidden Valley Averts Mishap', *Chicago Tribune*, 21 June 1945, p. 5.
231 panning for gold: Ibid, p. 122.
231 cases of beer: C. Earl Walter Jr, CEW, dated 9 June 1945.
231 'too overcome to write': Ibid.
231 deliver personal messages: Unbylined story, '*Tribune* Sending Kin's Notes to "Hidden Valley"', *Chicago Tribune*, 15 June 1945, p. 3.
232 'Robert was killed instantly': Letter from John McCollom to Rolla and Eva McCollom, quoted to the author by Robert's daughter, Dennie McCollom Scott, 30 May 2010.
232 'dropping me some panties?': Walter Simmons, 'WAC, 2 Yanks Marooned in Hidden Valley', *Chicago Tribune*, 8 June 1945, p. 1.
232 'begging for a pair of pants': Margaret Hastings, SLD, Part Fifteen.
233 'Tropic skin diseases': Margaret Hastings, SLD, Part Fifteen.
233 'Mumu' and 'Mua': Interview with Helenma Wandik, 1 February 2010.
234 lengthy thoughts about the natives: C. Earl Walter Jr, CEW, Miscellaneous Notes on the Natives.
234 'some pictures of pinup girls': Ibid.
234 couldn't quite fill his gourd: Ibid.
235 'many curving lines on the paper': Ibid.
235 'white gods dropped out of the sky': Unbylined Associated Press story, 'Three in "Shangri-La" May Quit Peak Today', *New York Times*, 14 June 1945, p. 4.
235 'the happiest people I've ever seen': Walter Simmons, 'Hidden Valley Dwellers Hide Nothing, But All Wear Smiles', *Chicago Tribune*, 16 June 1945, p. 1.
236 'They lived well': Interview with C. Earl Walter Jr, 6 July 2009.

236 'the best-looking girl': C. Earl Walter Jr, CEW, Miscellaneous Notes on the Natives.

Chapter 21: Promised Land

237 'headlines all over the world': C. Earl Walter Jr, CEW, dated 11 June 1945.
237 'my prayers on the future': Ibid, dated 13 June 1945.
237 'My last news of Dad': Ibid.
238 'I will not risk': Ibid, dated 10 June 1945.
238 delayed their departure: Ibid, dated 15 June 1945.
238 kept after his journalistic prey: US Army air-to-ground transcript from 15 June 1945, reprinted in Imparato, pp. 79–80.
240 'two Filipino medics': Walter Simmons, 'WAC, 2 Yanks Marooned in Hidden Valley', *Chicago Tribune*, 8 June 1945, p. 1.
240 reacted angrily in his journal: C. Earl Walter Jr, CEW, entry dated 22 June 1945.
241 'you gonna use any of this?': John McCollom, unaired interview with Robert Gardner, Dayton, Ohio, October 1997.
241 'farewells to Pete and his men': Margaret Hastings, SLD, Part Fifteen.
241 weeping at their departure: Ibid.
242 bestowed another *maga*: Interview with Yunggukwe Wandik, 3 February 2010.
242 glanced back over her shoulder: Margaret Hastings, SLD, Part Fifteen.
242 'break off a bite and eat it': John McCollom, unaired interviews with Robert Gardner in Dayton, Ohio, October 1997.
242 'Nobody knew what the food was': Interview with Tomas Wandik, 1 February 2010.
242 a place of magic: Interview with Yunggukwe Wandik, 3 February 2010.
242 McCollom's offer of a machete: His son, Helenma Wandik, fondly remembered the machete sixty-five years later, as did his niece and nephew, Tomas and Yunggukwe Wandik.
243 'Some people were getting mad at Wimayuk': Interview with Helenma Wandik, 1 February 2010.
243 'They loved them': Margaret Hastings, SLD, Part Thirteen.
243 It remained in use: Author's visit to a village near the site of Uwambo in February 2010. Yali and Dani villages tend to move over the years, and Uwambo was no longer a village site.
244 'up and down and crevice to crevice': Interview with C. Earl Walter Jr, 6 July 2009.
244 'I thought I was well': Margaret Hastings, SLD, Part Fifteen.
244 'Hats off to Sergeant Decker': C. Earl Walter Jr, CEW, dated 15 June 1945.
245 'plenty rugged': Ibid, dated 16–18 June 1945.
245 'Are they hostile?': US Army air-to-ground transcript from 16 June 1945, reprinted in Imparato, p. 82.
245 'Our main trouble is water': Ibid.
245 'My main concern': Interview with C. Earl Walter Jr, 7 July 2009.
245 'We are rolling too well ...': C. Earl Walter Jr, CEW, dated 16–18 June 1945.
246 'like a million dollars': Margaret Hastings, SLD, Part Fifteen.
246 'we instantly named "Bob Hope"': Ibid.

247 running up the trail: C. Earl Walter Jr, CEW, dated 16–18 June 1945.
247 'the best damn field soldiers': Ibid.
247 jumped up and down: Far East Air Service Command Report, dated 18 June 1945, reprinted in Imparato, p. 87.
247 sitting beside him: Ralph Morton, 'Survivor Trio of Shangri-La Safe in Valley', *Sarasota Herald-Tribune*, 20 June 1945, p. 2.
247 'Surely the followers of Moses': Margaret Hastings, SLD, Part Sixteen.

Chapter 22: Hollywood

248 'there it lies today': Margaret Hastings, SLD, Part Sixteen.
248 'ever make a jump before': John McCollom, interview with Robert Gardner, Dayton, Ohio, October 1997.
249 'a rank amateur': Margaret Hastings, SLD, Part Sixteen.
249 'Pull your legs together!': Ibid.
249 'Pull on your risers!': John McCollom, interview with Robert Gardner, Dayton, Ohio, October 1997.
250 'This man is drunk!': Interview with C. Earl Walter Jr, 6 July 2009.
250 'Drunker than a hoot owl': John McCollom, interview with Robert Gardner, Dayton, Ohio, October 1997.
250 'The valley is going Hollywood': Unbylined Associated Press story, 'Shangri-La Trio Eat Pork Chops, Await Rescue', *Sarasota Herald-Tribune*, 21 June 1945, p. 2.
250 Canadian House of Commons: Ernest J. Chambers, *The Canadian Parliamentary Guide* (Ottawa, Canada: The Mortimer Company, 1908), p. 143.
250 helped to launch the Federal Reserve Bank of New York: Unbylined story, 'H.V. Cann Returns to Canada', *New York Times*, 3 March 1917, p. 12.
250 study structural engineering: Interview with Alexandra Cann, 15 August 2009.
251 gamble away his sizeable inheritance: Ibid.
251 small movie roles: www.imdb.com resumé of Alexander Cross, retrieved 15 August 2009. Also, interview with Alexandra Cann, 15 August 2009.
252 drinking buddy Humphrey Bogart: Interview with Alexandra Cann, 15 August 2009.
252 front-page story: Unbylined story, 'Actor Confesses Theft of Gems At Palm Springs', *Los Angeles Times*, 28 March 1937, p. 1.
253 'Nobody likes to prosecute a friend': Unbylined story, 'Mrs. Hearst Not to Prosecute Cann in Gem Theft Case', *Los Angeles Times*, 29 March 1937, p. 8.
253 'Host's Jewels Are Stolen By Thespian': Unbylined Associated Press story, 'Host's Jewels Are Stolen By Thespian', *Brownsville (Texas) Herald*, 29 March 1937, p. 7.
253 a Hearst and a heist: Special To The New York Times, 'Ex-Wife of Hearst Jr Robbed', *New York Times*, 28 March 1937, p. 27.
253 married and divorced three times: Interview with Alexandra Cann, 15 August 2009.
254 broken back: Interview with playwright Keith Dewhurst, Alexander Cann's son-in-law, 15 September 2009.
254 'a great deal more about filmmaking': Interview with Alexandra Cann, 15 August 2009.

254 Netherlands Indies Government Information Service: David J. Snyder, 'The Netherlands Information Service Collection: An Introduction', *HAOL*, No. 8, 2005 (Otoño), pp. 201–209.
254 'War Correspondent and Cinematographer': Correspondence between Robert Gardner and John Daniell, son of Fred Daniell of the Dutch East Indies Film Unit, dated 17 December 1997.
254 his charm and Canadian accent: Ibid.
254 slammed full-speed into the *Australia*: Australian War Memorial publication, 'The first kamikaze attack?' www.awm.gov.au/wartime/28/article.asp, retrieved 2 March 2010.
255 'smoke already pouring out': Unbylined Associated Press story, 'Jap Plane With Dead Pilot Rips Allied Cruiser', *Los Angeles Times*, 2 November 1944, p. 2.
255 flew from Melbourne to Hollandia on 17 June: Alexander Cann, 'Chuting Photog Pictures Life In "Shangri-La"', *Chicago Tribune*, 2 July 1945, p. 5.
255 'six quarts of whisky and a party': US Army air-to-ground transcript from 22 June 1945, reprinted in Imparato, p. 117.
255 'obviously dangerous': Interview with Alexandra Cann, 15 August 2009.
255 'whether I jumped or was pushed': Alexander Cann, 'Chuting Photog Pictures Life In "Shangri-La"', *Chicago Tribune*, 2 July 1945, p. 5.
256 aspirin supply: Margaret Hastings, SLD, Part Sixteen.
256 chow mein and fried potatoes: Ibid.
256 'a full fifth of Dutch gin': Interview with C. Earl Walter Jr, 6 July 2009.
256 'not until another story comes along': US Army air-to-ground transcript from 24 June 1945, reprinted in Imparato, p. 122.
256 'the most magnificent survivor': Unbylined story, 'Hidden Valley', *Pulse Supplement*, undated newsletter of the USS *Barnstable*, which took Walter and his men to Manila. A slightly different version of this quote appears in the unbylined story, 'Modern Legend of Shangri-La', *Jungle Journal*, newsletter of the Far East Air Service Command, Vol. 1, No. 4, 20 June 1945, p. 3.
256 'I ... will give up my crown': US Army air-to-ground transcript from 24 June 1945, reprinted in Imparato, p. 122.
256 became fast friends: Interview with C. Earl Walter Jr, 6 July 2009.
256 'experience and hard knocks': C. Earl Walter Jr, CEW, dated 21 June 1945.
256 'really learn something': Ibid, dated 23 June 1945.
257 'a swell egg': Ibid, dated 29 June 1945.
258 'thought she was a dog': Margaret Hastings, SLD, Part Sixteen.
258 'I wanted to cry': Ibid.
258 insisted that his bed go to Decker: Ibid.
259 'laid down in agony': C. Earl Walter Jr, CEW, dated 20 June 1945.
259 recreate the last leg of the journey: C. Earl Walter Jr, CEW, dated 21 June 1945. Also, Robert Gardner interview with C. Earl Walter Jr and John McCollom, in Seattle, 13 May 1998.

Chapter 23: Gliders?

261 Navy Construction Battalion: Don Dwiggins, *On Silent Wings* (New York: Grosset & Dunlap, 1970), p. 109.

261 L-5 Sentinel: Gerard M. Devlin, *Silent Wings: The Saga of the U.S. Army and Marine Combat Glider Pilots During World War II* (New York: St. Martin's Press, 1985), p. 354. Also, website of the National Museum of the US Air Force, www.nationalmuseum.af.mil/factsheets/factsheet.asp?id=519, retrieved 5 March 2010.
261 consume all its fuel: Devlin, p. 254.
261 lanky country boy: Interview with Margaret Palmer Henry, daughter of Henry Palmer, 12 March 2010.
262 headed straight for a blackboard: Devlin, pp. 354–355.
262 'no second chances': Ibid, p. xi.
263 A leader in glider technology: Ibid, pp. 29–36.
263 quiet war machines: Ibid. Also, David T. Zabecki, *World War II in Europe* (New York: Routledge, 1999), pp. 1471–1472.
264 one thousand glider pilots: Major Michael H Manion, 'Gliders of World War II: "The Bastards No One Wanted"', unpublished thesis presented to the faculty of the School of Advanced Air and Space Studies, Air University, Maxwell Air Force Base, Alabama, June 2008, p. 56.
264 watched with interest: Robert Gardner interview with John McCollom, Dayton, Ohio, October 1997.
264 furniture company and a coffin maker: Manion, p. 53. Also, Don Dwiggins, *On Silent Wings*, p. 78.
265 wingspan of 25.5 metres: Waco CG-4A specs come from the National Museum of the U.S. Air Force, www.nationalmuseum.af.mil/factsheets/factsheet.asp?id=504, retrieved 7 March, 2010.
265 fourteen thousand Wacos: *World War II Glider Pilots*, edited by Turner Publishing (Paducah, Kentucky: Turner Publishing, 1991), p. 16.
265 fifteen thousand dollars: Ibid.
265 seventeen deluxe, eight-cylinder Ford sedans: Marvin L. Arrowsmith, 'OPA Set New Car Price Ceilings Near 1942 Averages', Associated Press story published in St Petersburg *Evening Independent*, 19 November 1945, p. 1.
266 stop within two hundred metres: *World War II Glider Pilots*, p. 16.
266 'suicide jockeys': Lloyd Clark, *Crossing the Rhine: Breaking into Nazi Germany, 1944 and 1945* (New York: Grove Atlantic, 2008), p. 87.
266 a mordant toast: National World War II Glider Pilots Association website, www.pointvista.com/WW2GliderPilots/GliderPilotHumor.htm, retrieved 7 March 2010.
267 'don't go by glider!': Walter Cronkite, foreword to John L. Lowden's *Silent Wings at War: Combat Gliders in World War II* (Washington, DC: Smithsonian Institution Press, 2003), p. ix.
267 nearly five hundred glider retrievals: Keith H. Thoms et al, 'Austere Recovery of Cargo Gliders', www.ndu.edu/inss/Press/jfq_pages/editions/i48/29.pdf, retrieved 9 March 2010.
267 retrofitted as medevac aircraft: Leon B. Spencer, former World War II Glider Pilot, and Charles L. Day, 'WW II U.S. Army Air Forces Glider Aerial Retrieval System', www.silentwingsmuseum.com/images/Web%20Content/WWII%20USAAF%20Glider%20Aerial%20Retrieval%20System.pdf, retrieved 20 October 2009.
269 scattered all over: Imparato, p. 59.
270 a pilot with United Airlines: William Samuels, *Reflections of an Airline Pilot* (San Francisco: Monterey Pacific Publishing, 1999), p. 46.

270 most experienced glider pickup pilot: Ibid, p. 72.
270 turned over his own quarters: Ibid, p. 73.
270 *Leaking Louise*: Samuels, p. 72.
270 a three-day case of dysentery: Samuels, p. 74.
270 *Fanless Faggot*: Sergeant Ozzie St George, 'Rescue From Shangri-La', *Yank: The Army Weekly*, 17 August 1945, p. 6.
271 'What do you think, Mac?': Samuels, p. 73.
271 thirty to sixty centimetres high: US Army air-to-ground transcript from 19 June 1945, reprinted in Imparato, p. 110.
271 toilet paper: Unbylined story, 'Reynolds Allen Clears Up Several Hidden Valley Facts Related in Prior Articles', *Silent Wings*, newsletter of the National World War II Glider Pilots Association, Vol. 1, No. 4, September 1974, p. 16.
271 a huge winch: Ibid. Details on glider snatch technique and equipment also came from Spencer; Imparato; Lowden; Thoms et al; Devlin; and Roy Gibbons, 'Brake and Reel Device Used in Glider Snatch', *Chicago Tribune*, 1 July 1945, p. 3.
272 within three seconds: Lowden, p. 17. Also, Leon B. Spencer, former World War II Glider Pilot, and Charles L. Day, 'WW II U.S. Army Air Forces Glider Aerial Retrieval System', www.silentwingsmuseum.com/images/Web%20Content/WWII%20USAAF%20Glider%20Aerial%20Retrieval%20System.pdf, retrieved 20 October 2009, p. 5.

Chapter 24: Two Queens

275 after we get out of here: Frank Kelley, 'Weather Delays Rescue of Shangri-La Shutins', *New York Tribune*, datelined 23 June 1945. Found in C. Earl Walter's scrapbook; no page given.
275 five cowrie shells: Margaret Hastings, SLD, Part Sixteen.
275 Sixty-two arrows and three bows: C. Earl Walter Jr, CEW, dated 23 June 1945.
275 four shells: Frank Kelley, 'Weather Delays Rescue of Shangri-La Shutins', *New York Tribune*, datelined 23 June 1945. Found in C. Earl Walter's scrapbook; no page given.
275 pigpen ... collapsed: John McCollom, unaired interviews with filmmaker Robert Gardner, Dayton, Ohio, October 1997.
276 ruining the local economy: Ibid.
276 At a funeral: L. Heider, pp. 132–133.
276 'don't take the shells': Interview with Lisaniak Mabel, 2 February 2010.
276 'be careful': Interview with C. Earl Walter Jr, 6 July 2009.
277 'quite a money monger': C. Earl Walter Jr, CEW, dated 30 June 1945.
277 Gerlagam Logo: Interviews with Narekesok Logo and Dagadigik Walela, 3 February 2010.
277 'eggs that landed unscrambled': Ozzie St George, 'Rescue From Shangri-La', *Yank: The Army Weekly*, 17 August 1945, p. 6.
277 'believers in mankind': US Army air-to-ground transcript from 21 June 1945, reprinted in Imparato, p. 117.
278 'Natives not very fast': C. Earl Walter Jr, CEW, dated 24 June 1945.
278 'shot through the heart': Margaret Hastings, SLD, Part Seventeen.
278 found the skeleton: C. Earl Walter Jr, CEW, dated 27 June 1945.
279 'a dying race': C. Earl Walter Jr, CEW, dated 22 June 1945.
279 'You could see where the cuts were': Interview with Narekesok Logo, 3 February 2010.The story of the pig was confirmed in interviews

with Dagadigik Walela on the same day, and with Ai Baga and Lisaniak Mabel on 2 February 2010.

279 'smeared their heads with mosquito repellant': Walter Simmons, 'Glider Takes Six More Out of Shangri-La', *Chicago Tribune*, 1 July 1945, p. 3.

279 infection on her breast: US Army air-to-ground transcript from 21 June 1945, reprinted in Imparato, p. 114.

279 'a wonderfully carefree people': Walter Simmons, 'Glider Takes Six More Out of Shangri-La', *Chicago Tribune*, 1 July 1945, p. 3.

280 'the captain forbade it': Margaret Hastings, SLD, Part Seventeen.

280 'a man of dignity and authority': Ibid, Part Sixteen.

281 'a word of each other's language': Ibid, Part Seventeen.

282 'a royal guest': Ibid.

282 'the rest of us': US Army air-to-ground transcript from 21 June 1945, reprinted in Imparato, p. 114.

282 'a wise people': Margaret Hastings, SLD, Part Seventeen.

282 an ornate necklace: C. Earl Walter Jr, CEW, dated 20 and 21 June 1945.

284 severed the nylon tow rope: Samuels, p. 74. Also, Margaret Hastings, SLD, Part Eighteen.

284 compass mast was knocked off: Ozzie St George, 'Rescue From Shangri-La', *Yank: The Army Weekly*, 17 August 1945, p. 6.

284 the steel cable: Devlin, p. 357.

284 'The winch just blew up': Walter Simmons, 'Glider Rescue Test Again Fails', *Chicago Tribune*, 26 June 1945, p. 1.

284 Winston Howell: A dispute exists over the first name and rank of the winch operator. Some accounts call him Private James Howell. However, stories by Sergeant Ozzie St George of *Yank* and Walter Simmons of the *Chicago Tribune*, both of whom covered the mission, identify him as 'Master Sergeant Winston Howell'. In his memoir, *Reflections of an Airline Pilot*, William J. Samuels identifies him as 'Frank' Howell.

284 certain they'd have no trouble: Ralph Morton, 'Survivor Trio of Shangri-La Safe in Valley', *Sarasota Herald-Tribune*, 20 June 1945, p. 2.

284 'A shower of aluminum': Samuels, p. 74.

284 'badly rusted': Unbylined story, 'Reynolds Allen Clears Up Several Hidden Valley Facts Related in Prior Articles', *Silent Wings*, newsletter of the National World War II Glider Pilots Association, Vol. 1, No. 4, September 1974, p. 16.

285 cancel the glider snatch: Walter Simmons, 'Glider Rescue Test Again Fails', *Chicago Tribune*, 26 June 1945, p. 1.

285 inviting the Seabees: Unbylined Associated Press story, 'Five More Rescued At Shangri-La', *Miami News*, 30 June 1945, p. 4.

285 'any haphazard attempt': US Army air-to-ground transcript from 19 June 1945, reprinted in Imparato, p. 111.

285 'possibility of a bad accident': Ibid.

285 'if the glider pickup didn't work': C. Earl Walter Jr undated interview with Sonny Izon.

285 'I said my Rosary': Margaret Hastings, SLD, Part Eighteen.

286 asked a chaplain to pray: Ibid. Also, Samuels, p. 74.

286 'might have been dead': Margaret Hastings, SLD, Part Seventeen.

287 'one of us handsome guys': Ibid.

288 their name for Margaret was Nuarauke: Interview with Ai Baga, 2 February 2010.

288 'Sleep with this woman': Interview with Hugiampot, 2 February 2010.
288 Caoili was called Kelabi: Ibid. The names were confirmed by others in the valley including Lisaniak Mabel, Narekesok Logo and Dagadigik Walela, in interviews from 1–3 February 2010.
289 'appreciate our help': C. Earl Walter Jr, CEW, dated 19 June 1945.
289 'our first uneasy night': Ibid, dated 22 June 1945.
290 on his terms: Interviews with Ai Baga, Lisaniak Mabel and Hugiampot, 2 February 2010.
290 'the enemies talked': Interview with Ai Baga, 2 February 2010.

Chapter 25: Snatch

291 overload the glider: US Army air-to-ground transcript from 22 June 1945, reprinted in Imparato, p. 116. Also, Walter Simmons, 'Clouds Defeat Hidden Valley Rescue Effort', *Chicago Tribune*, 29 June 1945, p. 2
291 sat in the co-pilot seat: Walter Simmons, 'Clouds Defeat Hidden Valley Rescue Effort', *Chicago Tribune*, 29 June 1945, p. 2. Also, Imparato, p. 72.
291 reflected confidence: Pilot William J. Samuels was certain Elsmore's act was a mark of confidence in the C-47 crew. See Samuels, p. 74.
292 'puffs of cigar smoke': Walter Simmons, 'Glider Saves Yanks Marooned in Shangri-La Valley', *Chicago Tribune*, 30 June 1945, p. 1.
292 'Does the queen': US Army air-to-ground transcript from 28 June 1945, reprinted in Imparato, p. 139.
292 a B-25 bomber: Don Caswell, 'It's Not Exactly Shangri-La', United Press story datelined 1 July 1945, found in C. Earl Walter Jr's scrapbook.
292 'my prayers on the future': C. Earl Walter Jr, CEW, dated 13 June 1945.
293 'I will not be on the first glider': US Army air-to-ground transcript from 28 June 1945, reprinted in Imparato, p. 139.
294 glider's tail rose: Alexander Cann's film, *Rescue from Shangri-La*, copy provided by Robert Gardner.
294 'jumping up and down': Margaret Hastings, SLD, Part Eighteen.
294 whooping and hollering: Transcript of 29 June 1945, press conference, reprinted in Imparato, p. 189.
295 'gas or time': US Army air-to-ground transcript from 28 June 1945, reprinted in Imparato, p. 141.
295 lighten the load: Report of Major William Samuels, reprinted in Imparato, p. 143.
295 'a damn good day': Ibid.
295 'better not try a dry run': Ibid, p. 142.
295 'ready to go?': Margaret Hastings, SLD, Part Eighteen.
296 'they understood that we were going': Margaret Hastings, SLD, Part Eighteen.
297 'We had a crying ceremony': Transcript of interview with Binalok Logo conducted by Buzz Maxey, 1997, no month given. Binalok had since died when the author visited the Baliem Valley, but his explanations were confirmed during discussions with other witnesses quoted throughout the book.
297 a more traditional style: Ibid. A man named Lolkwa joined Binalok during this part of the discussion.

297 'insured for ten thousand dollars': Margaret Hastings, SLD, Part Eighteen.
298 'survived a hideous plane crash': Ibid.
298 'I don't think I can pick up': Unbylined story, 'Corporal Margaret Hastings and Two Companions Are Rescued By Glider', news clipping in Margaret Hastings' scrapbook, at TCHS.
298 'This is the best weather': Ibid.
298 'Are you nervous': Report of Major William Samuels, reprinted in Imparato, p. 143.
298 220 kilometres per hour: Unbylined United Press story, 'Glider Rescue Almost Ends in Second Tragedy', *Schenectady* [NY] *Gazette*, 2 July 1945, p. 7.
299 'Oh boy, Oh boy': Ozzie St George, 'Rescue From Shangri-La', *Yank: The Army Weekly*, 17 August 1945, p. 6.
299 slowed the *Leaking Louise*: Ibid.
299 about one thousand feet: Unbylined United Press story, 'Glider Rescue Almost Ends in Second Tragedy', *Schenectady Gazette*, 2 July 1945, p. 7.
299 through the upper branches: Ibid.
300 grazed a tree top: Margaret Hastings, SLD, Part Eighteen.
300 'into our line of vision': Ibid.
300 hands sweating: Ibid.
300 'as far as she can go': Associated Press story, unbylined but written by Ralph Morton, 'Trio, Snatched Out of Valley, Arrive Safely', from the scrapbook of C. Earl Walter Jr.
300 cut the glider loose: John McCollom, unaired interview with Robert Gardner, Dayton, Ohio, October 1997.
300 'Let 'em heat up': Ibid.
301 a persistent slap-slap noise: Margaret Hastings, SLD, Part Eighteen.
301 tried not to look: Ibid.
301 one more task: John McCollom, unaired joint interview with C. Earl Walter Jr, conducted by documentary filmmaker Robert Gardner in Seattle, 13 May 1998.
301 cylinder heads ... overheating: Report of Major William Samuels, reprinted in Imparato, p. 144.
302 'brushing the mountain tops': Unbylined United Press story, 'Glider Rescue Almost Ends in Second Tragedy', *Schenectady Gazette*, 2 July 1945, p. 7.

Epilogue: After Shangri-La

303 Landed 400 metres away: Ozzie St George, 'Rescue From Shangri-La', *Yank: The Army Weekly*, 17 August 1945, p. 6.
303 'Get a haircut and shave': Transcript of press conference, reprinted in Imparato, pp. 184–189.
303 'The Four Musketeers': C. Earl Walter Jr, CEW, dated 30 June 1945.
304 'We were excited to go': Interview with Lisaniak Mabel, 2 February 2010. This account is supported by a passage in a story printed in the *Jungle Journal*, the newsletter of the Far East Air Service Command, Vol. 1, No. 5, dated 4 July 1945: 'One boy the Filipinos were reluctant to leave behind was a chap whom they named Smiley ... For a few minutes, they thought they had him talked into a great new future, but in the end he backed out.'

305 'The identity of the valley': *Science*, New Series, Vol. 102, No. 2652 (26 October 1945), p. 14.
309 letters to the victims' families: Letter to Mr Rolla McCollom, father of Robert and John McCollom, from Lt Col Donald Wardle, chief of the Army Disposition Branch, Memorial Division, dated 1 May 1959. From Robert McCollom's IDPF.
309 'segregation was not possible': Ibid.
310 honorary pallbearers: Lieutenant Colonel Anne O'Sullivan, 'Plane Down, WACs Aboard', *Women's Army Corps Journal*, October–December 1974, Vol. 5, No. 5, p. 16.
310 a lei of vanda orchids: Ibid.
310 Robert McCollom's wedding ring: Letter to Mrs Cecelia A. McCollom, the widow of Robert McCollom, from Lt Col Donald Wardle, chief of the Army Disposition Branch, Memorial Division, dated 13 May 1959. (Coincidentally, fourteen years to the date after the crash.)
310 his best friend: Interview with Melvyn Lutgring, 9 January 2010.
311 larger historical event: Interview with Margaret Harvey, Henry Palmer's daughter, on 12 March 2010. Also, Obituary of Henry Earl Palmer, *The Watchman* of Clinton, Louisiana, 28 October 1991.
311 offered a choice: Samuels, p. 76.
311 military honours: Special to the *New York Times*, 'Ray Elsmore, 66, Helped M'Arthur', *New York Times*, 19 February 1957, p. 31.
311 An obituary: Ibid.
312 obituary of George Lait: 'George Lait, Coast Publicist, Dies at 51', *New York Times*, 13 January 1958, p. 29.
312 Ralph Morton: Associated Press obituary, 'Ralph Morton, Former War Reporter', *Newsday*, 20 October 1988, p. 41.
312 Walter Simmons: Trevor Jensen, 'Walter Simmons: 1908–2006; Editor and War Reporter', *Chicago Tribune*, 1 December 2006, obituary, p. 18.
312 'stopped off to be an alcoholic': Tony Stephens, 'Talented agent loved his actors', obituary of John Cann, *Sydney Morning Herald*, 25 September 2008, retrieved 14 August 2009, at www.smh.com.au/news/obituaries/talented-agent-loved-his-actors/2008/09/24/1222217327095.html.
313 returned to acting: Reuters obituary, 'Canadian Actor Dies', *Ottawa Citizen*, 22 December 1977, p. 36. Also, interview with Alexandra Cann, 15 August 2009, and follow-up emails.
313 Lucille Moseley: Unbylined story, 'Filipino Scout Weds U.S. Girl', undated news clipping in the scrapbook of C. Earl Walter Jr. Accompanied by a second unbylined, undated clipping, headlined, 'Shangri-La Hero Here'.
313 dissolved the 1st Recon: Commendation letter signed by Douglas MacArthur, dated 15 August 1945, found in Margaret Hastings correspondence file at TCHS.
314 'Did you earn that?': Interview with C. Earl Walter Jr, 1 March 2010.
314 last entry in his journal: C. Earl Walter Jr, CEW, dated 3 July 1945.
314 'the highlight of my life': Interview with C. Earl Walter Jr, 1 March 2010.
315 married late in life: Interview with Betty McCollom, 1 August 2009.
315 a telephone call every year: John McCollom, unaired interviews with filmmaker Robert Gardner, Dayton, Ohio, October 1997.

316 tears to his eyes: Letter from John S. McCollom to retired Colonel Edward T. Imparato. See Imparato, p. 160.

316 left the Army in 1946: John S. McCollom's obituary, published in the *Dayton Daily News,* 21 August 2001, p. 10, provided by Betty McCollom.

316 'Why wasn't I killed instead of them?': Ibid.

316 'a baby daughter he had never seen': Undated John McCollom letter to Colonel Edward T. Imparato, reprinted in *Rescue from Shangri-La*, p. 160.

317 Robert, waiting for them: Pat Pond, 'Reunion: Thirty Years After', *Women's Army Corps Journal*, October–December 1974, Vol. 5, No. 5, pp. 18–19. During his unaired interview with John McCollom, Robert Gardner tried sensitively to raise the subject of Robert McCollom's death, but each time John McCollom changed the subject or said something along the lines of, 'I was lucky.'

317 too weak to carry him: Interview with Betty McCollom, 1 August 2009.

317 his own obituary: John S. McCollom's obituary, published in the *Dayton Daily News,* 21 August 2001, p. 10, provided by Betty McCollom.

318 'most celebrated young woman': James R. Miller, 'Reconversion of a Heroine', *Los Angeles Times Magazine*, 7 July 1946, p. 5.

318 'She's blonde': Unbylined story, 'Read Shangri-La Diary', *Boston Sunday Advertiser*, 15 July 1945, no page given. Located in Margaret Hastings' scrapbook at TCHS.

318 fielding offers: Unbylined editorial, 'The Price of Fame', apparently from the *Owego Gazette,* dated 14 July 1945, located in Margaret Hastings' scrapbook at TCHS.

318 'true comic': Letter from Frances Ullman, editor of *Calling All Girls* magazine, to Margaret Hastings, dated 19 July 1945. Located in Margaret Hastings correspondence file at TCHS.

318 dined at Toots Shor's: James R. Miller, 'Reconversion of a Heroine', *Los Angeles Times Magazine*, 7 July 1946, p. 5.

318 Some three thousand people: Stuart A. Dunham, 'Shangri-La WAC Home, Finds Every Girl's Dream Come True', *Binghamton Press*, 20 July 1945, p. 1.

319 'alligator pumps': Unbylined story, 'Owego Welcomes WAC Home', *Owego Gazette*, 20 July 1945, p. 1.

319 movie offers: Ibid.

319 Loretta Young: Sidney Skolsky, 'Hollywood is my Beat', undated gossip column clipping in Margaret Hastings' scrapbook, at TCHS.

319 waving their handkerchiefs and crying: James R. Miller, 'Reconversion of a Heroine', *Los Angeles Times Magazine*, 7 July 1946, p. 5.

319 fourteen different states: Tour schedule contained in Margaret Hastings correspondence file at TCHS.

320 letter is chaste: Letter from Don Ruiz to Margaret Hastings, dated 10 October 1945. Located in Margaret Hastings correspondence file at TCHS.

320 'I have the deepest sympathy': Letter to Margaret G. Nicholson from Colonel Luther Hill, dated 21 July 1945, provided by Major Nicholson's family.

320 'my commander's widow': Interview with John McCarthy, 13 September 2009.

321 'overwhelmed with war stories': Interview with Rita Callahan, 1 August 2009.

321 'if he didn't drown': Associated Press story, 'Former WAC Recalls 47-Day Jungle Ordeal', *Los Angeles Times*, 26 November 1961, p. E2.

321 honorary members: Unbylined story, 'Hidden Valley Survivors to be Honored', *Silent Wings*, newsletter of the National World War II Glider Pilots Association, Vol. 1, No. 4, September 1974, p. 1.

322 'doing what has to be done': Pat Pond, 'Reunion: Thirty Years After', *Women's Army Corps Journal*, October–December 1974, Vol. 5, No. 5, p. 19.

322 'You bet!': Ibid, p. 18.

322 'a good fight': Interview with Rita Callahan, 1 August 2009.

SELECT BIBLIOGRAPHY

Alexander, Larry. *Shadows in the Jungle: The Alamo Scouts Behind Enemy Lines in World War II*. New York: NAL Caliber, 2009.

Brown, Jerold E. *Historical Dictionary of the U.S. Army*. Westport, CT: Greenwood Press, 2001.

Clarinbould, Michael John. *The Forgotten Fifth: A Photographic Chronology of the U.S. Fifth Air Force in World War II*. Hyde Park, NY: Balus Design, 2007.

Connolly, Bob and Robin Anderson. *First Contact: New Guinea's Highlanders Encounter the Outside World*. New York: Viking, 1987.

Devlin, Gerard M. *Silent Wings: The Saga of the U.S. Army and Marine Combat Glider Pilots During World War II*. New York: St Martin's Press, 1985.

Diamond, Jared. *Collapse: How Societies Choose to Fail or Succeed*. New York: Viking, 2005.

Diamond, Jared. *Guns, Germs, and Steel: The Fates of Human Societies*. New York: W.W. Norton, 1997.

Dwiggins, Don. *On Silent Wings: Adventures in Motorless Flight*. New York: Grosset & Dunlap, 1970.

Flannery, Tim. *Throwim Way Leg: Tree-Kangaroos, Possums and Penis Gourds*. New York: Grove Press, 1998.

Gardner, Robert. *Making Dead Birds: Chronicle of a Film*. Cambridge, MA: Peabody Museum Press, 2007.

Gardner, Robert and Karl G. Heider. *Gardens of War: Life and Death in the New Guinea Stone Age*. New York: Random House, 1968.

Hampton, O.W. 'Bud'. *Culture of Stone: Sacred and Profane Uses of Stone Among the Dani*. College Station, TX: Texas A&M University Press, 1999.

Harrer, Heinrich. *I Come From the Stone Age*. London: The Companion Book Club, 1964.

Hayward, Douglas. *The Dani of Irian Jaya Before and After Conversion*. Sentani, Indonesia: Regions Press, 1980.

Heider, Karl G. *The Dugum Dani: A Papuan Culture in the Highlands of West New Guinea.* Chicago: Aldine Publishing, 1970.
Heider, Karl G. *Grand Valley Dani: Peaceful Warriors.* 3rd ed. Belmont, CA: Wadsworth Group, 1997.
Hilton, James. *Lost Horizon.* New York: Pocket Books, 1960.
Hitt, Russell T. *Cannibal Valley.* New York: Harper & Row, 1962.
Imparato, Edward T. *Rescue from Shangri-La.* Paducah, KY: Turner Publishing, 1997.
Keats, John. *They Fought Alone.* New York: Pocket Books, 1965.
Lowden, John L. *Silent Wings at War: Combat Gliders in World War II.* Washington, Smithsonian Institution Press, 1992.
Manchester, William. *American Caesar: Douglas MacArthur, 1880–1964.* New York: Little, Brown & Co., 1978.
Matthiessen, Peter. *Under the Mountain Wall: A Chronicle of Two Seasons in Stone Age New Guinea.* New York: Viking, 1962.
Meiselas, Susan. *Encounters with the Dani: Stories from the Baliem Valley.* New York: Steidl/International Center for Photography, 2003.
Morison, Samuel Eliot. *History of U.S. Naval Operations in World War II, Vol. 8: New Guinea and the Marianas, March 1944–August 1944.* Champaign, IL: University of Illinois Press, 2002.
Morse, Roger A. *Richard Archbold and the Archbold Biological Station.* Gainesville, FL: University Press of Florida, 2000.
Rottman, Gordon L. *U.S. Special Warfare Units in the Pacific Theater, 1941–45: Scouts, Raiders, Rangers and Reconnaissance Units.* New York: Osprey Publishing, 2005.
Rottman, Gordon L. *World War II Pacific Island Guide: A Geo-Military Study.* Westport, CT: Greenwood Press, 2001.
Samuels, William. *Reflections of an Airline Pilot.* San Francisco: Monterey Pacific Publishing, 1999.
Sandler, Stanley. *World War II in the Pacific: An Encyclopedia.* New York: Garland Publishing, 2001.
Sargent, Wyn. *People of the Valley: Life with a Cannibal Tribe in New Guinea.* New York: Random House, 1974.
Sheehan, Susan. *A Missing Plane: The Dramatic Tragedy and Triumph of a Lost and Forgotten World War II Bomber.* New York: Berkeley Books, 1986.
Souter, Gavin. *New Guinea: The Last Unknown.* Sydney: Angus & Robertson, 1964.
Treadwell, Mattie E. *The Women's Army Corps.* Washington: Office of the Chief of Military History, Dept. of the Army, 1954.
Weise, Selene H.C. *The Good Soldier: The Story of a Southwest Pacific Signal Corps WAC.* Shippensburg, PA: Burd Street Press, 1999.

INDEX